Date Due

MAR 1 5 1971			
AUG 2 6 1983			

CORNELL STUDIES IN ANTHROPOLOGY

HUAYLAS

An Andean District
in Search of Progress

Cornell Studies in Anthropology

This series of publications seeks particularly to provide descriptive accounts and interpretations of cultural process and dynamics, including those involved in projects of planned cultural change, among diverse cultures of the world.

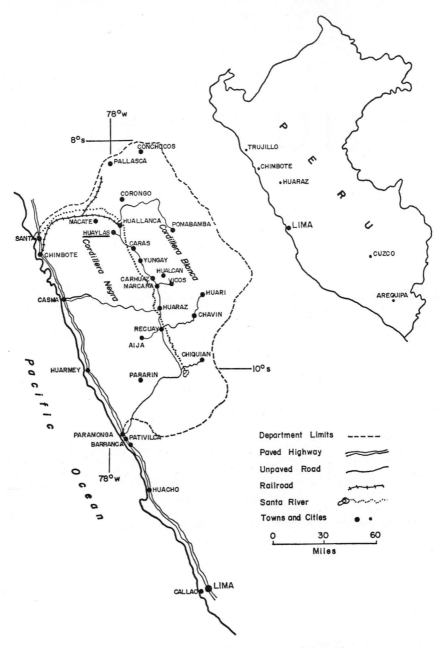

Map 1. Peru and the Department of Ancash

HUAYLAS

An Andean District
in Search of Progress

By PAUL L. DOUGHTY

with the collaboration of
MARY F. DOUGHTY

Cornell University Press

ITHACA, NEW YORK

Library of Congress Catalog Card Number: 68–14969

PRINTED IN THE UNITED STATES OF AMERICA
BY KINGSPORT PRESS, INC.

To ALLAN R. HOLMBERG

(1909–1966)

to whom so many owe so much

Preface

Selecting a Community for Study

My general interests took me in search of a community outside the traditional manor environment; the narrow intermontane valley of the Callejón de Huaylas, in the Department of Ancash, seemed to be an appropriate region in which to make the kind of study I had in mind. Since the Cornell-Peru Project had already sponsored several studies there,[1] my research would make a distinct contribution in supplementing the body of data previously collected.

Accompanied by my wife, I first spent a few days at the Cornell-Peru Project headquarters then at Vicos. From there, we visited most of the small towns and cities in the Callejón. Mr. Lucio Vásquez, a teacher at Vicos, was good enough to accompany us, introducing us to various persons and generally helping us to become acquainted with the area.

On Sunday, March 13, 1960, with Mr. Lucio Vásquez, Dr. Mario C. Vázquez, and his wife, Aida Milla de Vázquez, we paid our first visit to Huaylas (pronounced, Wy-lahs). An uncle and a former classmate of Lucio Vásquez lived there, and we went in search of them. We found the ex-classmate, Don Máximo Rojo, at work in the garden behind his house which also functioned as a hotel and store. I was introduced as an anthropologist, interested in the life and customs of Peru. Mr. Rojo promptly offered to show us around the town of Huaylas and to introduce us to various persons. Our first stop was at the church which had just been refurbished through local efforts. We then went to the office of the Concejo Distrital, the district government, where the mayor was conducting a meeting. This was interrupted by our presence, and the mayor, Dr. Enrique Villegas Acosta, after welcoming us,

[1] For a bibliography of this material to 1963, see Dobyns and Vázquez, 1964.

described some of the activities in which the district was engaged at the time. Under his direction, the people of the district were undertaking the installation of a new electrical system to utilize the current from the hydroelectric plant at nearby Huallanca. Upon hearing that I was interested in studying the life and customs of the area, he suggested that we take up residence in Huaylas.

With the mayor and Mr. Rojo, we then visited the Eusebio Acosta Library, which occupies a corner of the plaza, to see the collection of 3,000 volumes which was the gift of a Huaylino who has resided in New York City for about forty years. Don David Flores, the librarian, related the story of the library with much elaboration of detail and ended by having us sign the visitors' book. As we were to discover later, this particular ritual is de rigueur for almost all visitors to Huaylas.

On returning to Vicos and weighing the various merits of the places visited, I decided that it would be wise to pay another and more extended visit to Huaylas under less formal circumstances before making a decision about the choice of a site for study. Our first impressions of Huaylas were favorable from the point of view of the study: it was definitely mestizo in character; it was a small farming community; there was the prospect that changes occurring in Huaylas would be of particular interest from the point of view of the research. Among other things, the electrification project was of interest, since the Cornell-Peru Project had first initiated studies in the Callejón with the idea of studying the impact of the hydroelectric plant and the electrification of the Callejón. Because no other town in the valley enjoyed the use of the current from the plant at that time, it seemed a happy fortuity that we should have the opportunity of witnessing the first installation.

In addition, the town of Huaylas was a district capital and thus afforded us an opportunity to observe the relationship between the government and the people at the "grass roots," since a district is the smallest administrative unit in Peru. There were other advantages as well. The fact that Huaylas was the capital of a district meant that certain statistical data, such as the national census, birth, death, and marriage records, and certain tax records which are reported from the district level, would be available. Furthermore, the town was the seat of the parish of Huaylas and had a resident priest. In short, Huaylas was representative of the smallest institutionally complete unit of Peruvian society. This being the case, it would be possible to evaluate the importance of the official organizations and their role in the process of culture change, particularly with regard to the breakdown or maintenance of traditional cultural values and organization.

The geographical setting also offered certain advantages. Situated somewhat apart from the rest of the Callejón, the town of Huaylas is encircled by a multitude of *chacras*, compactly arranged in a sloping valley and set like an amphitheater against the mountainsides. Everything considered, Huaylas seemed to be a complete ecological unit, geographically independent of the rest of the Callejón and, because of this, lending itself more readily to the study of change, since outside forces impinging on the life of Huaylas could perhaps more readily be discovered and evaluated.

Our second visit to Huaylas, under less formal conditions, reinforced my original impressions, and I decided to choose it as the locale for the study. Accordingly, with the assistance of Don Máximo Rojo, I rented a house in the center of the town, and after making final visa arrangements in Lima we took up residence in Huaylas on April 2, 1960.

The Role of the Investigator

From the first, it became apparent that not only would we be permitted to participate in community affairs in the best anthropological tradition of participant observation, but that the community would encourage us to do so. This came somewhat as a surprise, since I had been warned that outsiders frequently encountered closed doors and generally chilly receptions in highland mestizo communities. On our second night in Huaylas, a parade of men, led by the mayor and the governor, swept by the house. They motioned for me to accompany them, and I found myself dancing up the street, together with about forty jubilant men, to the music of the *cajas* and *roncadoras*.

The merriment was in celebration of a successful day's work on the electrification project by men of the *barrio* of Yacup. We were entertained at the house of the *barrio inspector*, and I was introduced to the men as an anthropologist interested in the life and customs of Huaylas, whose studies would possibly be of benefit to the people of Huaylas. These remarks by Dr. Villegas were greeted with cheers, and a dozen or more men from the *barrio* welcomed me to Huaylas with *abrazos* (embraces).

Such a straightforward introduction and the enthusiastic reception it evoked were a little surprising, to say the least, since the first few days are almost always a delicate period in the anthropologist's attempts to establish rapport with the subjects of his study.[2] It proved to be my good fortune that both the mayor and the governor were extremely popular figures at the time of our arrival, and their sanctioning of my presence and objectives was the best possible introduction into the community.

Later, Mr. Rojo also arranged for me to meet the parish priest so that, as he phrased it, "there would be no misunderstandings about my intentions," since Huaylas was *"muy católico"* ("very Catholic"). A few days later, we found ourselves immersed in the celebration of Semana Santa (Holy Week). By Huaylas tradition, all the officials and important men of the district are assigned seats in the church for Easter week, and attendance is considered obligatory. I was advised that my name would be placed on one of the chairs and that I would be expected to accompany the procession of important persons to the church from the offices of the municipality which served as the meeting point. On this most solemn of occasions, I arrived at the church and, with the other men, looked circumspectly about for the chair assigned to me. I found it, my name tag clearly reading: "Sr. Paul Potty." On Jueves Santo (Holy Thursday) my wife and I were asked to be *padrinos* (sponsors) for the mantle of the image of the Virgin Mary.

This immediate participation in the life of the community was slightly breath-taking, since I had, at first, almost no control over the course of events. It seemed best, under the circumstances, to go along with the arrangements, despite some of my misgivings, and to handle emergencies and delicate situations as they arose. Fortunately, none appeared.

The major result of this venture was our widespread acceptance in Huaylas as residents who presented no particular threat to the established religion (since we were obviously not Protestant missionaries, as some had originally thought) and who were willing to share in the life of the community. We met a great many persons, and others, from all over the district, heard of our presence and aims in positive terms. We began to receive dinner, tea, and picnic invitations, at least one a week during the first month and more than three per week throughout the rest of the time we spent in Huaylas. In May 1961, our last full month of residence in Huaylas, we received twenty-two invitations for

[2] Lewis, 1951:xv, or Stein, 1961:vii–xi.

meals. During the first month we also received four gifts of bread, three of fruit, and eight of vegetables—mostly corn, which was in season. This, too, was a continuing pattern.

Thus, we were quickly involved in a network of social obligations, reciprocating in the best way we could (although most inadequately) the generous hospitality which the various townspeople and rural residents offered us. Living in the town we had the benefit of electricity supplied by the diesel generator, at first for four hours each evening. After the installation of the new system, there was electricity twenty-four hours a day. Each householder was required to pay the Concejo (council) according to the number and wattage of the bulbs in his house, but when I attempted to pay my bill at the district office, the lieutenant mayor, with a grin, informed me that the Concejo had voted, "some time ago," to give us free electricity.

All was not sweetness and light, however. In May 1961, I was reported to the police for "stealing the riches of the land of the sun." [3] This occurred after a trip that several Huaylinos and I had made to see some archaeological remains and some "mummies," which had been found in the *barrio* of Iscap. The police investigated and were convinced that nothing was amiss, particularly when we were able to show a schoolboy's essay describing how he and his classmates had salvaged the "mummies" from a tomb which had been previously violated by *huaqueros* (archaeological treasure hunters).

The ebb and flow of life in Huaylas did not impose any great hardships upon us, except that the tempo of research sometimes slowed to the pace of village activities. With the repetitiveness of daily chores and events, the cycle of the townsman's life becomes one's own: arising at 6:30 A.M. to see if there would be meat for sale in the market and perhaps making another trip to the market later for vegetables; fetching two or three buckets of water for use during the day; sweeping the cobblestoned street in front of one's house in accordance with municipal regulations; cooking and making bread; retiring to bed at 10:30 P.M. or so along with almost everyone else when the electricity was cut

[3] This is a romantic way of saying archaeological remains, envisioned as being gold and silver artifacts of inestimable value. The government of Peru requires that all foreign archaeologists obtain permits, signed by the President, to carry on work, and it is against the law to remove archaeological remains from the country. At the time of this incident, a cache of such remains had been uncovered in Lima as they were about to be smuggled out of the country. The case received a great deal of publicity in the nation as a whole.

off (except the die-hard billiard players who played by candlelight).

Nevertheless, our presence in the town was a source of some wonder to visitors to Huaylas. "How can you possibly manage here?" was a question we were often asked by visitors from Lima. "What do you eat? Don't tell me that you can find enough here?" Yet, while outsiders tended to regard our role in Huaylas as a difficult one, the Huaylinos themselves both expected and encouraged us to participate actively in their life, and, by becoming their *compadres*, thus establish human ties which are enduring and sincere. Within the framework of relationships established on this basis, we found that Huaylinos reacted positively to our presence, extending their cooperation and support to our research efforts and making our stay in Huaylas a memorable and enjoyable one.

Research Procedures and Methods

In gathering data, a number of techniques and resources were employed, supplementing the basic method of participant observation. For the most part, interviews were conducted in an informal, "natural" setting, preferably in surroundings familiar to the informant. Thus I spent a great deal of time visiting Huaylinos in their homes, stores, or places of work. The few times that I arranged for interviews in our house proved generally unsatisfactory either because informants grew restless after a short time or because there were interruptions that prevented the development of extended conversations.

On some occasions, notes were taken in the presence of informants. On other occasions, they were not, either because I felt that the informant would be offended or disturbed or because it was inconvenient to write. Thus, during church services, dinners, dances, and the like, facts had to be remembered until time could be found to jot down key points. On several occasions I used a tape recorder to record conversations or to dictate notes, especially when there was a great deal of material and little time for writing. Notes were normally transcribed from the tapes as quickly as possible.[4]

In these various aspects of the research, my wife, Mary French Doughty, was of great assistance to me, especially in conducting interviews with women with whom I would not have been so free to talk,

[4] Potential users of tape recorders for such purposes should be warned, however, that dependence on tape can be a "booby trap," if one does not transcribe the data fairly soon after recording. Because it may take a long time to do this, the tendency is to put off the job. As I write, there are still three tapes awaiting transcription.

and in copying archival data. In addition to the data obtained from observation and interview, I drew upon archives housed in the Concejo office. These included the register of vital statistics (births, deaths, and marriages) and numerous volumes of correspondence, official orders, fines, meeting reports, and so on, dating from the year 1889, as well as the official *Libro de Actas* (Book of Acts) kept by the District Council, or Concejo Distrital, which provided an interesting historical overview of events in Huaylas from 1889 onward. The archival work, although rewarding, was particularly time-consuming because much of the material was unorganized. As a result of my interest in the archives, two young men from the town, Mr. Nilo Acosta Ruíz and Mr. Libio Villar Lopez, assisted me not only in putting the documents in order, but also in extracting the statistical and other information I needed. Because of their interest and the quality of their work, I employed both of these young men from time to time, particularly Mr. Acosta, in mapping the settlement pattern of the district.

In addition to the municipal archives, I was also given access to the files of the local tax office (Caja de Depósitos), police station (*puesto*), and Comunidad Indígena. The Caja de Depósitos collects taxes both on businesses and on property in the district and keeps a register of all taxpayers, land sales, importation of alcoholic beverages, *coca*, and cigarettes, among other things. From the police archives it was possible to obtain records of all commercial traffic in and out of Huaylas for the past several years and also to obtain a copy of the "blotter," in order to arrive at a picture of the major kinds of crimes and problems handled by the police.

In addition to these records, I took microfilms of the school matriculation books and class registers for the past seven years for the light they would shed both on the formal education process and on the relationships of the people in the various sectors of the district to the schools. I also sponsored an essay contest in the boys' and girls' schools in the town in an attempt to obtain more information about *repúblicas* and children's knowledge about these public works projects. While this did not turn out quite as I had anticipated, it provided many extremely valuable insights into the educational system and the ethos surrounding it.

The records of the Comunidad Indígena were made available to me and microfilmed, as were local provincial newspapers, which I did not have the time to examine closely while in Huaylas. The only body of archival data to which I did not have free access was that in the church. While I was permitted the use of the volumes containing baptismal, funeral, and marriage records—dating from 1604—it proved impossible to complete the work because the parish was left without a priest during the final months of our stay in Huaylas, and the parish house was closed by order of the bishop.

During the months of January and February, 1961, I made a census of the District of Huaylas. I supplemented it with a questionnaire, dealing with migration and agriculture, which was administered to some 22 per cent of the family heads throughout the district. The census and survey of Huaylas were undertaken with the advice of and with financial assistance provided by Dr. J. Mayone Stycos. In exchange for his aid, I supervised, in addition, the administering of a questionnaire dealing with fertility among the women of Huaylas, employing five anthropology students (men) from the National University of San Marcos and eight students (women) who came from the National School of Social Service in Lima to Huaylas to administer it. By special arrangement with the two schools, the students were to be given credit for field research performed under my direction.

In preparation for the census and the other questionnaires, maps were drawn, and every occupied house was located and given an identifying number. Because the district is divided into *barrios*, these were used as the basic units for enumeration and analysis. The census forms were printed on IBM "mark sense" cards, which were used in the field and later perforated and partially analyzed in Lima. The data collected on the family-head questionnaire was transferred to Unisort marginal punch cards for analysis.

As a result of the interest created in the district by these studies, I was asked to give a talk and report the results to the people in the district and to give another in Lima before the Huaylas District Association. Both these talks were reported in the Lima newspapers, principally because Huaylinos work as reporters on them.

During the summer months (July and August) of 1960, I served as Field Instructor for the Columbia-Cornell-Harvard-Illinois Summer Studies Program. Five undergraduates from these universities came to Peru and worked under my supervision, two staying in Vicos and three living with families in Huaylas. During the course of the summer, the three students in Huaylas, James Fox (Harvard), Alice Kasokoff (Radcliffe), and Gary Parker (Cornell), studied religious organization, the educational system, and the Quechua language respectively. In addition to these studies, they also made general observations which they recorded on 5-by-8-inch pages in the style that I had adopted, as described below.

Field notes were recorded on 5-by-8-inch Unisort marginal punch cards and were classified as soon as possible according to the system developed for the Human Relations Area Files.[5] I made some modifications in this system in order to accommodate my own interests and the punch code for the Unisort cards. The use of the Unisort cards permitted much greater freedom in taking notes and also proved to be timesaving because the marginal punch system allowed the recording of unrelated data on the same card, thus avoiding both the necessity of making several copies of the card to be filed as in the HRAF system and the necessity of placing each datum on a separate card.

From the first, I experienced a great deal of difficulty in remembering the names of all the persons we met, and confusion soon crept into my notes. Frequently, in transcribing a day's notes, it was necessary to refer to the actions of some individual whose name I either did not know or could not recall. Another problem stemmed from the fact that, as a general policy, our doors were left ajar so that people would feel free to knock and come in for a visit. This sometimes led to the potentially embarrassing and delicate situation in which an informant might see his name or that of someone he knew written in the notes and ask me to explain what had been said, in violation of the informant's anonymity.

To avoid problems of this kind and to facilitate the accurate recording of names, the following system was devised. All informants were listed as they appeared in the notes, like actors in a drama, and assigned a number. Whether I knew his name or not, the person was briefly described so that he could be identified at a later date. Even in the event that his name was unknown, the person could still be correctly identified and discussed. If such a person's name was learned at a later date, it was filled in next to the number.

The notes contain only the numbers assigned to the individuals and not their names. Hence, an alphabetical list was also kept to make it easy to locate the number of any given person. Finally, in addition to solving the three problems mentioned above, the use of numbers in-

[5] Murdock, 1950.

stead of names in writing up the notes afforded a saving of space, since it is more economical to write 489 than "Arquemedes Rodriguez Chuquillanqui" several times in any given page.

Acknowledgments

The basic research for this book was conducted from February 1960 through September 1961 under the auspices of the Cornell-Peru Project, supported by the Carnegie Corporation of New York. Additional assistance was also received when I twice acted as field instructor for the Columbia-Cornell-Harvard-Illinois Summer Field Studies Program for undergraduates for periods of two months in 1960 and 1961. The product of this research constituted the basis of my doctoral dissertation completed at Cornell University in 1963.

On a second trip to Peru, from December 1962 through August 1964, for the Cornell-Peru Project under Peace Corps contract PC-(W)-155, I had an opportunity to gather supplementary materials about Huaylas.

I would like to express my appreciation to the many teachers and colleagues who have helped me in various ways. My debt to Dr. Allan R. Holmberg is very great. As Chairman of my graduate study program and Director of the Cornell-Peru Project he generously shared his knowledge with me, giving his support and friendship at every turn. It was he who first suggested that I consider Huaylas as a site for my research.

Dr. Robert A. Polson and Dr. Richard B. Fisher as teachers and members of my graduate committee made important contributions to my knowledge of society and the natural environment.

Dr. Mario C. Vázquez and Aida Milla de Vázquez were of great assistance to my wife and me during our first sojourn in Peru. As this work was prepared for publication, Mario Vázquez with untiring goodwill, reviewed, criticized, and suggested pertinent changes or additions to the manuscript.

In return for advice, board and room, friendship, and immeasurable quantities of practical assistance on many occasions, this expression of appreciation to Dr. Henry F. Dobyns and his wife, Dr. Cara E. Richards, is wholly inadequate.

Dr. J. Oscar Alers offered many helpful comments on the manuscript, particularly with respect to the sections on demography. During the initial period of research, Dr. Pelegrín Román Unzueta, head of the

National Plan for Integrating the Aboriginal Population of the Ministry of Labor and Indian Affairs (now, Communities) and his staff provided us with assistance in a number of ways.

In the process of conducting a census and survey of Huaylas, an enterprise made possible by Dr. J. Mayone Stycos, I had the invaluable assistance of Dr. Humberto Ghersi Barrera and Messrs. Hernán Castillo Ardiles, Humberto Rodriguez Pastor, Mario Vallejos B., Cesar Ramón Córdova, and Arcenio Revilla Corrales of the Department of Anthropology of the National University of San Marcos; and of Misses Ida Gonzales Ismodes, Emma Fujii A., Aurora Garfias R., Bertha Monge D., Ernestina Estella E., Gaby Seminario L., Carmen Bernales U., and Adela Romero L. of the Social Service School of Peru.

For the preparation of the original census maps and other materials I am indebted to Mr. Nilo Acosta Ruíz and Mr. Libio Villar Lopez of Huaylas who assisted me in numerous ways, as mentioned earlier.

Mrs. Bertha Basurto de Escobar lent her expert hand in the preparation of the charts and maps which appear here, and Mrs. Shirley Watkins was responsible for typing the draft of the manuscript. I am grateful to the Society for Applied Anthropology, Duke University Press, and Quadrangle Books, Inc., for permission to quote material from George M. Foster, *Culture and Conquest: America's Heritage* (Chicago, 1960).

The debt which I owe to the people of Huaylas is greater than any other. With dignity, patience, and understanding, they responded positively to the onslaught of our many questions and pardoned our errors, teaching us more than can be adequately summarized on the following pages. I wish particularly to thank the mayor of Huaylas, Dr. Enrique Villegas Acosta, and the members of the District Council in the name of all those Huaylinos who so generously gave us their friendship and cooperation.

Of those Huaylinos who may read this, and of those who cannot as well, I ask their forbearance for this effort to describe and interpret their society in the hope that, despite any errors it may contain, it will aid them, as it has me, in understanding the complex times in which we live.

P. L. D.

Lima, Perú
March 1967

Contents

Illustrations

MAPS

Plates appear following page 34

FIGURES

Tables

HUAYLAS

An Andean District
in Search of Progress

Introduction

Peruvian society has characteristically been described in terms of dichotomies. No work fails to distinguish between the coastal and highland regions. The position of the Quechua-speaking Indians vis-à-vis the Spanish-speaking mestizo has continued to occupy the research energies of social scientists and other observers of the Andean scene for many years, and rightly so. The socio-cultural hierarchy has remained intact, in large degree, since colonial times. Although personalities and reform programs come and go on the political fronts, the fundamental cultural backdrop with all its props, models, and values has only recently begun to show signs of wear.

The Indian has always been the problem child in the New World milieu dominated by European men. The Indians were too numerous and too essential to the colonial economy to ignore. The Spaniards and their creole successors in Peru institutionalized Indian culture and the Indian caste in accord with the ethnocentric hierarchical view which they held. In their status as serfs and servants, the Indians have survived in provincial aloofness, rarely affected by the vicissitudes of time, politics, society, and technological innovations which have so stirred Western civilization and the rest of the world. Yet they have long been controlled and exploited by people whose interests and motivations came from outside the Andean valleys. In this state (particularly on the manors) the Indians "belonged" to whoever controlled the land they lived on and who gave them orders, as Saenz lamented three decades ago.[1] Culturally, they were foreigners in their own country and denied

[1] Saenz, 1933: 172. For a description of how such a system operated, see Holmberg *et al.*, 1965:3–33.

access to the means by which their situation could be altered. It is little wonder that through the years, Peruvian society has been termed one of the most rigid in Latin America [2] and that the continued existence of the economically impoverished and socially discrete Indian masses constitutes the single greatest obstacle to the emergence of Peru as a full participant in modern Western civilization.[3]

The negative stereotype by which the Indian has been, and continues to be, classified is fortified by the Indian's visibility—his distinctive manner of dress, speech, and comportment. The Indian has traditionally been treated paternally and abusively, always as a social inferior of the mestizo. He is kept in his place, while the mestizo monopolizes the power, positions of respect, economic advantage, and whatever technological improvements that exist in the rural environment that make life more enjoyable and less arduous.[4]

Attention has been called to the fact that this situation is not unlike the social system of the southern United States, particularly with regard to interpersonal relationships between Negroes and whites.[5] But this similarity has its limitations. The social distinctions with regard to the Andean Indian are essentially cultural in nature, although certain racial (in the biological sense) undertones are discernible. The Indian can, under certain conditions and with some tutelage, lose his visibility and thus become more "acceptable" to the national society.

It is not easy, however, for the Indian to change his social status—his ascribed one—without considerable risk and sacrifice. Emigration from one's community is often the path chosen by those who seek to change their status and to satisfy their needs. Indeed, this seems to be the major road by which one may gain access to cultural, social, and economic alternatives.[6] Experience has shown, nevertheless, that even though migrants adopt national culture to a large degree, one's "superiors" in

[2] Beals, 1952:334.

[3] Arthur D. Little, Inc., 1960:3; Holmberg, 1960:71; Owens, 1963:90; Ford, 1955:103–117.

[4] Holmberg *et al.*, 1965. For a more general treatment of this situation in the Andean regions, see Nuñez del Prado, 1955; Vázquez, 1961a; Rycoff, 1946; International Labour Office, 1953.

[5] Stein, 1961:41. Numerous situations and hypotheses presented, for example, by Dean and Rosen (1955) appear to describe most adequately the predicament of the Andean Indian.

[6] With regard to this specific point, see Alers *et al.*, 1965:336; Bradfield, 1963:75. For a review of the internal migration patterns in Peru, see Dobyns and Vázquez, eds., 1963.

his place of origin may refuse to accept this as representing a change in status.[7]

The pressures that augur for change in the highland society have intensified greatly over the last twenty years. The national population has increased by 59.6 per cent since 1940,[8] a fact which has led to correspondingly greater demands on the limited arable lands. Numerous industrial developments in the coastal regions, particularly in Lima, have created new labor needs. The spectacular growth of the fishing industry in nearly every coastal port and city (particularly along the north coast) is most notable.[9] Mining developments in the southern coastal regions of the country have been similarly expansive.[10] The labor force for these enterprises has been drawn primarily from the highland regions of the country. Many new aspirations and wants, titillated by radio broadcasting, politics, and the educational system, have now taken root in even the most isolated of hamlets.[11]

The strictly dichotomized society, with its patronal and rigid social structure, has thus been challenged. The new generations of highlanders—both Indian and mestizo—are restless, rejecting many of the old ways, yet reaffirming others and combining them with newer traits and ideas. A struggle for a share of the things they feel should be theirs is thus in progress.

The Indians involved in this transculturation process have become bilingual. They have put aside their homespun uniforms or combined them with clothes and other items of more contemporary tastes. They

---

[7] Joan Snyder, 1960:162–165, 475–489, 491–497. In the small community she studied, Joan Snyder found that returning migrants and others who were socially mobile were generally not accepted in the nearby mestizo town. Yet the former Indians from the village she studied wore mestizo-style clothing, adopted mestizo mannerisms, and maintained a set of "superior" and discriminatory attitudes toward people whom they defined as Indians. R. N. Adams (1959:106) describes the case of a well-educated and widely traveled "Indian" from Muquiyauyo in central Peru, who, upon returning to his native town, found that he was still considered an "Indian" by some of the older mestizos.

[8] Perú, Instituto Nacional de Planificación, 1964:xxvii.

[9] Between 1952 and 1962 the Peruvian fishing industry moved from seventeenth to first place in world rankings, based on the volume of fish caught (Banco Central de Reserva del Perú, 3, 1963:12).

[10] Banco Central de Reserva del Perú, I, 1963:86–89.

[11] One such community was Chaquicocha, Junín. As a result of temporary employment in the mines at La Oroya, members of the community galvanized the people into a working unit, initiating many rapid changes (Castillo *et al.*, 1964a:34–35, 77–91). Also see Organización de los Estados Americanos, 1961:98–109.

work for wages and engage actively in petty commerce; they travel, acquire modern technical skills, and actively seek an education. They constitute a people neither mestizo nor Indian, but one increasingly influenced by modern Western civilization as mediated by Lima. Yet they are inevitably bound, in various degrees, to their respective local and regional traditions. It is this ubiquitous and highly diversified human being who has been popularly and scientifically referred to as the *cholo*.[12]

In the southern highlands, generally considered the bastion of the traditional Indian population, it was estimated that 38 per cent of the population could be classified as *cholo*.[13] In the central highlands and Mantaro Valley regions, studies indicate that *cholos* probably form a much greater percentage of the population.[14] The dynamism, unity, and progressiveness he observed in the Mantaro Valley Comunidad of Muquiyauyo caused Adams[15] to wonder whether or not these features occurred elsewhere, and if so, why.

This was the question that motivated me to seek a community that might be experiencing similar changes. It seemed important that this newly emerging Andean culture with its concomitant social adjustments be charted over a greater territory for both comparative and predictive purposes. It was of interest to document the nation's influence, through its various formal institutions, on the lives of the Andean people insofar as that was possible. This book, therefore, represents an attempt to describe and analyze some of the new ingredients of Peruvian national culture as it is presently evolving in a highland district.

[12] This term has many, often subtle meanings, the most important of which can be briefly summarized here. In Vicos, Ancash, for example, the word *cholo* refers to an Indian boy. Elsewhere, in mestizo society, it is utilized to mean "buddy" or "pal," and in a derogatory sense to mean "upstart" or "hick." In some usages, *cholo* may reflect upon one's Indian cultural background. Historically, the word has had varying significance and degree of use (Varallanos, 1962:1–36). Social scientists, both Peruvian and foreign have chosen to use it with reference to individuals or classes of individuals of Indian origin from the highland regions who represent this new, still changing synthesis of Andean and modern Western cultures. See, for example, Vázquez, 1951; Mangin, 1955:174–189; Schaedel, 1959:15–26; Escobar, 1959:1–21; Fried, 1961:24–25; and Bourricaud, 1962. The term "cholificación" has been coined to refer to this process of transculturation (Schaedel, 1959:19–23; Bourricaud, 1962:215–228).

[13] Schaedel, 1959:15.

[14] Organización de los Estados Americanos, 1961:89–109; Escobar, 1947; Adams, 1959; Arguedas, 1953:101–124; Alers-Montalvo, 1960; Sabogál Wiesse, 1961; Maynard, 1964; Castillo *et al.*, 1964a; Castillo *et al.*, 1964b.

[15] Adams, 1959:216.

CHAPTER I

Huaylas and Its Valley

Callejón de Huaylas

The Callejón de Huaylas is acknowledged to be one of the most impressive and beautiful of Andean valleys. Along its eastern flank is the Cordillera Blanca, whose heavily glaciated peaks range up to 22,205 feet at the summit of Peru's highest mountain, El Huascarán. On the west, the valley is delimited by the Cordillera Negra, a range of rugged mountains with altitudes up to 16,500 feet at its northern extreme in the District of Huaylas.[1]

The valley itself is rather hilly and narrow, having been carved out by the Santa river and innumerable avalanches and floods.[2] The Santa rises from a glacial lake on the high, grassy *puna* (region above the timber line) at Conococha and flows rapidly in a northerly direction for about 125 miles; it then slices through a spectacular, narrow defile, called the Cañon del Pato (Duck Canyon), and angles abruptly down to the coast near Chimbote. The Santa is the only major sierra river which belongs to the Pacific drainage system.

As implied by its name, the Cordillera Negra does not have a glacial or snow cap, a fact of utmost importance for agriculture. The Callejón

---

[1] A beautifully illustrated geographic description of the Callejón de Huaylas has been published by Kinzl and Schneider (1950). The geology of the District of Huaylas and the Cordillera Negra is described in Bodenlos and Straczk, 1957:3–10, 147–149.

[2] For an account of a recent avalanche, see McDowell and Fletcher, 1962.

de Huaylas can thus be divided into two distinct agricultural regions: the slopes to the east of the Santa river, which have an abundant supply of water the year round from the melting snows of the Cordillera Blanca, and those to the west, which depend upon the short rainy season and the husbandry of this water for irrigation. On the western slopes, dry farming is a common practice.

The Callejón de Huaylas is densely populated despite its rural character. Homesteads and tiny hamlets are scattered over the slopes up to the *puna* on both sides of the river. Some of the settlements, particularly at the southern end of the valley, are at altitudes of over 13,000 feet. Most of the population, however, is concentrated in some twenty-three villages and small cities which border the Santa river. Eight more villages and towns lie further up the slopes. Huaylas is one of these, being located at an altitude of 9,118 feet in the Cordillera Negra.

The highway system in the Callejón is typical of Peruvian highlands. Two roads enter the valley from the coast, uniting at Huaraz to form the main route along the east bank of the Santa and passing through most of the towns which border the river. It is a one-and-a-half-lane-wide dirt road, which covers the traveler with dust from April through December and mires him in mud during the rest of the year. During the rainy season, because of frequent slides and washouts, the maintenance of the road would be difficult even with adequate equipment. In 1961 there were only two modern road scrapers occasionally in use over the entire route from Caraz to Pativilca (a distance of about two hundred miles), so the condition of the road was rough at best.[3] In spite of this, there is considerable daily traffic to the coast, consisting mainly of trucks, which double as buses, and taxis, called *colectivos*. From the department capital, Huaraz, the trip to the coast takes about seven hours, with another two to three hours needed to reach Lima.

Going north, past the city of Caraz, the road crosses over the Santa to the west bank. Here desert conditions prevail due to the lack of water, and there is almost no cultivation on the lower slopes, except at the village of Mato. Higher in the Cordillera Negra, numerous yellowish patches mark the presence of wheat fields which are dry farmed. At

[3] A project to improve this road was begun in 1962 when a short segment near Huaraz was paved prior to the national elections. Since then, portions of the road have been widened and leveled so that the section between Huaraz and Caraz can be paved.

Mato the road divides: the main branch continues through the Cañon del Pato, with its forty-two tunnels, to Huallanca and the rail depot; the other branch goes through Mato, climbing precariously up into the Cordillera Negra for ten miles toward Huaylas.

District of Huaylas

As a geographical unit, the District of Huaylas is composed of three distinct ecological zones, which are vertically ranged: the *puna,* the irrigated farmlands, and the arid, uncultivated land on the lower slopes. The road which leads to Huaylas travels upward through the desert region for about eight miles, winding through the deeply eroded *quebradas,* or gorges. The slopes are very steep and rocky, with occasional limestone outcroppings exposed where extensive blasting was necessary to create the narrow roadbed. Visitors describe the ride to Huaylas as spectacular, or even thrilling, in the sense of dangerous.

Except during the rainy season and the months of May and June, the rather abundant plant life of the desert is sere, and the landscape presents a somewhat dreary appearance. There are several varieties of succulents and a few hardy *molle* trees scattered among the small zerophytic plants which dominate the scene. Ascending rapidly, the road attains an altitude of nearly 10,000 feet at a place which Huaylinos call Curcúy, a pass through which the road descends into the irrigated valley. The panorama of the fertile fields of Huaylas set against the backdrop of the Cordillera Negra comes as a surprise after the approach through the arid countryside. From the pass, the hanging valley or terrace appears to be almost flat, sloping gently up into the mountains.[4] Hundreds of eucalyptus trees (planted since 1930) obscure the farmhouses in the rural areas and provide a permanent verdant touch to the landscape.

From Curcúy, the road descends quickly to the town of Huaylas, which occupies the southernmost rim of the little valley. The square with its fountain in the center is bordered by the newly refurbished seventeenth-century church, the balconied municipal buildings, and several private residences built in the same style. From the Plaza de Armas, narrow cobbled streets go off at right angles, between the white-plastered, two-storied houses. Like most of the towns of the

---

[4] This impression is probably responsible for the name Atun Huaylas by which the district was officially known until very recently. Atun Huaylas means great meadows, or fields.

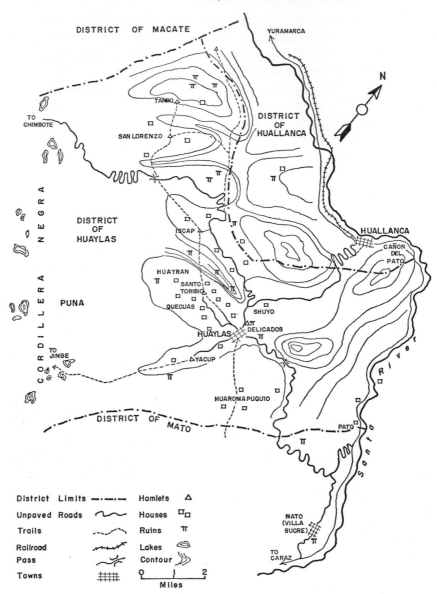

Map 2. District of Huaylas

valley, Huaylas is laid out in the classic grid pattern, which the Spaniards imposed as the model for city planners in colonial times.[5] The
town is long and narrow, rather than square, sloping gently upward

[5] Foster, 1960:34–49.

from north to south. The two principal urban facilities which the town offers its inhabitants, in addition to cobbled streets, are electricity and water. Strung along the streets on poles, or on supports attached to the roofs, the wires show through the torn insulation at many places. At the corners, naked fifty-watt light bulbs are suspended over the intersections. In the upper half of the town, there is a public water spigot at each corner, but in the lower or northern half of the town numerous wells and springs provide the water.

Although houses line the streets, giving the town an urban air, behind them are the *chacras,* the small cultivated plots which invade the town, some being adjacent to the plaza itself. Away from the center of town, the houses are more widely separated by the fields. The rural settlement pattern is one of dispersed, but not isolated, homesteads, rather evenly spaced over the countryside. Outside the town, within a radius of three miles, there are four tiny hamlets, each centered about a rural school and chapel. A heavily settled rural area, called Santo Toribio or La Campiña, is about a mile from town. Here the houses conform to an urban settlement model along four streets, one of which is cobbled. Two large primary schools (complete through the fifth grade), one for boys and one for girls, are the nuclei of the settlement (see Plates 1, 2, and 4).

A Synopsis of the Past

The name Huaylas[6] appears with tantalizing frequency in historical writings. Available accounts, nevertheless, provide only glimpses of the history of Huaylas. The pre-Columbian record is, with one exception, unsubstantiated by archaeological investigation.[7] The fragments of history which have been pieced together here raise more questions than they answer, pointing to the necessity of conducting a major research effort to resolve them.

Huaylas has long had an intimate and direct relationship with the Callejón de Huaylas. Huaylinos recount that their ancestors were a proud race that dominated the area prior to the arrival of the Incas, sometime between 1463 and 1471.[8] It is thought by some Huaylinos that Pachacutec may himself have played a role in this conquest,[9] an

---

[6] Also to be found written as Atun Huaylas, Hatun Huaylas, Atunguaylas, Gatunguaylas, Huaylas, Huailas, Guaylas, Guaiglia, Atun Huaylla, and in other variations. Today, the spelling, Huaylas and Huailas, are used interchangeably.

[7] Thompson, 1962.   [8] Mason, 1957:36–37.   [9] Martinez, 1961b:30–31.

event which Huaylinos say is commemorated in a stone carving depicting two snakes, one of which is biting the other.[10]

More obvious are some of the other stone sculptures. Two feline heads are mounted on either side of a doorway of one of the houses in town. In front of the library on the plaza are two more large Chavinoid stone sculptures which serve as benches.[11] Other, smaller pieces are embedded in various walls or adorn patios throughout the district. Numerous doorsteps appear to have been shaped by pre-Columbian hands.

Several impressive ruins are located in various parts of the district. Chupacoto is a three-hundred-yard-long temple mound which presently forms the northern boundary of the town (see Map 3). A large townsite, called Huantar, covers the long ridge that bisects the valley between the *barrios* of Shuyo and Huayrán and Iscap (see Map 2). The extensive ruin called Pueblo Viejo lies near the *barrio* of Tambo. Its complex system of terraces is crowned by what would appear to have been an Incan *tambo* or inn and some fortifications. The agricultural terraces are now unused. Other terraces, *chullpas*, or mausoleums, and ceremonial mounds cover a large area at a place called Parián in the *barrio* of Iscap. The abundant remains indicate that Huaylas has been densely populated since Chavín times at least, or 1000 B.C. They also hint that the population during pre-Columbian times was at least as great as if not greater than it is at present.[12]

The first Spaniards entered the Callejón de Huaylas on January 17, 1533, when Hernando Pizarro and Miguel Estete passed through the district of Huaylas, then known as Hurin Huaylas, lower Huaylas, on their way to Pachacamac, the great religious center on the coast near Lima. Estete left the following account of their passage through Huaylas.

The next day [January 17, 1533] before noon we arrived at a large town [Huaylas] that is in a valley with many cornfields between the mountains.

[10] The stone, which is about four feet square, has been embedded in the inside wall of an irrigation tank (called San Andrés, in the *barrio* of Yacup). Its position makes it difficult to observe but quite safe from theft.

[11] A brief description of these was published by Donald E. Thompson (1962:245–246). According to him, "They represent a style so far unreported from the Callejón. The closest stylistic similarities are to be found in the Chavín style and in the unique monoliths at Cerro Sechín temple in the Casma Valley."

[12] See Dobyns (1963) for a recent estimate of the size of the aboriginal population of Peru.

Halfway along the road there is a large and furious river [Santa river]; it has two bridges next to each other made of netting in the following manner: they raise a great foundation from the water to a good height and from one side of the river to the other are cables made of woven lianas as thick as a man's thigh and are anchored to great rocks. It is as wide as a cart from one side to the other and plaited cords cross it [forming the floor of the bridge]. . . . Over one of these bridges pass the common people and it has a gatekeeper who collects tolls; by the other bridge pass the gentlemen and the captains; it is always closed though they opened it so that the Captain H. Pizarro and his retinue and horses passed all right. In this town, called Guayllasmarca [Huaylas], they rested two days because the horses were tired from the difficult road and so that the people on foot and Indian porters could rest. We were well received by the chief and Indians of the town and were served meals and all that we needed; the chief is called Pumapaccha.

Saturday the twenty-first of the month, the captain left the town of Guayllasmarca and went to lunch at another town [Villa Sucre, Mato], governed by the former where they gave us all that was necessary. Later near this town he passed another net bridge made as the former and we slept two leagues from there at another town [Caraz] subject to Guayllasmarca.[13]

The following August, Francisco Pizarro and his company stayed a week in Huaylas before continuing on through the Callejón. At this time, Pedro Sancho reported that the Spaniards heard Mass and found good houses.[14] One imagines that the settlement to which they refer is the ruin called Huantar, mentioned above. Of particular note is the fact that Francisco Pizarro took as his mistress, Inés Yupanqui Huaylas (Inés Huaylas Ñusta), the teenage daughter of the Inca Huayna Capac and Contarguacho, daughter of the lord of Huaylas.[15]

[13] Quoted from Gridilla, 1933:192–194, with notes which are added to my translation. The translation by Sir Clements Markham published by the Hakluyt Society (Estete, 1872:77–78) was edited, omitting pertinent material.

[14] Sancho de la Hoz, 1917:135. The supposed site where this first Mass was said is located just north of the town at a place called Oratorio.

[15] The history of this union is both long and complex. Inés Yupanqui Huaylas left Pizarro after the birth of the children and married Francisco de Ampuero. He became mayor of Lima in 1574 and held other high posts in the colonial administration. The children were cared for by the Alcántara family. Gonzalo died while still very young, but Francisca went in 1551 to Spain, where she was to marry her uncle, Hernando Pizarro, who was imprisoned at the time. Further details of these events may be found in Porras Barrenchea, 1936:56–65; Martín-Pastor, 1938:8–14; Arciniega, 1941:330–360; Alba *et al.*, 1945:26–27; Martinez, 1961a:20; and Palma, 1953:32, 35–37.

Inés Yupanqui Huaylas bore Pizarro two children, Francisca and Gonzalo. In 1540, Pizarro gave the *repartimiento*[16] of Huaylas to the former. At this time, the *repartimiento* consisted of 3,000 Indians in Huaylas, plus 1,800 more in Conchucos. The *encomienda* of Huaylas included all of the present-day province of Huaylas and much of what are now the provinces of Yungay and Carhuaz—this corresponding to the territory formerly known as Hurin Huaylas—in addition to the area of Conchucos to the north. The tribute was to be delivered to the *encomendera*, Francisca Pizarro y Yupanqui, every four months.[17] Because Francisca was only six years old at the time, the management of the *encomienda* was entrusted at first to Contarguacho, her grandmother, who still resided in Huaylas.[18] The extent of her control over the operation, however, is not known. The *encomienda* passed into other hands, apparently sometime after 1550.

The textile mills, first reported to have been established about 1550, were still in operation in 1585. One of these was operated by Gerónimo de Guevara, the *encomendero* for much of the Callejón de Huaylas area. The other was in the hands of the Indian community.[19]

The present town of Huaylas was apparently founded by the Spanish after 1550, perhaps under the Viceroyalty of Toledo (1569–1581), who formalized the colonial regime in Peru and forced the Indians to live in new settlements called *reducciones*. The church had already been established by the time Archbishop Mogrovejo made his pastoral visits there in 1585 and 1593. The Archbishop reported on his first visit that Huaylas had a fine climate, a good city plan, and a good church.

---

[16] This term refers to the Indian labor provided under the *encomienda* system. The *encomienda*, a grant of rights to collect tribute, was designed to make the Indians subject to the King of Spain through their conversion to Catholicism, payment of tribute, and so on. Tribute was paid by the Indians through work in such activities as mining and in the textile mills (*obrajes*). The person to whom the *encomienda* was given was called the *encomendero*. Additional material on the operation of this and other colonial institutions can be found in Rowe, 1957:155–199; and Silva Santisteban, 1964.

[17] The tribute consisted of the following: 200 pairs of rope-soled sandals, 100 pairs of a different type of sandal, 60 (each) halters, bridles, cinches, and hobbles, 20 lassos, 20 cargo packs, rope, 20 large sacks (*costales*) made of maguey fiber, 6 horse blankets of maguey fiber, 15 woolen dresses, skirts, shawls, and blouses, 2 woolen cushions, 1 woolen mattress, 3 yards long and 2 yards wide, and, finally, 10 dresses made of finely spun wool (Porras Barrenchea, 1936:56–65; Gridilla, 1937:427–429).

[18] Porras Barrenchea, 1936:63–64.   [19] Gridilla, 1937:267–268.

He also noted that the district was divided into nine *estancias* (outlying settlements or populated areas), five belonging to the Indian community and four others pertaining to the *encomendero* Guevara and the *caciques* (chiefs) Diego Cachachi, Pedro Barba Vilcas, and Pedro Vilca Rupay. Mogrovejo's activities in the Parish of Santo Domingo de Huaylas were to baptize 1,513 persons during his first visit and 222 on his second visit.[20]

By this time, Huaylas had its own *cabildo* or council and was subject to the Corregimiento de Huaylas (the regional government), whose seat was in Huaraz.[21] In these newly established towns, the Indians were divided into upper and lower sectors, often representing the old *ayllu* groupings (consanguineal kin groups, sometimes identified with specific places).[22] The present-day *barrios* of Huaylas may have derived from the aboriginal *ayllus,* but there is no record of this. The history of Huaylas after this point is extremely sketchy and uncertain, aside from the fact that the entire area became part of the Intendencia of Tarma in 1784, when the Corregimientos were abolished.[23]

The written accounts of Huaylas during and after the War of Independence from Spain are, unfortunately, equally fragmentary in nature. Some amusing anecdotes involving Simon Bolivar's activities in Huaylas are recorded by Ricardo Palma and often retold by Huaylinos at the present time.[24] Bolivar, however, officially established the District of Huaylas in 1825 and this designation was reaffirmed in 1857.[25]

The development of the present social system and pattern of land tenure probably took place during this period of the eighteenth century. Ford has summarized the actions of San Martin and Bolivar with respect to this in the following manner.

While the War of Emancipation was yet in progress, San Martin in his role as Protector of the Liberty of Peru issued several decrees in August of 1821, proclaiming the Indians to be full citizens of the new Republic. The

[20] Gridilla, 1937:365. The first baptismal records that I found in the church bore the date 1604. I did not have sufficient opportunity, however, to conduct a thorough search for other such materials which were said to have been taken to Caraz, Huaraz, and Lima.

[21] Vargas Ugarte, 1949:186–191.   [22] Varallanos, 1959:187, 203.

[23] Varallanos, 1959:180–181.

[24] Palma, 1953:1009, 1012–1015. Huaylinos say that Bolivar stayed a week in Huaylas, resting in the fine climate. The house where he is said to have stayed is pointed out to visitors.

[25] Stiglich, 1923:191–192.

decrees specifically abolished personal tribute and involuntary servitude of the autochthonous group. With Bolivar's rise to dictatorship of the country in 1823, several more decrees were issued with the intention of converting the Indians into small landowners and of abolishing the system of *reducciones.* The first of these decrees, published in April of 1824, ordered that all state lands with the exception of those occupied by the Indian population be offered for sale. The lands of the *reducciones* were to be distributed among the inhabitants, who were entitled to full ownership of their apportionments. Preference was to be given to those who were already located on the sites, but it was specified that no Indian should remain without a share of land. Bolivar's intent, in keeping with the new liberal thought of the period, was to establish a democratic nation of small, independent farmers.[26]

For the most part, the governmental machinery was ineffectual in carrying out this policy, and through much of the country the Indians lost their land to greedy officials, local *caciques,* and others who exercised power. A succession of *caudillos* (bosses) presided over the chaotic first decades of the Republic as a "large and rapid concentration of land in the hands of a few owners" took place.[27]

What happened in Huaylas is, again, unreported. Nevertheless, the description of the district made by Raimondi, based on his visits there in 1860 and 1868, leaves the strong impression that the land was, as Bolivar had intended, a community of small farmers.

Huaylas enjoys a certain fame because of its countryside, and actually the nickname *cosecha* (harvest) is applied to them. Slightly inclined, the land throughout its entire extension is covered with green plantings and bounded by a shelter of mountains, which rise like an amphitheater to form the beautiful Huaylas countryside. Innumerable little houses are found scattered among the fields and an infinity of narrow paths cross the cheerful fields in all directions, forming a real labyrinth where they turn, confusing everyone who is not of the place. . . .

Scarce streams which come down from the nearby hills serve for irrigation: but the quantity of water which they bring is not sufficient for all the country in the time of the year when it doesn't rain; they collect the water from all the springs in small reservoirs and distribute it with equity and economy measured by what is needed. . . .[28]

This description could just as well have been made in 1967 as it was a hundred years ago. There are no large estates in the district at the present time and Huaylinos deny the existence of any in times past.

[26] Ford, 1955:43.   [27] Kubler, 1952:1.   [28] Raimondi, 1873:104–106.

During the last two decades of the nineteenth century Huaylas was witness and victim of armed conflict. In 1883 the district found itself host to a battalion of soldiers under General Andrés Cáceres, seeking to escape the Chilean armies during the fateful War of the Pacific.[29] After this incursion came the Indian rebellion led by Pedro Pablo Atusparia. This uprising of the Indian masses began in Huaraz in 1885 and spread down the Callejón, the Indians capturing most of the towns. A force of Indians lead by Pedro Cochachín took Huaylas and remained there until driven out by a vigilante group from Caraz. The vigilantes, called the Azules (Blues), did considerably more damage than the invading Indians, sacking and burning many houses. Several Huaylinos died at their hands as well.[30]

The only lasting effect of these armed intrusions, however, was the destruction of the municipal archives. The keeping of systematic records was not resumed until 1889, from which point pertinent historical data will be summarized in the ensuing chapters.

[29] Basadre, 1946:200–201.　　[30] Garcia-Cuellar, 1945:156.

CHAPTER II

The Population of Huaylas

Population Dynamics

One of the major results of the Spanish conquest was the formation of a new, complex, racial and social milieu.[1] Another consequence was that the Peruvian population was ravaged, during the colonial period, by exposure to contagious diseases formerly unknown in the Americas: the common cold, smallpox, bubonic plague, typhus, measles, and various others.[2] Because of their early and continued contact with the Spaniards, it can be assumed that the people of Huaylas did not escape these afflictions.

Estimates of the size of the early historic population of Huaylas are difficult to make because the territory to which the name Huaylas is applied is not clear, as previously indicated. There are some census materials available, however, dating from the early years of the Republican period, which, although they cannot be considered precise, serve to give some idea of the growth of the population since the end of the colonial period. According to Kubler, the population of Peru reached its lowest point at that time and has since increased continuously.[3]

Table 1 illustrates this growth from 1836 to 1961. It is evident that the population increase in Huaylas has not kept pace with that of the rest of the country. Since 1940, the Huaylas population has increased

---

[1] Belaunde, 1957:48–90.   [2] Dobyns, 1963:493–515.   [3] Kubler, 1952:34.

by only 116 persons, and since 1876, by only 522 persons. This numerical stability, in sharp contrast to the population of the rest of the country, can be readily noted in the percentage of population increase from 1836, as shown in Table 1.

Table 1. Comparative population growth: District of Huaylas, Department of Ancash, and Republic of Peru, 1836–1961

	1836 *	1876 †	1940 ‡	1961 §	Per cent increase 1836–1961
District of Huaylas	3,322	4,873	5,379	5,495	65
Department of Ancash	121,462	284,091	424,975	582,598	379
Republic of Peru	1,373,736	2,699,945	6,207,967	9,906,746	621

* Kubler, 1952.

† Perú, Ministerio de Gobierno, 1878.

‡ Perú, Ministerio de Hacienda y Comercio, 1944.

§ All census data for the District of Huaylas, 1961, unless otherwise noted, are taken from my census of Huaylas, January-February of 1961. The Peruvian national census was taken in July of 1961 (Perú, Instituto Nacional de Planificación, 1964) and the following results were reported for Huaylas:

> Male   (urban),   586, and (rural), 2,130 = 2,716
> Female (urban),   672, and (rural), 2,432 = 3,104
> Total   (urban), 1,258, and (rural), 4,562 = 5,820

The national census results for the District of Huaylas are not utilized here for two reasons. First, the results at the district level have not been fully published as yet. Second, the national census was conducted at the time when the Fiesta of St. Elizabeth was taking place in Huaylas (see Chapter X). Several hundred Huaylinos customarily return to Huaylas from the coast for this occasion, thus inflating the population temporarily. Despite the fact that the national census was carefully administered in Huaylas, for purposes of this work, these figures will not be utilized unless necessary. The results obtained by the national census for areas outside the district of Huaylas have been incorporated for comparative purposes.

The birth and death rates in Huaylas have dropped since 1949 (Table 2 and Figure 1). The extremely high death rate has been more than halved during the past twenty years, thus creating the typical picture of a population explosion, despite the lowering of the birth rate.

The decrease in the number of deaths, as illustrated in Figure 1, is coincident with the increased activity of the Corporación Peruana del Santa which had initiated the construction of a hydroelectric plant in Huallanca in 1943. By 1946 the company offered medical services to its workers and their dependents. This was the first time that modern medical services were available, on a permanent basis, within the district. In addition, the company undertook campaigns to eradicate malaria and *verruga* [4] from the province of Huaylas. Streets, houses,

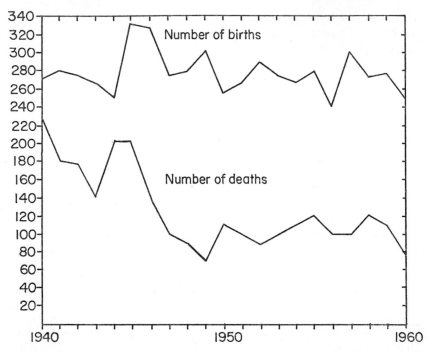

Figure 1. Number of births and deaths in the District of Huaylas from 1940 to 1960 (based on the Dataria Civil, Distrito de Huaylas, for 1940–1960)

stream beds, refuse heaps, and other breeding places of insect vectors were thoroughly sprayed with insecticides, with the result that flies, mosquitos, gnats, and other insect pests were all but eliminated for several years. This process was repeated again some years later.

The leading causes of death as recorded in the municipal registry of vital statistics (Dataria Civil) were respiratory ailments such as colds (142 in 1940) and infectious diseases such as measles and whooping

[4] Bartonellosis, also known as Carrion's disease, *verruga* is a crippling disease and is sometimes fatal. Some of its symptoms are similar to those of malaria. The disease is confined largely to the Santa and Rimac (Lima) river valleys. Transmitted by a minute variety of mosquito, it may be regulated through spraying and control of breeding places and habitat.

cough. Also recorded as causes of death were post partum accidents, stomach-aches, fevers, dysentery, paralysis, liver and kidney problems, "weakness," heart attacks and fright (*susto*)—there were two cases in 1959. The incidence of all causes of death, of course, varies from year to year for natural reasons. It also varies according to the sophistication of the person reporting the death and the attitude of the recording secretary. Thus, what may appear as "fevers" in one year, in other years might well be recorded as grippe. Unless they succumb at the hospitals in Huallanca, Caraz, or Yungay, Huaylinos are not attended at

Table 2. Birth and death rates per 1,000 persons in the District of Huaylas, 1940–1960 *

	1940		1960	
	Number	Rate †	Number	Rate †
Births	272	50.5	242	43.8
Deaths	222	41.2	76	13.8

* Figures taken from *Dataria Civil*, Distrito de Huaylas, 1940 and 1960.

† Birth and death rates computed as follows.

$$\text{Rate} = \frac{\text{no. of births (or deaths)}}{\text{total population}} \times 1,000$$

the time of death by physicians or other trained medical personnel. Hence, the actual cause of death may bear little relation to what is recorded.

There is a strong undercurrent of distrust connected with the hospitals in the region. Many people, particularly those with little experience outside Huaylas, resist delivering themselves into the care of strangers whose methods are not well understood. Because of this, many delay seeking hospital care until their illness is advanced, by then too late to be cured by the meager resources of the doctors or hospitals. Thus hospitals tend to be associated with death rather than with physical salvation and many people prefer to exhaust the capabilities of local talent before venturing outside the district for assistance.

There are a number of persons, both male and female, who practice what is called "empirical medicine." These people, who are called *curiosos* or *curanderos* (both male and female), utilize a varied and somewhat exotic assortment of folk and scientific medicinal techniques and remedies. A variety of herbal compounds is commonly used and sold in the stores.[5]

The most common types of remedies administered either at home or by a *curioso* include the following: teas brewed from a number of local and imported plants, massages such as *ron de culebra* (alcohol in which a snake has been preserved) and Vicks Vaporub, headache and cold remedies such as aspirin, and, especially, injections. The latter seem to be the preferred, almost magical, technique for curing all ills. Indeed, if the same medicine is offered in both oral and injection form, the latter will invariably be selected. Because a great many persons (in addition to the *curiosos*) give them for a small fee, and because the sanitary precautions taken are primitive at best, injections are a likely source of contagion.[6]

The *cuy* (guinea pig) is frequently used by experts in such matters to diagnose an unexplainable illness or malady. The live *cuy* (a male animal for men, female for women) is first rubbed over the body of the sufferer by the *curioso* and then killed. An "autopsy" is then performed on the animal to see which part of its body is diseased. The results of this exercise indicate which part of the patient's body is ailing and requires attention.[7] Some Huaylinos referred to this as the "guinea pig X-ray."

Several women have the specialty of midwife (called *partera* or *comadrona*). Children are customarily delivered at home with a midwife and members of the family assisting as necessary. Few children are born in the regional hospitals, although a growing number of upper- and middle-class women would prefer this.

A small, poorly equipped first-aid station (Botiquín Popular) is maintained in town by the national government and dispenses, at cost, a small assortment of medicines. The two employees are equipped to give only minimal assistance to ailing persons or accident victims. Serious

[5] Most herbal remedies come from the forested eastern slopes of the Andes, the *montaña*, or from the Amazon jungles. Such supplies are commonly sold in the market places of the Callejón de Huaylas and are distributed by itinerant vendors who specialize in this business. During the Fiesta of St. Elizabeth (Chapter X), several vendors from Huánuco and Pasco Departments sell these items in quantity.

[6] Syringe kits and extra needles are available in the stores, as is a variety of medicines in injection form.

[7] This practice is common throughout the Callejón and Andean area generally. For further discussion of this, see Chadbourn, 1962; Stein, 1961:86; and Andrews, 1963:372.

treatment necessitates a trip to one of the regional hospitals, the closest being a difficult one-hour drive away at Huallanca. During 1960 and 1961 a drugstore was operated by a Huaylino who had worked as a pharmacist in Lima. He quickly became the "doctor" of the district, only to leave in 1962 to return to Lima. The lack of immediate medical facilities is keenly felt in Huaylas among all sectors of the population, and there has been interest expressed in establishing a clinic in the district.

Table 3. Infant mortality rate per 1,000 live births in the District of Huaylas, 1940–1959 *

Year	Infant mortality rate †
1940	435
1945	365
1950	205
1959	179

* Figures taken from *Dataria Civil*, Distrito de Huaylas, for 1940–1959.

† The infant mortality rate is calculated as follows.

$$\text{Rate} = \frac{\text{no. of deaths of infants less than 1 year old}}{\text{no. of live births}} \times 1{,}000$$

The relatively high crude death rate of 13.8 per 1,000 is the result of these circumstances. This represents, nevertheless, a sizable decline from the 1940 figure (Table 2). By the same token, the infancy mortality rate of 179, which is very high, again marks a vast improvement over the 1940 figure (Table 3). The decrease in the number of deaths in the district is dramatically reflected in Figure 1. The lines of the graph clearly show the response to the relatively simple public health measures taken by the Corporación Peruana del Santa and the increasing, if still somewhat hesitant, use of modern medical facilities.

The crude birth rate (Table 2) for the district, as in the case above, shows a decline from the 1940 figure of 50.5 births per 1,000 persons, which was extremely high. The decline in birth rate cannot be attributed to any widespread use of modern contraceptive devices, however, because knowledge of such techniques was limited to a handful of persons in the district at the time of study. A number of native contraceptive techniques employing herbs were known and sometimes utilized by women. For most persons, however, pregnancy could be avoided only by foregoing sexual relations. It should be noted, nevertheless, that relatively little resistance to the idea of contraception was discovered. The present birth rate of 43.8 falls well within the pattern for Latin American countries, although it still must be considered high.

The fertility ratio of 430 (Table 4) is not particularly remarkable. At the time of the census there were 1,290 women in the district over

Table 4. Fertility ratio for women fifteen to forty-four years of age in the District of Huaylas, 1961

	1961
Number of women, 15–44 years of age	1,864
Number of children under 5 years of age	803
Fertility Ratio *	430

* The fertility ratio is computed as follows.
$$\text{Ratio} = \frac{\text{no. of children 0–4 years of age}}{\text{no. of women 15–44 years of age}} \times 1{,}000$$

fifteen years of age who had borne children. The 631 women over forty-five years of age had had an average of 5.9 live births. Of this group, 14.5 per cent of the women had "given light" (*dar a luz*, to give birth) to nine or more children. A number of women in the rural areas, particularly those who have had the least amount of outside contact, say that it is woman's duty to bear a dozen children—"in order to finish the task" (*para cumplir la tarea*)—one for each of Christ's apostles.

Be this as it may, it appears that being married in the church is a sign of greater marital permanence. Such unions tend to produce more offspring. Table 5 demonstrates this point rather well. Of the four types of marital arrangements, persons mated in consensual unions have fewer children than the others. This is largely due to the greater insecurity of the marital situation and the lesser degree of permanence. Persons who are not formally married often enter into two or three such relationships before they finally marry, if they marry at all. Despite the tendency to have numerous progeny, the "task" does not usually begin until after the twentieth year. Only eighteen out of 232 women in the fifteen- to nineteen-year age group had borne children.

Table 5. Marital status and number of live births for women over fifteen years of age, District of Huaylas, 1961

	Totals	Civil wed- ding	Church wed- ding	Civil and church wedding	Con- sensual union	Sepa- ration from spouse	Single	Widow *
Number of women bearing children	1,290	65	114	467	218	70	158	198
Number of chil- dren born	6,498	316	720	2,699	895	281	468	1,118
Average number of children	5.0	4.8	6.3	5.7	4.1	4.1	2.9	5.6

* Twenty-two widows are under 45 years of age.

The graph in Figure 1 combines the number of births and deaths, giving the profile of the increase in the population, despite the lowered birth rate. With this picture in mind, one anticipates a spectacular overall increase in the size of the Huaylas population. The natural increase in the population between 1940 and 1961 amounted to 3,187 persons (Table 6). The fact that this increase is not reflected in the 1961 population of Huaylas is testimony to the great geographic mobility of Huaylinos. Huaylas has exported the results of its population "explosion," principally to Lima and Chimbote on the coast. At the moment, there is nothing to indicate that this firmly established pattern will be altered in the near future.

Table 6. Natural increase in the population and population loss in the District of Huaylas, 1940–1961

Population, 1961 *	5,495
Population, 1940 *	−5,379
Net increase	116
Total births, 1940–1960 †	5,769
Total deaths, 1940–1960 †	−2,582
Natural increase	3,187
Population, 1940	5,379
Natural increase	+3,187
Projected population 1961	8,566
Population, 1961	−5,495
Population loss, 1940–1961	3,071

* Perú, Ministerio de Hacienda y Comercio, 1944.
† Figures taken from *Dataria Civil*, Distrito de Huaylas, 1940–1960.

Distribution of the Population

As a direct result of the emigration of Huaylinos from the district, the population pyramid (Figure 2) portrays a great imbalance. The population is almost halved after the age of fifteen years, the time when most children finish primary school. The relation of formal education

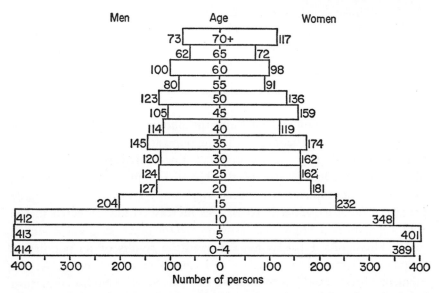

Figure 2. Population distribution by age and sex in 1961 for the District of Huaylas

to the emigration is, as will be seen in Chapter IX, an extremely important one. The high infant mortality rate eliminates whatever numerical superiority that might otherwise be shown in the zero-to-four-year-old age group.

The large number of children, 43 per cent of the total population, when combined with that portion which is sixty-five years of age and over, means that exactly half of the population of Huaylas falls into a category that is usually classified as dependent.[8] Based on Table 7, a dependency ratio of 96.6 dependents per 100 persons of "working age" is obtained for Huaylas.[9] This figure contrasts markedly with that for

[8] Barclay, 1958:266–268.   [9] Computed as follows:

$$\text{Dependency ratio} = \frac{\text{population } 0-14 + 65 \text{ and over}}{\text{population } 15-64} \times 100$$

Table 7. Number, sex ratio,* and percentage of the population according to major age groups, 1961

Age group	Number of men	Number of women	Sex Ratio	Number of men and women	Per cent of total population at each age level
0–14	1,238	1,138	108	2,376	43
15–64	1,250	1,545	80	2,795	50
Over 65	135	189	71	324	7

* The sex ratio is computed as follows.

$$\text{Ratio} = \frac{\text{no. of men}}{\text{no. of women}} \times 100.$$

the community of Vicos, which, in 1963, had 83.1 dependents per 100 persons of "working age." [10] The difference is accounted for in the migration patterns of the two places. In Vicos there is little emigration, whereas in Huaylas the opposite is true.[11] The degree to which those classified as dependents actually fulfill this statistical role is, of course, relative. Children and older persons are expected to work according to their capacity to do so in both Vicos and Huaylas.

The composition of the population by sex (Tables 7 and 10) again illustrates the role of emigration in the demographic process. The more frequent departure of men than women from the highland towns and hamlets is strikingly shown in Table 8, particularly for 1940, when

Table 8. Comparative sex ratios,* 1940 † and 1961 ‡

Year	District of Huaylas	District of Caraz	Province of Santa	Dept. of Ancash	Province of Lima	Perú
1940	82.9	81.0	125.0	86.0	104.0	97.0
1961	91.3	89.8	110.5	93.2	99.0	98.0

* The sex ratio is computed as follows.

$$\text{Ratio} = \frac{\text{no. of men}}{\text{no. of women}} \times 100$$

† Derived from Perú, Ministerio de Hacienda y Comercio, 1944, Vol. III.
‡ Derived from Perú, Instituto de Planificación, 1964.

there were only 82.9 men for every 100 women in the district. The destinations of these migrants at that time were the coastal plantations

[10] Alers, 1965. [11] Vázquez, 1963:93–102; Doughty, 1963:111–127.

Map 3. Town of Huaylas

of the Province of Santa and the city of Lima. The greater balance shown by the sex ratio in Huaylas in 1961 (91.3 men per 100 women) is due to the increased emigration of women rather than to a cessation of male participation in this process. The augmented female emigration from Huaylas is a significant measure of the reduction of the hiatus between male and female integration into the national economy and life.

Further detail with respect to the sex ratios can be seen in Table 7. The asymmetrical nature of the population is particularly noticeable between the ages of fifteen and sixty-four, which give a sex ratio of 80 men per 100 women. The significance of this is manifold. It means that marriage and family relations are probably interrupted by the absence of the husband. It also implies that many women are probably more actively engaged in providing support for the large "dependent" population than might otherwise be the case.

The definition of an urban population that is used here follows the Peruvian census classification.[12] The capital of each district, province, and department is automatically considered as urban, whatever its size. Other places, to be considered as urban, must present the appearance of an urban settlement (have streets, contiguous houses, public facilities) and have a population which is at least equal to that of the district capital.

This definition of urban is, of course, one which raises many questions. A review of the 1961 national census report, for example, reveals that there are 1,265 "urban" centers that have populations under 5,000 and whose average size is approximately 950 inhabitants.[13] Included in this group are many district capitals with populations of under 150 inhabitants.

In Huaylas there is clearly only one urban center under the census definition, although there are two other hamlets (Shuyo and Santo Toribio) whose physical characteristics might entitle them to be called urban. Their populations are, in each case, less than 150 persons. The town of Huaylas has a population of 1,156, representing approximately 21 per cent of the district population. The rest of the population is

[12] Perú, Instituto de Planificación, 1964:305.
[13] Perú, Instituto de Planificación, 1964:3–97. There were only 100 urban centers in Peru with populations exceeding 5,000 persons, but they accounted for 3,504,659 persons. There were 105 centers whose size ranged between 2,500 and 4,999 inhabitants; 1,193,519 persons were living in urban centers under 5,000 in size.

reported as rural (Table 9). In comparison with the figures given for
the 1876 census, the global picture has not changed very much, with
the exception that the rural sector of the population has increased
somewhat. The town has remained virtually the same size, declining by
226 over the span of years.

Table 9. Population of the District of Huaylas according to urban and rural residence
and *barrio* in 1876, 1940, and 1961

	1876 * Total	Percent- age of total	1940 † total	Percent- age of total	1961 total	Percent- age of total
Huaylas	4,973	100.0	5,379	100.0	5,495	100.0
Urban	1,382	27.8	1,246	22.0	1,156	21.0
Rural	3,591	72.2	4,368	78.0	4,339	79.0
Barrios						
Delicados ‡	1,382	28.4	1,229	22.0	736	13.4
Yacup ‡	415	8.3	441	8.0	876	16.0
Shuyu	895	17.6	695	11.0	671	12.2
Quecuas	972	19.5	892	16.0	889	16.2
Huayrán	941	18.9	977	17.0	924	16.8
Iscap	65	1.3	587	10.0	551	10.1
Tambo	204	4.1	557	10.0	363	6.7
San Lorenzo			236	4.0	236	4.3
Huaromapuquio					218	3.9
Others	99	1.9			34	.4

* Perú, Ministerio de Gobierno, 1878.

† Perú, Ministerio de Hacienda y Comercio, 1944, Vol. III.

‡ The change in population in 1961 is due to a reclassification of *barrio* limits. In
previous censuses, the whole town was included in the *barrio* of Delicados, whereas half
of the population belonged to the *barrio* of Yacup. Thus, in 1961 the *barrio* of Yacup is
credited with that portion of the urban population formerly assigned to Delicados.

In addition to the urban and rural sectors of the population, there is
the division of the district into nine geopolitical units, called *barrios*.
Most of the *barrio* of Delicados and approximately half of the *barrio* of
Yacup make up the town of Huaylas (see Map 3). The other *barrios*
are entirely rural in classification. The population development within
the district has apparently involved a steady growth of the rural
sectors, with people moving out from the established areas to form new
centers of population (Table 9). This pattern is demonstrated by the
growth of fringe areas in the district such as Iscap, Tambo, and San
Lorenzo between 1876 and 1940 and of Huaromapuquio between 1940

and 1961. Consequently, the district population is more evenly distributed over the territory than was previously the case.

The distribution of the population by sex in the *barrios* is irregular (Table 10), for various factors have been involved. While all regions

Table 10. Sex ratio of the population of the District of Huaylas according to urban and rural residence and *barrio* in 1876 and 1961 *

Area	1876 †			1961		
	Men	Women	Sex ratio	Men	Women	Sex ratio
Huaylas	2,384	2,589	92.0	2,623	2,872	91.3
Urban	642	740	86.7	657	752	87.3
Rural	1,742	1,849	94.0	1,966	2,120	92.7
Barrios						
Delicados	642	740	86.7	348	388	89.6
Yacup	190	225	84.4	402	474	84.8
Shuyu	430	465	92.4	317	354	89.5
Quecuas	485	487	99.0	417	472	88.3
Huayrán	445	496	89.7	435	489	88.9
Iscap	32	33	99.0	261	290	90.0
Tambo	107	97	110.3	189	174	108.6
San Lorenzo				116	120	96.6
Huaromapuquio				121	97	124.7
Others	53	46	115.2	15	12	125.0

* Unfortunately, the 1940 census does not furnish the data for analysis below the district level. Figures derived from Perú, Ministerio de Hacienda y Comercio, 1944, Vol. III, indicate that the ratio of men to women in 1940 was 82.9. The sex ratio is computed as follows.

$$\text{Ratio} = \frac{\text{no. of men}}{\text{no. of women}} \times 100.$$

† Perú, Ministerio de Gobierno, 1878.

have been affected by emigration, the *barrios* which are more thoroughly rural in character and which are farthest from the town, show a more balanced proportion of men to women. These are the *barrios* of Tambo, San Lorenzo, and Huaromapuquio. In each case the population shows a greater incidence of what can be called Indian characteristics, such as more monolingual Quechua speakers, lower literacy rate, and greater residential isolation. None of these *barrios*, for example, can be reached by an automobile, whereas this is possible in the others.

Although maintaining a high sex ratio (108.6), the *barrio* of Tambo has experienced a rather heavy emigration between 1940 and 1961—the Tambinos have formed a club in Lima called the Centro Social Tambo. The existence of two schools in Tambo (one each for boys and girls) has provided greater educational opportunities there, as compared to San Lorenzo and Huaromapuquio. This may explain why relatively equal numbers of men and women have emigrated from the *barrio*.

The migratory pattern as interpreted from Table 10 indicates that the district has been exporting important segments of its population at least since 1876. At that time, the principal impact was on the urban male sector (*barrio* of Delicados and in the *barrio* of Yacup). This pattern was apparently extended through much of the population by 1940 and has since come into greater balance with the participation of more women in the process.

Family and Household

Most of the households are comprised of the nuclear family, although many also include other relatives, particularly recently married sons or daughters, with their spouses and children, who do not yet have their own houses. This is the situation in 95 of the 1,195 households that were included in my 1961 census. In such cases, when either parent of a couple is in good health and able to work, he or she is considered the head of the household. In sixty-three cases, the household group included affinal relatives, usually the widowed mother of either the man or his wife. Aside from these, however, very few other relatives are to be found in Huaylas households. They rarely include collateral kin or godchildren, and no household was reported to include a *compadre* or *comadre* [14] of the head of the house.

Thirty-seven servants were reported as living within the households in which they were employed. In general, servants do not take full part in the activities of the family, except as employees. The majority of the families employing servants on this basis are of upper-class status.

Although the residence pattern is clearly neolocal, the nuclear family is large, and a man and his wife usually maintain their residence close to the home of some relative, most commonly a parent. As can be seen in Table 11, more than half of the population live in households containing six or more persons (51.7 per cent). Less than 2 per cent of the people live alone.

[14] Godsibs, male and female respectively. The *compadrazgo* system will be discussed below.

Of those residing in Huaylas, there are relatively few who are married to non-Huaylinos, but among the emigrants this pattern varies. Moreover, there is a strong tendency toward *barrio* and town endogamy, although marriages of persons of adjacent *barrios* are not unusual.

The marital status of the adult population is shown in Tables 12 and 13. It is evident that most couples who are married prefer to have both civil and religious ceremonies. The greater percentage of church wed-

Table 11. Size of households in the District of Huaylas, 1961

Number of members in household	Number of households censused	Percentage of households censused	Percentage of the population represented by each size household ($N = 5,495$)
1	97	8	1.7
2	149	13	5.4
3	188	15	10.6
4	184	14	13.5
5	186	15	17.1
6	151	13	16.6
7	113	9	14.5
8	58	4	8.5
9	29	2	4.8
10 or more	40	3	7.3
Total	1,195	100	100.0

dings among those who have only one ceremony indicates that being married by the church is considered more important than the civil wedding, although only the latter is held legal in Peru.

A greater percentage of couples living with parents than couples living independently are not formally married (that is, are living in consensual unions). Rural-urban differences are highlighted by the higher rate of consensual unions. Twenty-one per cent of the couples in rural areas, as contrasted with 10 per cent of those in town, live in consensual union.

Although couples begin living together at about twenty years of age, there is no haste to marry, since marriage would bind them to formal family responsibilities. A wait-and-see attitude often prevails. The woman particularly wishes to evaluate the qualities of the man and his

Table 12. Marital status of those over twenty years of age in urban and rural populations of the District of Huaylas, 1961 *

	Percentage of male population			Percentage of female population		
	Urban (N = 293)	Rural (N = 860)	Total (N = 1,173)	Urban (N = 382)	Rural (N = 1089)	Total (N = 1,471)
Marital Status †						
Civil wedding	8	5	6	8	4	5
Church wedding	8	11	10	6	9	8
Both civil and church wedding	45	42	42	31	33	32
Consensual union	10	21	19	8	15	15
Separated from spouse	6	1	2	7	3	3
Single	16	14	15	28	21	22
Widowed	7	6	6	12	15	15

* The population *under* twenty years of age included: men—one civil and religious wedding, one in consensual union; women—one civil wedding, nine consensual unions, six civil and religious weddings.

† Two men and one woman said they were divorced.

sense of economic responsibility in supporting her (and "her" children) satisfactorily. Young men, too, are reluctant to commit themselves to a permanent marital arrangement, and this fact helps to explain why, irrespective of social class, there are many women with children but no spouses. The common complaint of these women is that their husbands have deserted them. Because of the reluctance to "be tied

Table 13. Number and percentage of couples living together in independent households and living as dependent members of a household according to marital status in the District of Huaylas, 1961

	Couples living		Couples living as dependents in the household	
Marital status	No. of couples	Per cent	No. of couples	Per cent
Civil wedding	58	7.3	8	8.4
Church wedding	112	14.0	6	6.3
Both civil and church wedding	446	56.0	46	48.5
Consensual union	181	22.7	35	36.8
Total	797	100.0	95	100.0

down," most persons defer marriage (whether they are living in a stable union or not) until they have attained more mature years. According to many women, they wish to see if the men are "serious," that is, if the men are willing and able to support them for a lifetime.

When this stage is reached, however, the couple usually weds both legally and in the church in order to make the relationship doubly binding. It is relatively common, particularly among the middle and lower classes, for those not married in both ceremonies to separate and feel free to marry again by the other ceremony at some other place. In this highly mobile society it is not surprising, therefore, to find that the marriage ceremony, whether civil or religious, usually occurs at a late age. According to the records in the Dataria Civil, the average age at marriage is over thirty years for men and over twenty-eight years for women.

Considering the Huaylas population as a whole, the uneven sex ratio is not favorable for women who may wish to marry and remain in Huaylas. The factor which interrupts "normal" marital relations in Huaylas to a great extent is the heavy emigration and seasonal travel to the coast. At the time of our census, eleven men and twenty-eight women were temporarily separated from their spouses for this reason, and fifteen men and thirty-three women said that they were permanently separated. All but five of the separated women had children. The need to migrate for economic, educational, or medical reasons is one which is accepted by Huaylinos in a matter-of-fact way, for it is considered inevitable if one has any social or economic ambitions. In Huaylas the desire to "get ahead" (*superarse*) is frequently expressed. The great majority of Huaylinos have resided outside of the district for some period of time, and many, particularly in the middle and lower classes, work outside Huaylas for a few months annually in order to earn money for their families.[15]

All children born to couples who are not married in the civil ceremony are recorded in the register of vital statistics as *hijos naturales* (natural children), while those born to parents who are legally married (that is, married in the civil ceremony by the district mayor) are registered as legitimate children. The records of the Dataria Civil of

---

[15] Middendorf (1895:56–57) reported that this was a common pattern in Huaylas in 1886. He said that many Huaylinos worked in the Lima hotels, saving their money to take back to their families or to spend at the big July fiesta, which he erroneously identified as the Fiesta of the Patronness of Huaylas.

Huaylas reveal that the majority of births are registered as being "natural." The proportion of "natural" births between 1910 and 1950 ranges between 61 and 79 per cent for any given year. Since 1950, however, this high rate has steadily declined, and, in 1960, 52 per cent of the births were classified as "natural" and 48 per cent as legitimate. This change may be related to the increased prosperity in the district brought about by the construction of the hydroelectric plant in Huallanca.

Approximately 20 per cent of the "natural" children are later legitimatized when the parents marry in the civil ceremony at the municipal office, an event that often takes place thirty or more years after the children are born. It should be noted that until recently only legitimate or legitimatized children could legally qualify as heirs. Thus, in this district of small property owners, the pressure upon many parents to marry was probably considerable if disputes of land rights were in the offing. The fact is that the majority of persons who marry legally do so at about thirty years of age, just past the period of greatest fertility. Thus most children are born as "natural" children. This pattern of late marriage and high rate of "natural" children holds for all sectors of the society.

Further distinction should be made with respect to the "natural" children. Prior to 1933 the children of persons married in either civil or religious ceremonies were considered legitimate before the law. After this time, only the civil ceremony performed in the municipal office was classified as legal. In the sociological sense, children of persons married only in the religious ceremony would not be regarded as the products of casual liaisons, that is, "natural" or illegitimate.

The same reasoning would also apply to the case of "natural" children born to parents who are living in a stable conjugal relationship but who are not married in any formal manner. The children of consensual unions (*convivientes*) are also classified as "natural" children. Finally, the category of "natural" children includes the progeny of casual relationships. These are sometimes registered in the Dataria Civil as "spurious" (*espúrio*) children and are referred to in conversation by this term or as "children in the street" (*hijos en la calle*). Less than one per cent of the births, however, were so registered.

This does not mean that such "spurious" children are necessarily neglected or considered outcasts, although this is sometimes the case. "Spurious" children are often treated in the same manner as the others

1   The highland setting. The town of Huaylas nestles in the eucalyptus-covered valley.
The Callejón de Huaylas and the Cordillera Blanca are in the background.

2 The town of Huaylas and La Campiña

3 The *barrios* of Quecuas and Huayrán and the hamlet of Santo Toribio

4   Jirón Guia in the town of Huaylas

5   Don Carmen Espinosa plowing a small plot with his bullocks

6 Doña Juliana Conde Boca spinning wool

7 A man of many skills, Don Julio Corpus preparing the warp for a blanket

8   Don Felipe Espinosa and Doña Marina Boca de Espinosa watching a fiesta

9   Fresh bread from the oven of Inés Cano

10 The women of the Cotos family visiting in the kitchen

11 The changing generations: Helí Acosta and his grandfather, Don Gregorio Acosta

12 *Chicha* for the workers

13 Mayor Villegas conducting a public meeting in the municipal office

14 The *repúblicanos*. To the sound of the *roncadora*, a trail is opened to the electrical transformer station above the town.

15 Schoolboys at Mass on Flag Day

16   The baptism of Isabel Julia Ardiles Moreno

17   A *copita* of pisco to keep away the evening's chill in the store of Don Ricardo Espinosa

18 The baptismal party—parents and godparents

19 Don Jacinto Paulino sings a *huayno*, "The airplane that passed, went flying . . ."

20 Members of Don Florencio Lara's house-roofing bee in Santo Toribio working to the sound of the *roncadora* and the taste of *chicha*, passed around by his wife

21 The Morales brothers. In the church, they wait to strike a tune. Behind them is the altar of Saint Elizabeth.

22 Don Marino Liñan carrying his bullwhip, heading the *pashas* from Delicados *barrio* in 1960

23 Doña Bernadina Milla de Llamoca (center), home on vacation from Lima, dancing with the band during the fiesta of Saint Elizabeth

in the family. In some cases, a father may refuse to recognize such a child, thus denying any responsibility for its well-being, but this is generally frowned on as irresponsible. It is commonly felt that a man should acknowledge and accept the responsibility for all of his children. If the father is of the upper class and the mother of the lower or middle class, although supported financially by the father, the child may or may not enjoy the same privileges accorded his other children. This is, of course, at the discretion of the father.

Relationships of a casual or temporary nature are common at all levels of Huaylas society. Perhaps because of this, there is little stigma attached to them, although they may cause considerable strain upon the families involved. It was the consensus that most men in Huaylas indulged in premarital and extramarital relationships at one time or another, and that most men had had "spurious" children.

CHAPTER III

Atun Huaylas

The Huaylas Homeland

The District of Huaylas is divided into several political areas with overlapping social components. First, there is the political district of Huaylas, encompassing an ecological unit of remarkable geographic independence from the surrounding area. The main valley, where the bulk of the population resides, is laced together by innumerable trails. Even the one natural barrier which separates the *barrio* of Iscap from the rest is crisscrossed by a dozen paths. The basic geographic unity of the district, coupled with its independence from the rest of the Callejón de Huaylas, fosters a sentiment of oneness among Huaylinos. Throughout the district one hears such remarks as: "*We* Huaylinos celebrate *our* fiestas in this fashion," or: "How do you like the way *we* work in Huaylas?" or: "Over there in the Callejón, *they* do it differently."

When the time comes for dramatic expression, Huaylinos refer to themselves as the Atun Huaylas—the ancient name by which their district was known until the start of this century. Since it is a name with which all may identify and which has romantic, nostalgic appeal when speeches are made, Huaylas becomes Atun Huaylas. Huaylinos are wont to remember that their ancestors, before the Conquest, dominated the region and gave their name to both the Callejón de Huaylas and to the original Department of Huaylas.[1] They feel that the subse-

[1] According to F. Garcia Calderón (1879:121) the department name was changed to Ancash in 1839 in commemoration of the Battle of Ancash, a gorge

quent changing of names and the creation of new provinces and districts has capriciously neglected their prominence. The fact that the city of Caraz is the capital of the Province of Huaylas is particularly annoying for some of the townspeople who maintain that, because of its history, Huaylas should hold that position. They frequently consider the chances of Huaylas becoming the seat of a new province of that name, thus restoring Atun Huaylas to its rightful position. In 1935, in fact, they made a concerted attempt to have such a province created. At that time the Concejo took a census in order to "prove" that Huaylas had sufficient population to warrant such a position.[2]

The distinctiveness of Huaylas as a society is expressed in ways which typify the strong regional feeling common throughout Peru. There is, first of all, a great dedication and loyalty to one's *terruño*, the native land of birth. Identification with the homeland carries a feeling of allegiance and uniqueness which is rarely supplanted by long residence elsewhere. Once a Huaylino, always a Huaylino—it is simply a part of one's inheritance that cannot be, and is not, forgotten. When people discuss each other, the individual is first identified as a Huaylino, Carasino, or Huaracino, as the case may be. Even persons who have lived most of their lives in Huaylas are identified in this manner in conversation. One woman, about thirty years of age, who has lived in Huaylas since she was five, told my wife that she definitely considered herself to be from Pueblo Libre and, thus, not a Huaylina. Another, and much older, woman with over forty years' residence in Huaylas confided to me during my first week there that she still considered herself an outsider. "Loneliness," she said, "is the price one pays when he lives away from his place of birth." She predicted that we too would feel this and at times long to be at home. "At such times," she consoled me, "we can comfort each other."

The sacredness of one's birthplace is perhaps best expressed by the frequent references made to *"mi tierra"* (my homeland). It expresses a profound personal attachment that Huaylinos have for Huaylas, and it creates a fundamental, somewhat mystical, bond. After a man's kin and godsibs, the next allegiance is to his *paisanos* (fellow countrymen) or

---

near Yungay, where the War of the Restoration was decided, ending the Peru-Bolivia Confederation.

[2] The census recorded a population of over 7,000 for the district and seemed to be very complete. Because of the reasons for which it was taken, the data from it have been used with reservation, since it is likely that the roll was padded by the addition of names of persons who were not residing in Huaylas at the time.

co-distritanos (co-residents of a district). This does not, of course, apply to the children of Huaylinos who may be born and raised elsewhere.

The strong attachment to one's *tierra* is, in its present form at least, a sentiment probably derived from the basic Hispanic-Mediterranean culture infused by the Conquest into Peruvian life. G. M. Foster comments as follows:

The Spaniard's sense of attachment to his community is intense. When he travels within the region where his home is known, he identifies himself in terms of that pueblo. And if for any reason he settles in another pueblo, as likely as not, he will be known all his life by the prevailing nickname for individuals from that particular place.[3]

In Peru the regional associations in Lima owe their existence to the strength of this sentiment. Huaylas, like many other districts, provinces, and all the departments, has its representative organizations in Lima and Chimbote.[4] In 1964, there were seven clubs representing various segments of the Huaylas migrant population in Lima. The persevering kinship with one's *tierra* is a matter of deep emotion for many persons. Typical is the attitude of one of the many Huaylinos residing in Lima who had this to say about Huaylas in a short article:

This beautiful and tranquil city, cradle of illustrious personages, nestled in the slopes of the Cordillera Negra along whose base runs the famous "Callejón de Huaylas" is, without doubt, one of the most sublime and picturesque districts, that is called to exalt and lend distinguished note to the province of its name through its incalculable fountains of beauty with which nature has blessed it. Thus, there are many memories and anecdotes that you should know; small though this blessed land may be, full of traditional and modest life, it contains all that is wonderful, thus showing how Huaylas was in its first days full of glory and many hopes. For this reason, filled with affection towards her and guided only by the satisfaction and zeal to make it known, I am persuaded to fulfill this purpose.[5]

Appeals to the concept of *mi tierra* are thus made on every hand, for it is a national pattern. In the most popular vein, such regionalism is expressed in the style and lyrics of *huayno* music in the sierra, and also in the coastal *marineras* and the *vals criollo*. It is quite probable that

---

[3] Foster, 1960:35. Also see Pritchett, 1965:13–14.
[4] Mangin, 1959; Doughty, 1964.   [5] Morales, 1958:1 (my translation).

every town has been mentioned at least once in the lyrics of some song. The *huaynos* heard in Huaylas are performed in the "Ancash style" in contrast to those of Cuzco, Puno, or the central valley around Huancayo. The popular songs are recorded by singers who specifically identify themselves as Ancashinos, for example, La Pastorita Huaracina, El Jilguero del Huascarán, La Pallasquinita, and La Estrellita de Pomabamba.[6] At least two groups from Huaylas calling themselves the Lira Huaylina (Lyre of Huaylas) and the Conjunto Santo Toribio de Huaylas frequently played on the radio and in the theaters catering to highland migrants in Lima.

Huaylas and Its Neighbors

Regions, like families and individuals, are thought of as having unique qualities which are reflected in the behavior of all the *paisanos* of a given place. In this connection, Foster notes the continuance of an ancient Spanish custom in his recent survey of major cultural patterns of Spanish people and their relationship to new world customs.

As in Spanish America, a sometimes real and sometimes feigned enmity exists between neighboring towns, and this often gives rise to tales that ridicule the stupidity of the inhabitants of the "other" community.[7]

He later comments:

Literary exuberance as a manifestation of civic pride reaches its most developed form in the *dichos*, ubiquitous rhymes and sayings which eulogize the qualities the sons of a pueblo believe should make it the envy of the world and which ridicule all other places.

This has long been the case in the Callejón de Huaylas. The most common such *dicho*, or saying, which one hears in Huaylas is one attributed to the Italian geographer Raimondi, who visited the area in the 1860's.

Macate, remate	Macate, the end
Huaylas, cosecha	Huaylas, harvest
Mato, rastrojo	Mato, stubble
Caraz, dulzura	Caraz, sweetness

[6] Taken in order, they are: The Little Shepherdess of Huaraz, The Goldfinch of Huascarán, The Little Girl from Pallasca, and The Little Star of Pomabamba.

[7] Foster, 1960:36. In his ethnography of Alcalá de la Sierra, Pitt-Rivers (1961:9–13) provides a lengthy description of this pattern in Andalucia, Spain.

Yungay, hermosura	Yungay, beauty
Carhuaz, borrachera	Carhuaz, drunkenness
Huaraz, presunción	Huaraz, vanity
Recuay, ladronera	Recuay, thievery

The actual statement made by Raimondi concerning Huaylas seems to indicate, however, that these epithets had some currency in the region prior to his arrival there.

Its (Huaylas') inhabitants are all farmers. The countryside on the outskirts of Huaylas is very beautiful and presents a nice view; and it is not without reason that this people is called "harvest," for in reality very abundant harvests are obtained.[8]

Huaylinos say that they have always been noted for their good agriculture and their hard work in contrast to the other pueblos. They laughingly assert that it must be true—that there are many thieves in Recuay—for that town has the biggest jail in the Callejón. With tongue in cheek, they observe, over their own *copitas* (drinks), that there still is a great deal of drinking done in Carhuaz and that Yungay *used* to have beautiful women, but now it only has a good view of Huascarán. More seriously, they maintain that Huaracinos are still quite vain and pretentious. The town of Mato is referred to as "stubble," that part of the plant remaining in the field after the wheat has been harvested. As Huaylinos explain it, it means: "No hay nada" (There is nothing). Sweetness is attributed to Caraz because it once produced much sugar cane and *manjar blanco*,[9] and Macate is simply the end of the Callejón area, as it always has been. In this interpretation, only Huaylas receives favorable mention.

Much nostalgic sentiment for one's *tierra* is traditionally expressed in devotion to the patron saint of the district. It is good for the regional prestige of the district that the fiesta of the Patroness of Huaylas, the Virgin of the Assumption,[10] is suitably celebrated, for visitors from other towns inevitably comment upon the enthusiasm shown on this occasion. The Patroness (*La Patrona*) is considered the symbol of the district, and failure to celebrate her day with enthusiasm and in the prescribed manner suggests that the people lack unity, spirit, and

[8] Raimondi, 1943:122–123 (my translation).

[9] *Manjar blanco* (a candy of boiled milk and sugar) is still made in Caraz and in Mato in some quantity.

[10] Sometimes called in Huaylas "Nuestra Señora de la Asunción de Atun Huaylas" (Our Lady of the Assumption of Atun Huaylas).

respect for their spiritual guardian. Huaylinos remind outsiders, therefore, that the Virgin is *"bien venerada"* (well venerated), with four days of fiesta. They think of themselves as a Catholic people and wish to demonstrate their devotion.[11]

Yet, unlike other towns, the Fiesta of the Patroness in Huaylas is not the biggest popular celebration of the year. Rather, this honor in Huaylas goes to Saint Elizabeth, Patroness of the Harvests of Huaylas. It is this occasion, more than any other, which calls forth the greatest demonstration of regionalistic feeling, attracting almost a thousand Huaylinos home from the coast.[12] That Huaylas had the nickname "harvest" and that the biggest fiesta is in honor of the patroness of the harvests is probably not accidental. Although the historical record of this fiesta does not provide sufficient information, it is probable that both nickname and fiesta have their origins in pre-Conquest customs and that the Virgin of the Assumption was introduced in a Spanish attempt to wean the populace from ancient allegiances.

Be that as it may, Huaylas has two major fiestas, one in July and one in August, which mark major expressions of loyalty to the homeland. Of the two, the Fiesta of Saint Elizabeth is recognized by Huaylinos as being the most distinctive event on the yearly calendar, the one which distinguishes Huaylas from other towns of the Callejón whose fiestas differ in both style and organization.

There are other ways in which Huaylinos distinguish themselves from the people of the neighboring towns, whom they frequently either berate or ignore as we have seen. Something of the attitude of regional ascendency is conveyed by the following introduction to a story, describing an event which occurred in Huaylas in 1932.

I will tell you, dear reader, of what, in times past, was a traditional custom of pure Huaylas character, of that Republic that rests proud and great in one of the most beautiful lands of the Cordillera Negra. It is neither clever, nor fantasy or lyric invention; it is true, authentic and real like the very existence of the great people of Huaylas, whose sons, descendents of Apu-Capac, in spite of their *barrio* factions, have as a common denominator, the ridicule of Caraz.[13]

[11] The feast day of the Patroness is also celebrated by the "Colonia Huaylina" in Lima, which sponsors a Mass and procession, followed by a dance. According to a *huayno* about this occasion, "Huaylinos and devotees (of the Virgin) in greater Lima, all mix on this day of happiness . . ." (Cabellero, n.d.).

[12] The fiesta begins on July 1 and lasts until July 10. See Chapter X.

[13] Filgar, 1945:183 (my translation).

The relationship which Huaylas maintains with Caraz is that of a reluctant subordinate, since Caraz is the provincial capital and a city considerably larger than the town of Huaylas. Here, Huaylinos have many ties of kinship and *compadrazgo,* as well as political, social, and educational interests. Important legal proceedings are initiated in Caraz, and commercial ties are strong, too, since most merchants in Huaylas deal with wholesalers there. Thus, Huaylinos, particularly the townspeople, give much of their attention to events in Caraz. Occasions for trips there are frequent. Two buses (converted trucks) make at least one round trip daily from Huaylas, leaving at 7:30 A.M. and returning at about 4:00 P.M. Each may carry as many as sixty passengers in addition to cargo both to and from Caraz. Because of these many ties and because Caraz is the political center of the province, it is not surprising to find many Huaylinos in residence there and taking active roles in affairs. In fact, in 1960, a Huaylino was mayor of Caraz and another Huaylino was provincial clerk (*escribano*).

Yet relations between the town of Huaylas and the city of Caraz have not been without tensions, as indicated in Chapter I. As the second largest town in the province, Huaylas considers itself to be in competition with Caraz politically and, to some extent, socially. The fact that Caraz, as the capital, has continued to dominate the province is met with some resentment by Huaylinos, who consider Huaylas entitled to some of the power and prestige. That is why, in 1935, they made the effort to have a new province created in which the town of Huaylas would be capital. Although the attempt was unsuccessful, the desire continues to be expressed in the rivalry which Huaylinos feel with the Carasinos. For example, Huaylinos chide the people of Caraz for not being able to accomplish very much by themselves, citing the example of the "new" cathedral, which occupies one side of the Caraz plaza and was begun in 1895 but is still less than half completed. Overlooking their own difficulties, Huaylinos point out that the people in Caraz are always bickering and fighting among themselves to the point where nothing is accomplished.

The recent experience of Huaylinos has tended to reinforce, rather than diminish, the intensity of such feelings. When the lights are turned on during the evening in Huaylas, one is asked if he has ever seen the electric lights at night in Caraz, or, for that matter, in Yungay, or in any of the other cities in the Callejón. "The lights in Caraz look like oranges hanging from a string—you need a candle to find them," say Huaylinos, referring to the lack of adequate power. The electric current in Huaylas was, in fact, much better than elsewhere, and during our residence there the situation was improved through the installation of hydroelectric power from Huallanca, replacing the diesel generator which had formerly supplied the town with electricity. With an unlimited supply of power, Huaylinos undertook an ambitious rural electrification program.

They subsequently overlooked few opportunities for deriding Caraz' efforts to improve its system. While I was returning to Huaylas one evening from Caraz, in the company of a Huaylino and a man from Caraz, the former pointedly remarked, as we descended from the pass at Curcúy: "My, just look at all the lights in Huaylas! It looks like a big city." In contrast, the efforts to install a new system in Caraz foundered on the opposition of dissident elements. At last, when the Caraz project neared its finish, eight months after the inauguration of the new system in Huaylas, the Carasinos formally asked for the assistance of Huaylinos in making the final installations. Complying with the request, a team of Huaylinos went to Caraz on two occasions and supervised the final work in a sort of home-grown technical assistance effort. By so doing, the Huaylinos' sense of superiority seemed justified and was reinforced. Thereafter, several persons remarked to me, with obvious delight: "How the Carasinos must be burning up over this!" While some Carasinos may indeed feel challenged by Huaylas, it is doubtful that many are concerned. Generally, the people of Caraz regard Huaylinos as pretentious rustics or, at best, as small-town people who lack sophistication. The successful installation of electricity in Huaylas undoubtedly served, nevertheless, to goad Carasinos toward the installation of a better system of their own.

Such has not been the case with the town of Mato (also called Villa Sucre), which Huaylinos consider a backward and unprogressive place, inhabited by indolent and incompetent people. Although Huaylinos daily pass through Mato on their way to Caraz, there is relatively little social contact between the two towns, little intermarriage, and few ties of *compadrazgo*. The fiestas of one district pass largely unnoticed by the people of the other. Thus, in Huaylas, there is never any talk of attending the fiestas of Mato, although Huaylinos often attend religious celebrations elsewhere, in Huata or in Yuramarca, for example.

The attitude of Huaylinos toward Mato has its roots in recent history, as well as in certain basic differences between the two places.

The most important factor, however, is the fact that the people of Mato refused to cooperate with the Huaylinos when the latter were building their access road to the main highway. Since part of the Huaylas road had to pass through the town of Mato to reach the main road, the people of Mato reasoned that the Huaylinos would have to do the work. At this decision, the Huaylinos halted construction about two miles from the town of Mato and, making a right angle, built the road to the main highway via another route, by-passing Mato. The Huaylinos built a road more than ten miles in length over difficult terrain, but the Matinos continued without one, even though the main highway was less than two miles from Mato. This, and the fact that when the Matinos finally did build their road they requested assistance from Huaylas, contributed to the scorn which Huaylinos feel toward Mato.

The relationship between Huaylas and Huallanca is of a different nature. Prior to the early 1940's, Huallanca was a small settlement at the end of the railroad, officially dependent upon a part of the district of Huaylas. The geographical position of Huallanca is a peculiar one. It stretches along the banks of the Santa river at the bottom of a huge canyon whose barren and arid sides serve as great reflectors focusing the sun's heat onto the village (see Figure 3). This, in addition to its much lower altitude is responsible for its tropical climate. In the years before 1942, many Huaylinos had small plots of land there in which they grew tropical fruits and other produce, but since Huallanca was notorious for *verruga*, they seldom stayed longer than was necessary to plant or harvest.

With the advent of the hydroelectric project in 1942, however, Huallanca became the scene of intense construction activity, which continued until the major work on the plant was terminated in 1957. This work had an enormous impact on life in Huaylas for many reasons. Foremost, perhaps, was mere proximity. Huaylinos were brought into intimate contact with many outsiders, and a large percentage of the men of Huaylas were employed in a wide variety of jobs during the period of work. Thus new skills were introduced into Huaylas, and much money was injected into the local economy both through wages and separation pay. Currently nearly 40 per cent of the operating and maintenance staff at the hydroelectric plant are Huaylinos. In addition, much of the population of the village of Huallanca,

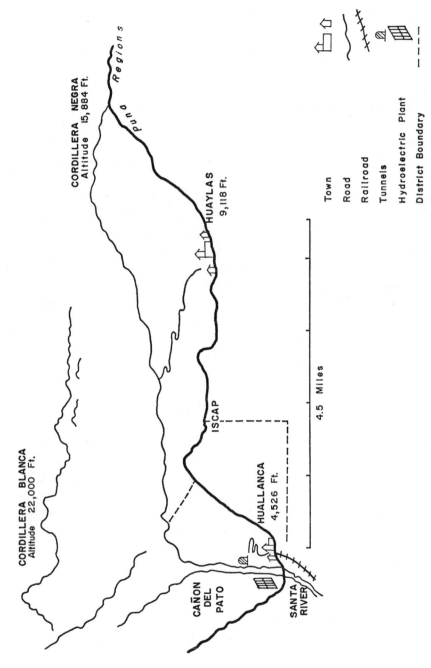

CORDILLERA BLANCA
Altitude 22,000 Ft.

CORDILLERA NEGRA
Altitude 15,884 Ft.

Puno Regions

HUAYLAS
9,118 Ft.

ISCAP

HUALLANCA
4,526 Ft.

CAÑON DEL PATO

SANTA RIVER

4.5 Miles

Town
Road
Railroad
Tunnels
Hydroelectric Plant
District Boundary

Figure 3. Profile of the Districts of Huaylas and Huallanca, looking south

which lies outside of the Santa Corporation grounds around the railroad depot, is made up of Huaylinos.

Because the activities during the construction of the plant brought so many people to the area, President Odria, in 1950, created the District of Huallanca, incorporating in it a sizable portion of Huaylas. Arbitrarily and hastily conceived, the new district boundary was drawn through the middle of the *barrio* of Iscap of Huaylas to include a portion of that population in the new district (see Figure 3 and Map 2). Regardless of boundaries, the Iscapinos involved continue to function as members of the *barrio* to which they have traditionally belonged and resent being officially considered part of another district. When my team of enumerators undertook the census in that *barrio*, the people who lived in the affected area beseeched us to consider them Huaylinos, apparently thinking that our doing so would officially join them to the district again. We did count this sector as part of Huaylas, since the *inspector* (leader) of the *barrio* of Iscap resided there. For the national census, which took place the following July (1961), to the dismay of the residents, the sector was counted as part of the district of Huallanca.

Despite this problem, which some Huaylinos find irksome, relations with Huallanca are without the frictions and the negative sentiments which characterize dealings with the people of Caraz or Mato. The ties are much closer, and there is a tendency among Huaylinos to think of Huallanca as their progeny. The people of the two districts participate in one another's activities and the Santa Corporation itself is intimately involved with life in Huaylas, even permitting the installation of a telephone in the Concejo office which is connected to their private system in Huallanca. The road to Huallanca from Huaylas is being completed, following the old, much-used foot and horse trail, part of whose course lies along the ancient Inca road. When this is finished, the association between the two districts will probably be even closer. As one Huaylino put it: "When the road to Huallanca is finished, good-bye Caraz." As he finished this remark, he drew his index finger across his Adam's apple.

Huaylas' relations with the towns throughout the rest of the Callejón increase in tenuousness as the distance becomes greater. Huaraz, of course, is important as the capital of the Department of Ancash. Aside from this official tie, however, Huaylinos have little to do with any activities there. Thus, Huaylinos delimit their district from surrounding areas and define some of the differences between themselves and their neighbors. In this context the feeling of district unity is strong.

Highlanders and Peruvians

Huaylinos proudly assert their regional allegiance as Ancashinos, that is, as people from Ancash. What is more important, perhaps, viewed in the perspective of the entire country, is their sometimes apologetic, but more often proud, self-identification as *serranos* or *provincianos*.[14] Sierra traits which are admired, or are considered to be particularly characteristic of Huaylas, are exalted. Thus, while eating some typical sierra dish, such as *picante de cuy* (guinea pig in hot sauce), one is often asked: "How do you like our food here in the sierra? This is something they don't eat on the coast!" *Cancha*, the parched corn served with meals on all occasions, is proudly identified as *pan serrano* (sierra bread). A special variety of corn, called *terciopelo*, considered peculiar to Huaylas, is highly prized for *cancha*. Huaylinos claim that it makes the very best *cancha* in the sierra, boasting that this variety of corn cannot be grown elsewhere. Indeed, elsewhere in the Callejón, corn of this color is sometimes called *cancha* or *maíz huaylino*, and is prized for this purpose.

The spirit of public work and cooperation in the *repúblicas* is considered a sierra trait, as are the use of Quechua and the distinctive style of dress, which includes *ponchos* and hats. *Ponchos*, which are often called *abrigo serrano* (highland overcoat) or the *abrigo de cuatro puntas* (overcoat with four corners), are considered distinctive of the real *serrano*. Almost all of the men in the district wear *ponchos* in the evening. Those on visits from Lima or Chimbote borrow them from relatives to re-establish their kinship with the sierra. Public work (or *repúblicas*) of which more will be said later, is given special emphasis by Huaylinos as a means of getting things done and demonstrating their progressiveness. In this regard, they feel themselves to be superior to their neighbors in Mato and Caraz, whom they say always require help from the government to accomplish something.

The same is true of the characteristic sierra music, the *huayno*. While other music may be popular, the *huayno* is danced by everyone with a special gusto. In Huaylas, everyone is expected to be able to

[14] These two terms—highlander and provincial—are used interchangeably in Huaylas. *Provinciano*, however, can mean any person from any district outside of Lima. But, *serrano* refers specifically to a highland dweller.

dance the *huayno*. If one who has resided on the coast declines, he will find himself admonished with remarks such as, "All *serranos* know how to dance the *huayno*," implying that even if one has lived on the coast for a while, he is still a *serrano*. The *huayno*, which is totally identified with the sierra, is coming to serve as a vehicle not only for expression of such typical sierra sentiments as regional loyalty, but also for complaints and demands of the government that changes be made. Hence one popular *huayno* heard in Huaylas went as follows:

Señor Senador	Mr. Senator
Mi pedido por favor	My request please
Quiero luz para mi	I want (electric light
pueblo	for my town).

The lyrics continue:

Pobre soy	Poor I am
Pobre nací	Poor I was born
Mi presencia le	(Perhaps) my presence
molestará	will bother you
Pero vengo por parte	But I come on behalf
De la humanidad.	of humanity.

Other *huaynos* proclaimed:

Soy serrana y bien	I'm a highland girl
Peruana	and real Peruvian.

and:

Argentina con sus tangos	Argentina with its tangos
Mexico con sus huapangos	Mexico with its huapangos
Los verdaderos peruanos	All real Peruvians
Con sus mulizas y	With their mulizas and
huaynos	huaynos
Adelante provincianos	Forward provincials
Para cantar nuestras	To sing our huaynos.
huaynos	

In content, the *huaynos* emphasize those aspects of culture which typify sierra life. In spite of the fact that highland culture has, over the years, been ridiculed by *costeños* (coastal people), the *huaynos* which one hears nowadays often exalt sierra ethnic unity and customs, for example, speaking Quechua, dancing *huaynos*, and even wearing Indian clothing.[15] As has been mentioned, *huaynos* make constant reference to particular towns, districts, or departments in the highlands. The fact that Huaylinos emphasize that they are *serranos* seems to reflect a growing highland "nationalism" throughout Peru, particularly in areas such as Ancash and in the Mantaro valley of central Peru. Being a *serrano*, then, is not something one need be ashamed of in Huaylas. Indeed, the opposite is more often the case.[16]

Considering the otherwise pronounced coastal influence on Huaylas culture and society, and the great impact which Lima and, more recently, Chimbote have had in Huaylas, this is, perhaps, surprising. Highland customs (both mestizo and Indian) have, until recent years, been subject to ridicule and derision by coastal people, particularly those from Lima. In the presence of such people, the phenomenon of the *serrano* denying his knowledge of Quechua, his preference for the *huayno*, or his eating of *cuyes* (guinea pigs) has been a common occurrence. It occurs in Huaylas, particularly among the youth, some of whom refuse to speak Quechua or deny knowledge of certain customs which they consider degrading.[17] Those who behave in this fashion, however, are considered to be extremely pretentious (*pretencioso*) and snobbish, qualities which Huaylinos do not value. On the other hand, it is claimed that most Huaylinos are bilingual, as indeed they are, in varying degrees of fluency. Among the townspeople, who

[15] Many *huayno* singers take Quechua names, such as Sipas Tika (Young Flower), Sumac Koya (Beautiful Princess), Raymi Ticka (Flower of the Winter Solstice). This is partly due to the international acclaim given Ima Sumac (Most Beautiful), who now resides in the United States and is a U.S. citizen (to the disappointment of many Peruvians).

[16] The movement to make the *serrano* respectable in a political sense, if not the epitome of what is good in Peru, is by no means recent. One of the earliest proponents was Manuel Gonzales Prada in the last century (1960:66–67). He was followed by José Carlos Mariátegui (1952) and others. One of the most outspoken champions of the downtrodden *serrano* is J. Guillermo Guevara in his *La Rebelión de los Provincianos* (1959), one of his numerous, militant essays on the subject.

[17] During the course of the census in Santo Toribio, I asked if anyone knew of some girls who might be willing to serve as interpreters and guides. Two sisters were suggested. The two, both about eighteen years of age, home from high school in Lima, agreed to go at their father's request. They refused, however, to speak any Quechua, denying knowledge of the language. The girls had been recommended by a neighbor, as well as by their father, because they had such excellent command of both Spanish and Quechua.

speak Spanish as a first language, there are several "Quechuistas"—persons noted for their ability and interest in speaking Quechua.[18]

Huaylinos at other times, however, express distress over the "backward" (*atrasado*) or rustic conditions in which they live. To the prominent outsider, they politely apologize for the lack of "facilities" in the town to which the visitor "must be accustomed," assuming that he notices their absence and misses them. By the same token, on being invited to someone's home, the host at once apologizes (*"disculpe usted"*) for the "inconveniences" of his dwelling and asks that you forgive him for not offering something better, the gist of his apology being: "That's the way we live here in the sierra." Thus, the outsider is thrust into a position of superiority and social prominence, vis-à-vis his host, and, if things are to proceed smoothly, his answers had best be made with considerable tact or ambiguity. Pat responses such as, "Don't bother" (*"No se molesta"*), "Don't worry" (*"No se preocupa"*), or "To the contrary" (*"Al contrario"*), pervade initial conversations. The final result of such verbal sparring is the establishment of certain criteria for judging the degree of social distance between the host and his guest. Being of the sierra is one such criterion. The acceptance of certain sierra customs decreases the social distance, while rejection increases it. The acceptance of sierra traditions peculiar to Huaylas, of course, decreases the social distance even more.

Among the other aspects of sierra life which receive special emphasis in Huaylas, agriculture and the system of land tenure are of great importance. It is common to hear Huaylinos make the claim that in the district all are farmers, urban and rural dwellers alike. Indeed, of the many families we came to know, only one claimed to derive nothing from agricultural pursuits, and even this one kept some chickens and some *cuyes,* and had a small vegetable patch in the patio. Unity is claimed on the basis of a common occupation, and it generates a certain degree of pride. Thus, one of the most ambitious men in town, one who runs a hotel, a store, and a mill, claims whenever he is asked, and on all public documents, that his occupation is that of *agricultor* (farmer).

A hundred years ago, Raimondi commented that the inhabitants of

[18] This amounts to more than mere fluency. Several persons pride themselves on poetry they have written in Quechua and take great interest in local and regional variations in the language. Their orientation is inclined, however, to be very sentimental or antiquarian.

Huaylas were all farmers. To the Huaylinos of today, it seems that they have always been and will always continue to be primarily *agricultores*. The *agricultor* must, in this case, be distinguished from *colonos* and *peones*, (serfs and farm workers), on the one hand, and *hacendados* (manor owners), on the other, who also engage in farming. In Huaylas, the farmer is the operator of a small family farm which, in most instances, he or another member of his family owns.

Hence it is asserted that "everyone, if you will, has food from his own field—here, we are all farmers." In other words, everyone is self-sufficient in Huaylas, at least in the popular view,[19] and this is said to account for the small daily market in Huaylas. Pride is expressed in the fact that most families own their own land, small though it may be, and that this results in economic independence for most.

In contrast to neighboring areas throughout the Callejón, there are no traditional haciendas [20] in Huaylas and, therefore, no monolithic class of serfs who are propertyless. The importance of this is recognized by Huaylinos, and it has contributed to a self-image which supports the transculturation process which is taking place in the district. This measured degree of sociocultural uniformity has certainly facilitated the greater incorporation of Huaylinos and Huaylas into the activities of the nation.

According to the distinguished diplomat and historian, Dr. Victor Andrés Belaunde, Peruvianness (*Peruanidad*) is a feeling of nationality based upon a unique bond among the people as a consequence of the great cultural, racial, religious, and political synthesis resulting from the Conquest.[21] In many areas of Peru, however, and among great numbers of the people, this bond is not recognized. Many people from Hualcán, for example, like other socially isolated Indian populations, have not identified themselves with the nation in which they live.[22] The question, "What is Peru?" may bring no reply, or, at best, a guess as to where it lies. The highlander's relationship to the president, deputies, and other government officials, and their functions, has been weak and

[19] E. W. Middendorf (1895:56–57) noted that this was the case in 1886, when he spent two days there during the course of his travels.

[20] For a description of the traditional hacienda, see Mario C. Vázquez, 1961a. There is one property called an hacienda in Huaylas and another adjacent to it in the district of Huallanca. Both of these were run on a share-cropping system and had very few resident peons.

[21] V. A. Belaunde, 1957:473–479.

[22] Stein, 1961:202.

surrounded by an aura of inaccessibility. This is, of course, a consequence of the plural nature of Peruvian society and the lack of social
integration.

In contrast, Huaylinos, as a group, are very conscious of their
national identity as Peruvians. The feeling of nationality in Huaylas is
not recent. The historical forces which have contributed to the development of Peru as a nation have impinged upon life in Huaylas from
early times, and, in addition, Huaylinos have long had direct contacts
with the focal point of national life in Lima. The mayor of Huaylas at
the turn of the century, Don Mariano Luís Alba, had served as a
representative in the Peruvian congress as have other Huaylinos since
then. At that time, many townspeople were accustomed to making the
long and arduous journey to the capital for work and education.[23] Since
then, these contacts have become increasingly important for all and not
merely for members of the upper class.

The nationalistic sentiments, however, are not all positive. Indeed,
among Peruvians who are conscious of their nationality, one is certain
to be impressed by the negative quality of many of the attitudes
expressed and by the feelings of alienation from the government. That
Huaylinos give vent to such sentiments, however negative, is nevertheless a measure of their involvement with their nation.

To some extent the alienation takes the form of latent fears that the
"authorities" or the "government" are but one step away from commit-
ting some grievous abuse of power. One of the census enumerators (a
young woman), for example, encountered a woman who had not
mentioned her infant daughter during the course of the interview. The
omission came to light when the child emerged from her hiding place
behind the mother's skirts. The woman said that she did not mention
the child's name because she feared that the enumerator would take her
away for the government. To what extent such incidents occurred is, of
course, impossible to say, but the hazard that such attitudes may pose
for census takers is clear.

Skepticism of the actions of governmental authorities, especially at
the departmental and national levels, is frequently given expression in
Huaylas. There were many tales of graft and corruption in government, invariably ending with the remark, "Well, that's the way we

---

[23] Middendorf (1895:59) notes that many young men went to the coast to work
in the Lima hotels around 1886 in order to make money to spend in the fiestas in
Huaylas. Others attended university there.

Peruvians are" ("*Así somos, los peruanos*"), while the listeners nodded in agreement. Malfeasance is anticipated and thought to occur, whether it actually does or not.

Perhaps the most common expression of alienation one hears in Huaylas is the complaint, "The government (all government outside of the district) has forgotten us." This is a lament heard over and over again (in 1960 and in 1967), not only in Huaylas, but in towns throughout the country. "They tell us that the government is going to do this and that thing for us, but it's just a bunch of lies. Even when they do send help, it's either too late or not enough to make any difference." Whether based on actual facts or not, such negative attitudes are a prominent feature of the national political folklore and tradition.

In many places, matters come to a rest upon the utterance of such a statement, for it is felt that only God, the President, or a *diputado* can do anything about the problem.[24] Indeed, some people in Huaylas feel this way, particularly about things over which they have little control or for which they lack access to the necessary information for resolving the problem.[25] When such things are discussed, Huaylinos express their displeasure and apparent resignation by observing, "How is it possible that the government remembers humble ones like ourselves? The government doesn't interest itself in such small problems." The deliberate reduction of the significance of the difficulties faced, however, betrays the muted conviction that the opposite should be the case.

Huaylinos have not always been content to wait for government action. When they voice such opinions, they frequently conclude that, "If we wait for the government, we will wait forever. It is better that we do things for ourselves." Feelings of alienation in Huaylas have thus led to some measure of self-reliance and accomplishment which have often become the focal points of Huaylas unity. Although the government has, in fact, given assistance to Huaylas in several ways, Huaylinos invariably play down the importance of it, emphasizing their own contributions instead.

[24] See the *huaynos* quoted above. Another such song goes: "Sr. Diputado, quiero carretera para mi pueblo . . ." (Mr. Congressman, I want a road for my town . . .).

[25] This is especially true in Huaylas with regard to agriculture. Many feel that the government should help them improve their production through improving the irrigation system.

Another by-product of this attitude is that, when government (or other) aid is made available, people invariably feel that there are ulterior motives behind the offer. Thus, while a gift may be received with apparent satisfaction, the giver is at the same time suspected of pursuing some secret and selfish ends. Indeed, this is considered to be the natural state of affairs because, they say, "We are such egoists" ("*Somos muy egoistas*").

For this reason, many persons who have offered their assistance in one way or another feel spurned or disillusioned because recognition is withheld from them. Sincerity is not taken for granted; it must be proved. On the other hand, those persons who are felt to have made basically sincere and disinterested contributions toward the betterment of life in Huaylas are shown great respect. Hence, aspirants to positions of leadership in Huaylas have long sought to demonstrate their loyalty to their *tierra* through deeds which will be interpreted in this manner.

Finally, these negative feelings are often manifested in nonpolitical ways as well. They frequently come into play when one must choose between the purchase of a nationally made product or something of foreign manufacture. In such instances, if one has the money at hand, it is the foreign merchandise which is inevitably chosen. The nationally produced items involved in this competition are ridiculed as being inadequate or of inferior quality, the products of untrained hands. The concept of an "underdeveloped" country has thus entered the minds of those who hear of it on the radio or read it in the Lima newspapers. The apology, "We are a poor and backward nation," is often repeated.

The establishment of schools in all sectors of the district around the turn of the century was instrumental in creating a feeling of national identity. The schools serve as instruments of policy designed to have this effect through the celebration of national holidays, the singing of the national anthem, and the teaching of Peru's history. The Huaylas district council, moreover, has sponsored the district-wide celebration of Fiestas Patrias (the Independence Day celebration) on the 28th and 29th of July for as long as records exist (1889). It has been the annual policy of the Concejo since that time to issue a municipal order that all houses in the district should be whitewashed, cleaned, or freshly plastered in honor of the occasion. Thus, in all sectors of the main valley, houses are duly whitened and many sport Peruvian flags or bunting.[26]

National politics are an important topic of conversation among up-

[26] Such preparations are observed in some districts of Lima and elsewhere as well.

per-class men, and knowledge of the political situation is general, since national political movements have had local influence since the last century. Thus, in the early years of the APRA party,[27] several middle-class children in Huaylas were named after Victor Raúl Haya de la Torre, its founder. Other local APRA members have, in times past, been chased into hiding or imprisoned. Several Huaylinos have served as provincial representatives in the Chamber of Deputies, the most recent being in 1948. This focused attention and interest on the course of national affairs, just as the formation of the District of Huallanca did in 1950 and as the near creation of a District of Santo Toribio did in 1954. In 1962, a former mayor of Huaylas was a candidate for representative from the Province of Huaylas.[28] People of the district gave him strong backing, for, as one man put it, "It behooves us to have a real Huaylino as deputy." It is felt that if a Huaylino becomes a member of congress, the possibility of receiving assistance will be greater. Huaylinos feel that otherwise they have no voice in national government and no real opportunity to obtain aid.

The image and position of Peru on the international level likewise concerns many Huaylinos, although this interest finds its greatest expression among the townspeople, particularly those of the upper class. Revival of the old border dispute with Ecuador in 1960 stirred considerable interest in Huaylas and evoked demonstrations of patriotic conviction, both privately and publicly. The District Council sent a representative to a patriotic rally in Caraz, supporting the country's stand against Ecuadorian "pretensions," as the claims on Peruvian territory were called. The occasion served as a reminder that some Huaylinos had actually taken part in the military action against Ecuador in the 1940's and that one middle-class man living in the Campiña had even been wounded. The acquisition of two cruisers from England by the Peruvian navy in 1960 was also the source of great interest and pride for some townspeople, who claimed that it gave Peru added stature in the face of the threats to national security posed by Chile and Ecuador.

The participation of Huaylinos in national affairs is further demonstrated by the number of men who have completed military service.[29] Even more important, however, is the number of persons who partici-

---

[27] Alianza Popular Revolutionario Americano.

[28] His campaign slogan was "Honor, Sacrifice, and Work."

[29] In 1961, 19 per cent of the men over twenty years of age said they had served in the armed forces, 41 per cent claimed to have had reserve training and the remaining 39 per cent had no military experience.

pate in national elections. In 1933 there were 651 registered voters in Huaylas.[30] In the recent election of 1962 almost 1,200 Huaylinos voted, or roughly 44 per cent of the population over twenty years of age. The political and social consequences of this fact will be considered in Chapter VII.

[30] Perú, Dirección Nacional de Estadística, 1933:8–9.

CHAPTER IV

The Elements of Cultural and Social Stratification

Town and Country

While there is feeling of community and unity vis-á-vis the outside world, there are strong internal divisions which mold and structure the day-to-day life of all Huaylinos and of Huaylas as a society. Underlying other more complex discriminations, is the fundamental dichotomy of town and country—urban-rural division—and the *barrio* divisions (see Map 3). That place of residence is a major criterion in determining the status of any person or group is due to the fact that residence is linked or associated with other characteristics that have more profound social implications. The *barrios* add an additional dimension to the rural-urban division which will be considered as well.

The town is the site of the parish church, the library, the municipal offices, police station, and the symbolic center of authority—the Plaza de Armas (the town square). As befits the capital of a district, it is also the center of commercial activity, the place from which the buses depart, and the locus of the principal modern facilities, such as post office, telegraph service, and, prior to the recent installation of hydroelectric power, electricity.

The people who live in the town thus have greater access to such advantages and comforts as are offered by urban life in the capital of a small sierra district. Furthermore, those who enjoy these benefits consider themselves, and are thought to be, more sophisticated, or even more civilized, than those who live in the countryside. The contiguous buildings with their many balconies, the stores, the cobbled streets, and the ebb and flow of human traffic through them, provide the intimacy of contact, however fleeting, which lends the flavor of urbanity to town life and induces uncomfortable feelings of being out of place in the rural dweller who may linger there.

The townspeople, linked by proximity to one another, kinship, and a network of social relationships and responsibilities, consider themselves apart from the countryman. Although they evince some aloofness and homogeneity, they are neither isolated from the people in the rural areas nor entirely alike.

While the local upper-class group is urban in residence pattern (with only five exceptions), this is also true of almost a thousand other Huaylinos—almost a fifth of the district population. Thus, while urban residence is not the only factor, the status it confers is extremely important. The significance of urban residence, both socially and politically, is reflected in the strong desire of the people of Santo Toribio to create an urban settlement there. Some kind of a population center is necessary to give focus to higher status. Thus, in each of the *barrios* there is the nuclear hamlet, with a rural school (some have two), a chapel, and a cluster of homes.

Within Huaylas, the relationship between urban residence and social status is illustrated by the lives of several persons who have moved from the rural setting to the town, where they have come to occupy prominent positions. Almost all activities of importance to the district are initiated and conducted in the town. When meetings of civic committees and *cabildo abierto* (open council meetings) are called, they take place either in the municipal offices or in the large hall of the Club Sportivo,[1] located on the town plaza. It is inconvenient for rural dwellers to attend relatively minor activities in town. The result is that when people are sought to assume responsibilities, the tendency is to select those who can be easily reached and whose presence at meetings is assured. Thus, residence in town tends to maximize the possibility of participating in important affairs in the district. It is possible that in the future, with improved communications between the town and the

[1] A social club.

principal rural areas (through the installation of telephones in the rural hamlets, for example), the participation in civic affairs of interested persons from rural areas will increase markedly. A first step in this direction occurred after the municipal elections in 1963 when open council meetings were held in the different *barrios*.

The centralization of activities in the town and the unequal access to authority lie at the root of the hostility which the people of the Campiña (*barrios* of Quecuas and Huayrán) feel toward the townsmen, and this has served to create a feeling of identity among them. The growth of rural opposition in Santo Toribio, the center of this area, was accompanied by a withdrawal from many district activities, even when participation was possible. This, in turn, had the effect of reinforcing the centralized character of district life. The spiraling of events in this fashion has led to attempts to develop duplicate institutions and activities in the Campiña, intended to create a rival, independent, urban environment. Streets were laid out (and one cobbled), schools built in the center of the area, a large area reserved for a plaza, a branch post office installed (1963), and municipal building begun (but not finished), a small chapel in honor of Saint Elizabeth constructed on the plaza-to-be and another next to the school in honor of Santo Toribio, the Patron of the hamlet.

Since the late 1940's, the people of Santo Toribio have celebrated the traditional festival of the harvests (the Fiesta of Saint Elizabeth) independently, in the same style as in town. In addition, social clubs, similar to those of the town, were established. The separatist movement culminated in 1954 with the near creation, by congressional act, of a separate district of Santo Toribio. This move was defeated only because the townspeople who opposed it were able to muster greater influence in Lima. Since that time, the drive to create the new district has cooled somewhat, and the people in the Campiña are themselves divided into two conflicting camps—those who wish to form the new district, and those who do not. Members of the latter group, as a result of this conflict, have grown closer to the town, and the leaders have begun to play active roles in district affairs. The hope of creating a new district is, nevertheless, still nourished by many who complain about the inaccessibility of facilities and services, particularly when they come to town in search of the mayor, the justice of the peace, or other officials, only to find them absent.

The terms used by Huaylinos to express rural-urban differences are listed below. Some, particularly those referring to the rural dwellers, carry strong implications of inferiority and may be considered derogatory. Those marked with an asterisk are not used unless some insult is intended.

URBAN

gente del pueblo	townspeople
los del pueblo	those from town
los de la población	those from the population
la población	the population
el radio urbano	the urban radius

RURAL

gente de la campiña	people of the countryside, specifically Quecuas and Huayrán
gente del barrio	people of the *barrio*
gente rústica	rustic people (rustics)
gente de las estancias (*caserios*)	people from the hamlets
gente del campo	country people
campesinos (rare)	farmers or country people
los del campo	those from the country
*chacrinos**	people from the fields (hicks)
*gente de la chacra**	people from the fields (hicks)
*gente de la colca**	people from the grain bin

Of these, the expressions, *los del campo* and *gente del campo*, are used most frequently by the townspeople to refer to the country dweller. The term, *gente rústica*, is used often and, while not necessarily derogatory, carries with it an implication of the inferiority of the country resident. All of the urban terms, however, require the addition of appropriate adjectives to insinuate disrespect or ridicule.

The Outline of Social Class

The social stratification of Huaylas, although related to the rural and urban distinctions just mentioned, is more complex than this simple dichotomy. In the highlands there seemed small likelihood that such a situation as described by John Gillin, in Moche on the north coast, would be encountered.[2] Previous studies had shown considerable class differentiation both in the Callejón de Huaylas [3] and elsewhere in the highland regions.[4] I have chosen to follow a modified version of the classification developed by Schaedel and Escobar,[5] since it does not rely entirely on ethnic terminology such as mestizo and Indian or *cholo* and *criollo*,[6] although such concepts enter into consideration. This allows discussion of changes in individual social, economic, and political status with less ambiguity arising over a person's cultural or racial background, a situation lamented by Fried.[7]

Thus, it is possible to describe a *cholo* who enters the local upper class without necessarily implying that he has become a mestizo. This is a dubious assumption in many if not most cases. The people of Huaylas are, for present purposes, described as falling into three groups called the upper, middle, and lower classes. All members of these classes in Huaylas would fall into the middle- and low-class categories described by Schaedel and Escobar, since there are no persons of great wealth or of national or departmental power and prestige in the district. On the other hand, there are very few, if any, Huaylinos who would clearly be classified as pertaining to the lowest class, that is, the Indians mentioned by those authors. All considered, Huaylinos constitute a rather homogeneous society, each class widely sharing the basic patterns of highland culture. Although the gap between the wealthiest and poorest Huaylinos is obvious, the economic and social differences between the classes are not sharply drawn.

[2] Moche was reported to be a society in which class distinctions were impossible to make, despite certain differences in wealth, residence, education and whether or not a person was a native Mochero (Gillin, 1945:113). In other coastal areas, however, the class distinctions are more clearly defined as in the Ica valley (Hammel, 1962) and in the Lurín valley (Matos *et al.*, 1964).

[3] Mangin, 1955; Ghersi, 1960; Patch, 1960:147–149; Mangin, 1967.

[4] Bourricaud, 1962; Schaedel, 1959a:15–26; Castillo *et al.*, 1964b:58–59; Adams, 1953:238–244; and Andrews, 1963:193–211.

[5] Schaedel, 1959:15–26 and Escobar, 1959:1–21. These authors describe the class system of the southern highlands as follows: The lowest class (Indians) with 51.4 per cent of the population; the low class (*cholos*) in both rural and urban areas with 38.3 per cent of the population; the middle class with 8.3 per cent of the population; and, the upper class with but 2 per cent of the population.

[6] This is a word of many uses in Peru. In this case, it refers to the cultural characteristics of coastal natives, particularly Lima and other coastal urban centers. It also refers to sly, sometimes deceitful, "nonconformist" behavior. For a fuller discussion of this, see Tschopik, 1948:252–261; and Simmons, 1955:107–117.

[7] Fried, 1961:26. See Patch, 1960:148–149, for further discussion of this point.

It was not long after we had taken up residence in Huaylas that the problem of delimiting the upper class was, in large part, resolved through what may be called the "participant-as-observer" technique.[8] During the Easter week celebrations, the most prominent residents (all men) were invited to attend three Masses as a group. I was included in this number, being a foreigner and guest in Huaylas.[9] The *notables* (notable persons), as members of this group were called, were selected by the parish priest with the assistance of some of his close lay associates. The criteria used in making the selection were relative affluence, education, family background, and political status.

The group consisted of schoolteachers, current and former high district officials (mayor, members of the Concejo, governor, justices of the peace, water administrator, and police commandant), owners of all the principal stores in the center of town, and others, such as "large" landholders, who were considered qualified. In all, fifty-two men were invited to occupy the reserved seats during the Masses on Holy Thursday and Good Friday.

Beginning with this group, it was possible, through observation and inquiry, to distinguish a group of 112 persons who, with their families, clearly constituted the local upper class. They comprise about 9 per cent of the total population. The *notables* or *visibles* (visible ones) are not formally organized, nor are they united by a single point of view, except perhaps, in religious preference. Nonetheless, they and their families constitute the *sociedad* ("society"), and their distinguishing characteristics are their greater control of, or access to, the power, wealth, and opportunities which exist in the district.

The differences between the upper and middle classes and between the middle and lower classes are ones of degree rather than of kind. Together, the latter constitute over 90 per cent of the population, in which the middle-class group is the larger, comprising approximately 60 per cent of the total population. The majority of the middle class are small property owners, engaged in farming and cottage-industry-type occupations. Taken as a group they are highly mobile in a geographic as well as social sense. Their individual shares of the wealth and power in the district come in smaller portions than those of the upper class.

[8] Babchuk, 1962:225–228.
[9] The selection committee assumed that I met all their criteria. More than that, however, Huaylinos expected me to participate and honored me with the invitation.

The lower class resembles the middle class to a great extent in its general patterns of living. Nevertheless, in economic terms, they are poorer, participate less in district affairs, and are more closely associated with the Indian cultural background in such matters as dress and speech than are persons of middle-class status. I estimate that they constitute 30 per cent of the total population.

Social status in Huaylas is, in part, measured by the level of participation in public affairs. The upper-class group refrains from direct participation in the *barrio* organization. For example, no member of the upper class accepts the position of *barrio inspector* (the principal official of a *barrio*) or any of the lesser *barrio* positions. These are filled by persons who do not consider themselves to be members of the upper class. It is in this sphere that the structure of the lower class begins to reveal itself. Those who are most active in directing *barrio* affairs approximate more closely the lifeways of the upper class and of national Peruvian society. Those who hold the lowest posts in the *barrio* structure, or who have not held any official position whatever, are generally poorer as well as less familiar with the ways of contemporary Western life.

The political and administrative positions, then, may be seen as corresponding to three levels or social classes (see Table 14).[10]

The divisions of responsibility among the social classes of Huaylas

Table 14. Political and administrative positions by class division

Lower class	Middle class	Upper class
Brazo (assistant to the inspector)	Brazo (assistant to the inspector)	
Cívico (assistant to Lt. Governor)	Teniente Gobernador (Lt. Governor)	Gobernador (Governor)
Repartidor de aguas (water distributor)	Repartidor de aguas (water distributor)	
	Subadministrator of waters	Administrator of waters
	Member of Irrigation Council	Member of Irrigation Council
	Concejal (councilman)	Concejal (councilman) Alcalde (Mayor) Juez (Judge)

[10] A detailed discussion of the political and administrative system follows in Chapter VII.

overlap but are still rather clear. The urban-centered upper class confines its political and administrative concerns to affairs of urban and district importance. Persons of middle-class standing hold positions of secondary importance in the district and assume the highest posts in the *barrios*. The most ambitious members of the middle class, however, can aspire to the district-level position of *concejal*, and even to that of *gobernador*, if they have the proper "connections." The lower-class group, which is primarily rural, takes part in the official organization at the lowest levels or not at all. The same kind of class division applies in all other organized activities, as in, for example, lay religious organizations, civic committees, and public works projects.

As in the case of the distinctions based on residence, Huaylinos themselves indicate the existence of these more complex differentiations through their classificatory terminology. Such expressions can be divided into two groups: the first emphasizes economic and occupational differences and the second refers to more general sociocultural characteristics (Table 15).

Table 15. Class terminology used as terms of reference

Economic and occupational distinctions		
Lower class	*Middle class*	*Upper class*
Gente plebe (common people)	Gente obrera (laboring people)	Los ricos (the rich)
Gente común (common people)	Gente trabajadora (working people)	Los mas ricos (the richest)
Gente pobre, los pobres (poor people)	Obreros (workers)	Adinerados (moneyed)

General sociocultural distinctions		
Lower class only	*Lower and middle classes*	*Upper class*
Gente indecente (rare) (indecent people)	Gente del barrio (people of the barrio)	Los visibles (the visible ones)
Gente humilde (humble people)	Cholos	Sociedad (the society)
Indios, gente indígena (rare) (Indians, Indian people)	Gente de poncho e llanqui (people of poncho and sandal)	Gente decente (decent people)
Clase indígena (rare) (Indian class)		Notables (notables)
		Caballeros (gentlemen)
		Mistis (rare) (mestizos upper class)

The proliferation of such terms is interesting. The words which one hears elsewhere in the Callejón, such as *indios, indígenas,* and *mistis,* are not commonly used in Huaylas and are usually avoided because of their negative connotations. Huaylinos stoutly insisted that there were no Indians in the district—at least, not like those of the *estancias* (rural areas) around Caraz or in Vicos.[11] Upper-class Huaylinos point out, when comparing the middle and lower classes with those of other districts, that there are no Indian serfs in Huaylas, that most Huaylinos speak Spanish, that there are few illiterates, and that the *gente humilde* do not wear the same sort of unique clothing which characterizes Indians elsewhere. Most of all, they note that Huaylinos are generally "progressive," not like the superstitious, conservative *indígenas* of other areas. Thus, the upper class is quite prepared, for the most part, to exempt the lower class from the Indian stigma that they may apply to this group throughout the rest of the Callejón.

Elsewhere, discrimination between the mestizo and the Indian has usually rested upon clearly distinguishable group differences, such as clothing, language, and, in some places, skin color, as well as distinct behavior. Both mestizos and Indians are "socially visible" to one another, and a glance or word is enough to classify anyone according to the hidebound stereotypes.[12]

Kubler's study of the early Republican population of Peru shows that the primary social distinctions, both in the colonial times and during the first years of independence, were the basis for establishing how much tax would be paid and who would pay it.[13] Thus, social category was of real importance for everyone. At first, obvious racial differences were brought into use as the basis for distinction. This was relatively simple, involving only the white Spaniards and the Indians. The offspring of racially mixed marriages were assigned the name mestizo. Eventually, many other terms came into use to designate persons of every type of racial heritage conceivable. That such a

[11] The schools of Vicos and Huaylas sponsored exchange visits in 1959. The Huaylinos' impressions were that the Vicosinos lived in very poor and "savage" conditions and that their lives were miserable. A Vicosino boy, who made the overnight trip to Huaylas and stayed with a lower-class family in town, said the Huaylas family lived "almost like Indians," because they spoke Quechua and ate the same kinds of food.

[12] As pointed out by Dean and Rosen (1955:8–9), visible characteristics serve as easy marks of identification and, consequently, provide the basis for stereotypes.

[13] Kubler, 1952:37–38.

system can become complex need scarcely be stated, but in Peru during the colonial period there eventually were dozens of such racial categories.[14]

The problem, so far as the interpretation of documents and census materials is concerned, lies in understanding what is meant by the terms used. Their meaning was, and still is, highly variable. For instance Kubler points out:

By Indian we have here accepted the census taker's or tax collector's judgment of who is an Indian, for it is with social attitudes towards race rather than with scientifically descriptive concepts of race that this paper deals.

The chief of these concerns is the self-identification of people who are being counted. They may or may not allow themselves to be called Indians, Mestizos or whites. The official taking the count, on the other hand, must in each case, given the extant attitudes towards race, form a judgment about the race of the individual before him. The aggregate of these attitudes and judgments as reported to the Government and public, affects the prevalent attitude towards "race."[15]

He adds:

Through four centuries of population mixture, these latter groups (Negroes, Whites, and Indians) have been so thoroughly mixed into the Peruvian gene pool that it is no longer possible or meaningful to discriminate among the crosses.

In light of this Kubler goes on to describe the waxing and waning of the Indian population vis-à-vis the mestizo population. In the District of Huaylas, there was a "reversion to Indian majority" in the early part of the nineteenth century and, in 1876 (Table 16) Huaylas was reported as having a considerable Indian population, although somewhat smaller than in previous years.[16]

[14] Varallanos (1962:66–71) presents a well-documented listing of such terminology, quoting Gregorio de Cangas' manuscript of 1762. According to this document, the racial classification system generated such human types as: the *mulato* from Spanish and Negro parents; the *tercerón* from Spaniard and *mulata;* the *cuarterón* from Spanish and *tercerón;* the *mestizo real* from Spanish and Indian parents; the *cholo* from *mestizo real* and *Indian parents;* the *chino* from Negro and Indian parents; the *rechino* from *chino* and Indian parents; and the *criollo* from *rechino* and *chino* parents. The list continues, seemingly, without end.

[15] Kubler, 1952:37–38.
[16] Kubler, 1952:40.

Table 16. Population of the District of Huaylas as classified by race in 1836, 1841–1842, and 1876 *

	1836 †		1841–1842 †		1876 †	
	Number	Per cent	Number	Per cent	Number	Per cent
Indians	1,188	35	1,243	34	1,582	28
Mestizos	2,134	65	2,359	66	3,859	72
Total	3,322	100	3,602	100	5,441	100

* Kubler, 1952:20.

† Population figures for the entire district, without taking into account subsequent boundary revisions.

The 1940 Peruvian census did not clearly define the various "races" for the census takers. According to the census instructions:

In 1940, the investigation of race, as expressed during the preparatory work, yielded a result of a sociological rather than ethnographic order. At no time has it pretended to make a scientific cataloguing of the population by its racial characteristics.[17]

In order to determine "race," respondents were asked: "Are you white, Indian, Negro, yellow, or mestizo?" Anyone who didn't answer, or didn't know, was assigned to the mestizo category. According to the census report 13 per cent of the answers to this question were made by the respondents and the rest—87 per cent—were filled in by the census takers. The census report states as a fact that because the question was asked by the census takers, and the information recorded, "it was clearly possible to differentiate between individuals of Indian, Negro, and yellow race, but that white and mestizo citizens were confused frequently." These two categories, therefore, were combined in reporting the results.[18]

Nevertheless, Kubler's notion that the "race" categories found in the

[17] Perú, Ministerio de Hacienda y Comercio, 1944, Vol. I:clxxviii (my translation).

[18] Perú, Ministerio de Hacienda y Comercio, 1944, Vol. I:clxxviii. Rowe (1947) recognizing this problem, made another analysis of the 1940 census, using language as the criterion for "Indianness." Although it is possible to concur with Kubler's statements quoted above, agreement ends when he speaks of "Indian gains" and "mestizo waves," as if populations were sweeping back and forth across the highlands. With reference to several provinces of the Department of Ancash, Kubler (1952:43) states: "The tendency is for the mestizo majority to move steadily into the mountains from coastal or montaña bases." This, of course, is false, as migration studies have shown (Dobyns and Vázquez, 1963).

census materials are measures of social attitudes and status is an extremely useful one. The fact that the 1940 census report recognizes this is of considerable help in the interpretation of the census materials.

According to Table 16, the Indian population of Huaylas remained relatively constant through the last century while the mestizos "gained" significantly in numbers. By 1940, however, the Indian population had all but vanished in Huaylas, in sharp contrast to the neighboring districts of Caraz and Mato. "Indians" constituted but 2 per cent of the total population of the district of Huaylas, while Caraz reported that 61 per cent of its inhabitants were Indians, and Mato, 62 per cent. The District of Huaylas reported the smallest percentage of Indians in the entire Department of Ancash, which assigned 55 per cent of its total population to this category in 1940. If Kubler's hypothesis is true, then the conclusion to be reached in the case of Huaylas is that a notable change in attitudes concerning "Indians" had taken place, or that the "Indians" of Huaylas recognized that "mestizo" status was more advantageous and insisted upon being classified as such. The figures may thus be taken as an expression of social attitudes, since the majority of the 1940 census takers were Huaylinos, just as they were for the 1961 national census.

To illustrate this point further, a brief review of local records presents an interesting picture of judgments concerning Indians in Huaylas. Marked changes appear in the registry of vital statistics whenever new municipal secretaries take office. Thus, in 1931, forty-three "Indians" were born; in 1932, none; in 1933, 114; in 1934, 234; in 1935, 185; and in 1936, one. One secretary recorded almost everyone as "Indian"—even some members of local upper-class families who would never so consider themselves. When that secretary was replaced (1936), "Indians" ceased to be born in Huaylas. Somewhat later the racial classification was officially dropped from its records by the census bureau, although the Ministry of Public Health requests it for their compilations.

While discussing the affairs of the Comunidad Indígena with one of its officers, we came across a partial census of its members, which, among other things, classified them according to "race" (Indian, mestizo, or white). After noting that one of the most fair-skinned men in the district [19] was classified as an Indian I inquired about the criteria

[19] He was also one of the most widely traveled. Being a former merchant seaman, he had spent several months in Europe as well as in the United States and the Far East.

used in establishing this classification. The man replied, "The lighter-skinned ones are the mestizos." Pointing to a swarthy young man who was passing the doorway, I asked what he was. The reply was that he was a mestizo. "How can that be," I asked, "if the first man mentioned is classified as an Indian, and the young man who just passed is so dark?" The man answered that the former liked to consider himself an Indian for political reasons because he was active in the Comunidad Indígena, but that the young man who had passed the door was mestizo because he wore a suit and "looked" cosmopolitan.

He went on to add that there are no longer any "real Indians" in Huaylas and that, unlike other places in the Callejón, most of the population spoke Spanish. He said that it had been so long since the typical Indian costume [20] passed out of use that no one could really remember the details of it. He added that he thought such clothing was last worn around 1870. He noted that the young people, especially those who go to Lima, do not want to be registered in the Comunidad Indígena because of the general connotation it carries of being "backward," that is, being an Indian.

In genetic terms, there are no pure representatives of any race in Huaylas, because the population has been thoroughly mixed for quite some time. Thus the range of phenotypes is wide and not at all uniform, as can be judged from the various plates. Nevertheless, some claim they can distinguish some unique racial differences among the population. Many persons prize fair complexions, light hair,[21] and other traits which are identified as non-Indian. Among these was a school teacher who claimed that she could tell the difference between the children of two *barrios* because those of one *barrio* had rounder faces with "eyes like Chinese," [22] while those of the other *barrio* (where she taught) had "finer, whiter faces." In spite of a wide acquaintance with the people of both *barrios*, this was a discrimination I was never able to make. It is to be noted, that the teacher's view coincided with the wider use of homespun garments in the one *barrio*, as opposed to the other. Thus, it would appear that style of dress and vested interest altered the

[20] From descriptions, the old Indian costume of Huaylas was similar to that worn in Hualcán today (Stein, 1961:86–90).

[21] Such physical characteristics are termed *rubio* (blond). The same term is also used to describe cigarettes made of light-colored tobaccos, such as U.S. brands. Inexpensive Peruvian brands are called *negros* (blacks) and are considered inferior.

[22] In the sierra, Indian girls are often called *chinas* by Indians, as well as by others. Indians are generally considered to have mongoloid physical traits.

teacher's perception of the racial status of her pupils. When not making comparisons, however, the same teacher asserted that the children she taught were "difficult" because they were "like Indians." Thus, the problem of distinguishing people according to visible characteristics is subject to the vagaries of individual attitude, perception, experience, and casual bias.

The problem of making such "racial" discriminations becomes more difficult as varying combinations of phenotype, dress, and language occur, and inconsistencies become common. For example, it is not unusual to find in such records as birth registers, in which there is classification according to "race," that at one time, a person has been listed as Indian, and, at another time, as mestizo.

The visible symbol of class membership most often encountered is that of dress. As noted elsewhere, the traditional Indian populations are identified by their style of dress, which in great part was instituted by the Spaniards in colonial times. The traditional dress of the region has been well described and need not be discussed here.[23]

In Huaylas, the clothing of even the most "Indian" of individuals differs from that worn in Vicos or in the uplands of Caraz. The principal difference is that lower-class men in Huaylas wear clothing tailored in modern Western style, whether or not the cloth is of homespun woolen *bayeta*. They do not wear distinctive woolen jackets, vests, or *bayeta* shirts. Instead they wear home-sewn or factory-made cotton shirts of modern style. Men's trousers are also modern in style (with pocket and buttoned fly, features which Indian clothes often do not have), made either of wool homespun, or cotton cloth. A common feature of men's pants in Huaylas is the familiar navy "bell-bottom" cut. This, just like sailor's attire, is functionally designed so that the pant legs may be easily rolled up to the knees, or above, when one is irrigating fields. Woven sashes (*fajas*) are used by many men instead of belts.

Most of the men wear *llanquis*[24] (sandals), but many also own and wear shoes, on occasion. No men go barefoot. The final items of the lower-class male wardrobe are the ubiquitous *poncho* and hat, which

[23] Stein, 1961:86–90.
[24] All sandals in Huaylas and elsewhere in the Callejón are made of discarded automobile tires, cut to the proper foot size and attached to the foot by rubber bands cut from old inner tubing. This constitutes, in all probability, the most durable footwear in the world.

are worn day and night. Woven of wool, the *poncho* is usually a walnut color [25] and may have vertical reddish stripes woven into the otherwise plain cloth. Completing the attire is a "Panama" hat, with a high, tubular crown and wide brim. These hats, which are made in Piura on the north coast of Peru, cost from eighty to three hundred *soles* ($2.50 to $10.50) each. New ones are usually purchased each year during the Fiesta of Saint Elizabeth from merchants who come from Piura for the occasion. The only other place in the Callejón where these hats are commonly worn is around the city of Yungay. No men in Huaylas carry the special pouches used elsewhere for *coca* (which is chewed like tobacco) and, if used, *coca* is carried in a handkerchief stuffed in one's pocket. Most of the men have their hair cut in modern style, although it often goes uncombed under the ever-present hat.[26]

For lower-class women, the clothing is simple and preserves many Indian elements. The basic style consists of a skirt and a loose-fitting cotton blouse of plain or print material which comes down to the hips. The most common skirt is the *pollera* made of heavy, homespun wool *bayeta* cloth. A very full skirt reaching to the shins of the wearer, Huaylas *polleras* are almost always some shade of red, from a deep garnet to a "shocking pink." The waist of the *pollera* is made of white cotton cloth, four or five inches wide, so that the skirt will not be too bulky at the waistline, as one woman explained it. Occasionally one sees a blue *pollera* or one of plain, undyed wool, but these are rare.

All women in Huaylas wear some sort of shoe. The most common type is of crudely tanned sheepskin and is made in Yungay. The style of these shoes is uniform: black leather with white leather trim, a laceless instep, and a very slight heel. Some lower-class women also own a pair of low-heeled shoes or oxfords for special occasions.[27] All lower-class women wear the *lliclla* (carrying cloth) over their shoulders, and this, too, is of wool homespun and usually matches the *pollera* in color. In addition, many women wear dark blue, fringed shawls (*pañolones*) which are manufactured in Lima. Completing the outfit is

[25] The color is called *nogál* (walnut), because the dye was usually derived from the walnut tree.

[26] Indian men at Vicos and elsewhere are distinguished not only by their heavy felt hats but also by their "bowl" haircuts.

[27] In the Huaraz area, high-top button shoes are fairly popular among Indian and *cholo* women. These are shoes made locally from ancient patterns which have been carefully saved over the years. This type of shoe is not worn in Huaylas. Elsewhere in the Callejón, most Indian and lower-class women go barefoot.

the ever-present hat of the same kind as that worn by the men. All the lower-class women wear their hair in twin braids, often interwoven with bits of colored cloth.

Fiesta wear is somewhat more colorful than the daily garb. Both women and men show a decided preference for bright cotton materials that have a satin luster for shirts, blouses, and dresses. The women may wear the *pollera* under the long cotton fiesta dress, but in no case do they wear more than one *pollera* at the same time.[28]

In contrast, upper-class persons wear modern Western fashions, either factory-made or home-sewn. Since many women are skilled at dressmaking, and since more than 80 per cent of the families have sewing machines, home-sewn or locally made clothes are most common, the patterns being copied from magazines and from old Montgomery Ward and Sears catalogues.[29] Suits, white shirts, and ties are worn on formal occasions by the men. Day-to-day attire consists of sport shirts and wool gabardine or cotton drill pants. Women wear a wide range of modern dress styles. Sweaters are very common and are often knitted at home. For outings and sports, some young women wear slacks (but no shorts—ever). The middle-aged or older women wear the dark *pañolones*, particularly in the evenings or in church. For daily wear, long beige cotton stockings are worn for protection from gnats. On dress-up occasions, high heels are worn, despite the difficulties posed by the cobblestone streets.

Certain lower-class items of clothing are worn by the upper class, because they are considered practical and appropriate sierra dress. These include *ponchos*, which are universally worn by men, and frequently the high-crowned "Panama" hats. The *ponchos*, however, are of a somewhat finer yarn than those of the lower class and tend to be of a lighter color, although this is highly variable. Such a *poncho* is thought to be of better quality and, consequently, is referred to as a *poncho de caballero* (gentleman's *poncho*). Upper-class men generally wear their *ponchos* only at night or on cold or rainy days. Because of the cold, many upper-class women wear *polleras* as petticoats, and they

---

[28] Indian women in neighboring areas in the Callejón wear as many as a dozen *polleras* at once, particularly during fiestas.

[29] These cherished possessions are purchased in Lima for about a dollar. In addition to their use by seamstresses and tailors, shoemakers also copy catalogue patterns on the request of their clients, who thumb through them to select the style they wish.

frequently use the Yungay shoes as slippers, although they rarely wear either outside the home.

Thus, the clothing styles of the upper and lower classes appear distinctive and easily recognizable, indeed almost as markedly so as anywhere in the region. The middle-class group, however, blends the two styles in various ways. The men, while usually wearing sandals, hats, and *ponchos*, also wear belts, shoes, creased pants, and, occasionally, suit coats. For work, however, they may wear the typical homespun clothing of the lower class. At other times, the combination of clothing worn by a given individual may vary in other ways. The same holds true of the women as well. On one occasion, they may wear a *pollera*, *lliclla*, hat, and Yungay shoes, and on another occasion, a cotton dress, nylons or long cotton stockings, shoes, sweater, and the inevitable hat. Women and girls of this class frequently wear cotton dresses over a *pollera* for daily work. Another very common item of their wardrobe is a kind of pinafore made of a close-checked, black and white cotton material. It is worn by both women and girls over their other garments.

In addition to these mixed fashions, there are other, older styles, worn primarily by elderly persons, particularly the women. Several of them (over seventy years of age) wear two-piece, ankle-length dresses, made of flowery cotton-print material, and high-crowned hats with wide black bands around them. Hat bands are not worn by anyone else, even for mourning.

Old photographs also indicate that fashions have changed with the times in Huaylas. It appears that at the turn of the century the style of clothing worn by the upper class was clearly Victorian—in both men's and women's clothing. The lower-class styles have also changed—at least insofar as the *ponchos* are concerned. The old photographs show a black *poncho* with wide vertical stripes to have been the vogue around 1901, whereas today this style is worn only by a few old men, and the plain brown, or *nogál*, color predominates.

The upshot of all this is a polyglot of fashions which is increasingly subject to change, especially among the lower and middle classes. Other items of wearing apparel, such as cardigan sweaters and open-toed shoes for women, and sneakers and blue denim pants for men, are the vogue for many of the young people. Construction helmets, such as those worn during the work on the hydroelectric plant installation at Huallanca, are very common among middle- and lower-class men, and even some of the upper-class men wear them on occasion. Changes in clothing styles are also prompted by one's relatives in Lima, who are a constant source of new fashion ideas and who send presents of clothing, catalogues, and magazines.

Abetting changes in fashion are seven of the main stores, which regularly carry stocks of ready-made clothing, and at least four stores which have a variety of shoes for sale. In addition, these same stores, plus several others, carry wide assortments of cotton cloth, thread, and other sewing supplies, such as patterns, for those who make their own clothing. One store also carries sewing machines in stock. As noted, there are many seamstresses, tailors, and shoemakers who are capable of making most of the items their clients may desire. Thus there are few obstacles—other than the lack of sufficient money, perhaps—to the adoption of new clothing styles or to the modification of old ones. Fashions are of great interest to the upper-class women who often talk about the new styles, and it is not unusual to observe lower-class women contemplating the purchase of new items in the stores or from clothing vendors during the Fiesta of Saint Elizabeth.

The matter of kinship is of continuing importance—that of having one's heritage defined as *de buena familia* (of good family). A few years ago, a young upper-class woman eloped with a schoolteacher from Santo Toribio because her father would not permit the marriage on social class grounds. Yet other men from the Campiña have married upper-class women from the town without difficulty. Thus there are signs that the situation is not as clearly defined as one might imagine, even in this most formidable and traditional sphere of social conservatism. The parish priest, who was not a Huaylino, half-complained to me that Huaylinos were just a "bunch of *cholos*" and that the "good" families were either decadent or had migrated to Lima. He said there were really no *blanco* (white) families left in Huaylas anymore. "Those we have today have all come into town from the hills," he stated. Analysis of the upper class at the present time shows that approximately 10 per cent of them have indeed come from the rural areas of the district and are not descended from the "good" families, thus indicating that although the situation is not as extreme as depicted by the priest, there is considerable social mobility.

The priests' opinion is echoed by some members of still-prominent "good" families, particularly by the women, who say that *sociedad* in Huaylas is not what it used to be fifty years ago when there were "real" gentlemen. "Then," one woman remarked, "the Indians knew their place and were not allowed into the offices of the Concejo Distrital." She continued, "Now, anyone can go there, and even work there." Such people in Huaylas—the would-be gatekeepers of an exclusive upper class—speak wistfully of the old days and not without some feeling of regret about the present situation. But more significant is their feeling that they can do nothing to alter the course of events. Thus, some either take little part in public life or remain as key figures in some small area of activity, usually connected with the church. Others, however, and they appear to constitute a slight majority, have fully accepted the developing pattern of social relations. Moreover, because the traditionalists are advancing in age, their influence is likely to continue its decline.

Social and Cultural Mobility

Some members of the upper class maintain that lower-class parents are reluctant to send their children to school and are not really interested in education or "getting ahead." Yet, in the next breath, many of these same individuals proudly assert that the *gente humilde* have built schools in each of the *barrios* by their own labor, that one finds few Huaylinos who cannot read, and that most Huaylinos have a real desire to *superarse* (to improve themselves). The lack of consistency is an indication that the ascribed characteristics that served as the basis for determining social status are being supplanted by other, more complicated criteria, such as amount of schooling, degree of technical training, or monetary wealth—things based upon achievement. While the traditional upper-class ideas about the "Indian" lower class persist, there is, nevertheless, an increasing awareness that these ideas are not valid and that the stereotypes no longer fit. Table 17 follows this line of analysis and is intended to give a somewhat more precise perspective of class characteristics.

At the present time, as contact between people of various cultural backgrounds increases, both in the Callejón and on the coast, so does the transculturation process, with the result that the traditional ethnic divisions become blurred, and economic, political, and other differences assume greater importance. A significant feature of social mobility in Huaylas is the fact that persons who have effected a change in their status have usually benefited from a reputation and experience gained outside the district. In Huaylas, migration or travel per se do not

Table 17. Social class and cultural characteristics of the population of the District of Huaylas according to selected criteria

Criterion	Class characteristics		
	Upper class (10%)	Middle class (60%)	Lower class (30%)
Residence	Almost entirely urban	Urban and rural	Primarily rural
Language	Spanish is the first language, Quechua is spoken by most	Use of Spanish and Quechua about equal	Quechua is the first language. Most men speak Spanish, but about one-third of the women speak only Quechua
Education	Complete primary schooling through university. No illiterates	Primary schooling, complete or incomplete. The few illiterates are almost all women	Primary schooling generally incomplete. Some men and about one-third of the women are illiterate
Dress	Modern Western styles. A few Indian items retained as practical	Predominance of Western styles, but many Indian items are common. Some homespuns; all wear sandals or cheap shoes	Homespun clothing in Western style is most common, but with many Indian features. Sandals and cheap shoes worn by all
Contacts outside Huaylas	Strong, particularly with Lima middle-class groups and comparable groups in Caraz and Huallanca	Strong, particularly with Lima and Chimbote working-class groups	Variable, contacts mostly with lower-class groups in Lima and Chimbote
Social mobility	Variable, mobility usually into Lima middle class, and becoming white-collar employees	Generally high mobility into coastal working class. Some mobility into local upper class	Variable, local mobility possible into middle class and, perhaps upper class, but only into lowest working-class groups on coast

Cultural orientation	Lima as well as regional and local	Coastal and local	Local, but coastal influence is considerable
Place of origin	Most are Huaylinos by birth but about ten per cent are from other places in the Callejón. Often immigrants are married to Huaylinos	Virtually all are Huaylinos. The few outsiders marry Huaylinos	Same as middle class. Some, however, have escaped from haciendas in the region
Migration rate	High, usually to Lima and usually permanent, but some return	High, particularly in Lima and Chimbote, but many return to Huaylas	Lower than the others; migration to Lima and Chimbote; some do seasonal work on coast plantations; many return
Occupation	Farming is often conducted for profit; almost all own farm land. Merchants, professionals and some artisans; having two or three secondary occupations is common	Self-sufficient farming and small business. Most are artisans, some have technical skills. Two or three occupations are common	Subsistence farming, part-time business (shopkeepers, vendors), day laborers, shepherds, weavers; multiple occupations are common
Economic status and capital	Wealthy in local terms. Generally own more land and equipment. Liquid assets available for small investments. Some use of banking facilities. Individual yearly income range: $900—$5,000 (U.S.) in 1961	Poor to moderately wealthy. Own land and equipment in lesser amounts. Availability of liquid assets variable, but usually limited. No use of banks. Individual yearly income range: $100—$1,500 (U.S.)	Poor, own land in very small units, and are poorly equipped. Almost no assets for investment. No use of banks. Individual yearly income range: $50—$500 (U.S.)
Economic enterprise	Variable. Generally conservative. High degree of independence, co-operative ventures involving three or more persons are rare	Variable. Often willing to take greater risks. Show considerable initiative, highly independent. Cooperative ventures limited to two or three persons	Generally conservative. Lack sufficient capital for anything but small home investments. Highly independent and cooperative ventures are rare

Table 17. (cont.)

| | Class characteristics | | |
Criterion	Upper class (10%)	Middle class (60%)	Lower class (30%)
Work patterns and attitudes	Both manual and nonmanual tasks are performed. Participation in agricultural work common. Wage labor used. Some preference for nonmanual tasks, but being a "good worker" is valued. Servants are common, but not universal	Mostly manual labor. Skill and reputation as a good worker is valued. Some use paid labor, but work with *rantín** also is used. A few have servants	Strictly manual labor. Being a good worker essential and valued. Little use of wage labor. More use of *rantín*
Level of living	Comfortable. Basic needs are satisfied. "Luxury" items are obtainable and common	Variable. But basic needs are generally satisfied. Few luxury items owned, but many are desired	Austere. Basic needs are usually met, but living conditions are very simple and poor. No luxury items to speak of
Political status and participation	Hold positions of town and district-wide importance. Some have regional influence in politics. No *barrio* posts held. Almost all vote	Hold high *barrio* positions and some district political offices. No regional influence. Many vote	Hold lower posts in the *barrios*. No regional influence. Few vote
Public and civic activities	Direction and active participation in civic projects and activities. Considerable initiative shown	Supporting leadership and active participation at lower levels. Considerable initiative shown in *barrio* work projects	Supporting or passive participation in public activities. Less initiative shown
Comunidad Indígena	Few participate or hold membership; those who are members have held top	Many are active members and hold high positions but many are also	Many are members, but most are not. Some hold or have held lower *barrio*

	positions. Most are hostile to the Comunidad	hostile to the Comunidad	offices
Kinship	Direct relationship with "good" families is usual but some are unrelated to them	"Poor relations" of the "good" families, but many are unrelated to them	Most are not related to "good" families—or such relationships are not given much weight
Family organization and structure	Family size is highly variable but is usually large. Many women are heads of families separated for a variety of reasons. Nuclear family and closest consanguineal ties most important	Same as upper class	Same as upper class
Marriage	Civil and/or religious ceremonies are usual, but there are a number of consensual unions. Average age at marriage for both sexes is over 28 years	Same, but there is some preference for religious over the civil ceremony. Many consensual unions. Average age at marriage is lower	Same as middle-class group
Compadrazgo *	*Compadres* chosen from upper class only or from prestigeful outsiders. Often serve as *protectores* for institutions	*Compadres* chosen from upper and middle classes, some outsiders chosen. Few serve as *protectores*	*Compadres* chosen from all social classes within the district. None serve as *protectores*
Religion	Roman Catholic. Understanding of formal practice and doctrine is usual. Formal support of church strong, but attendance nominal and mostly female. Few men receive communion or confess. Men tend to be anticlerical	Roman Catholic. A few Protestants of fundamental sects. Understanding of formal practice and doctrine somewhat less than that of upper class. Attendance at mass irregular, and more female than male. Few of either sex receive communion or confess	Roman Catholic. Fewer Protestants. Low comprehension of Catholic practice and doctrine. Attendance at mass very irregular. Almost none receive communion or confess

* See Glossary.

Table 17. (cont.)

Criterion	Class characteristics		
	Upper class (10%)	Middle class (60%)	Lower class (30%)
Religious activities	Women active in the *hermandades*,* but male participation highly selective. Fiesta participation on formal level and only in major celebrations	Some men and women active in *hermandades* and in teaching of catechism. Serve as *mayordomos** for small fiestas at rural chapels.	Few are active in formal organizations. General participation in rural and town fiestas
Health and medicine	Modern medicine accepted, but many folk practices and beliefs are common. Many wish to have a clinic or medical service in Huaylas	Modern medicine accepted in selective ways, but greater dependence on traditional medical belief and practice. Many would like a clinic in Huaylas	Much less acceptance of modern medical techniques. A few are interested in having a clinic in Huaylas
Hygiene and sanitation	Germ theory of disease poorly understood. Sanitation facilities primitive or nonexistent. Cleanliness and personal hygiene are valued. Some desire for improved sanitation, e.g., a sewerage system and water supply	No sanitary facilities. Less personal hygiene than upper class; otherwise the same. Little concern for improved facilities	The same. Personal hygiene poor. Residences are often extremely dirty or even squalid. None expressed concern for improved facilities
Food and nutrition	Relatively wide variety of foods. Intake of animal protein relatively good. Vegetables commonly used. Canned goods common. All cooking methods used. Home-produced items and cereals basis of diet. Many use recipe books	Less variety and lower animal protein intake. Greater dependence on home-grown items, mainly cereals. Some canned goods used for special occasions. Less variety in preparation	Similar, but with much greater dependence on cereals and home-grown products. Little meat. Little variety. Few vegetables

| Recreation and entertainment | Some coed recreation, e.g., volleyball, dances, picnics, and fiestas. Men play soccer, billiards, poker, etc. Dance is both modern and traditional. Men drink a great deal—all kinds of alcoholic beverages, but little pure *alcohol*. *Chicha** made by all. Most men smoke, and some women do. *Coca** not used. Men smoke more expensive Peruvian brands and some foreign brands | Coed activities limited to dances. Men play soccer, cards, and some billiards. Mostly traditional dances, but some are familiar with other. Heavy drinking, but less beer and more *alcohol* and *chicha*. Most men smoke, but women do not. Many men use *coca*, but the majority do not. Cheapest Peruvian brands smoked. | The only coed recreation is during fiestas. Men play some soccer, cards, but no billiards. Traditional dances almost exclusively. Men drink a lot—mostly *alcohol* and *chicha*. Most men use *coca*, but no women do. Men smoke when cigarettes are available—the cheapest brand |

---

*See Glossary.

enhance one's local prestige so much as does being able to point to some achievement, or to some prestigeful experience one has had while away which merits local recognition. Attaining a higher education (secondary or university), mastering some modern technical skill, or acquiring advanced business experience are particularly important. Although many sought to gain this kind of experience in Lima, the construction of the hydroelectric plant in Huallanca also provided many opportunities for Huaylinos during the past twenty years.

Beginning in 1944, the Santa Corporation and the many contractors engaged in the construction hired Huaylinos in all branches of their activity and provided them with advanced technical training in many fields. A brief review of the corporation's records revealed that over 600 Huaylinos had worked in the construction phase of the project and that, in 1960, almost 40 per cent of the operating staff of the plant were from the district. Many of these men, starting as laborers, were given opportunities to earn masters' ratings as carpenters, masons, plumbers, electricians, mechanics, and so forth.

An example of such talent mobility afforded by the hydroelectric plant construction was the case of a man from the Campiña who began work in 1945 as a peon, earning two *soles* a day ($0.08). During the course of the project, he worked as a carpenter and mason and, finally, became an electrician's assistant. Eventually, he achieved the rating of master electrician and today, after some correspondence-school courses, he has become the chief assistant to the head engineer at the plant. He is in charge of the technical management of the plant and earns a monthly salary in excess of 6,000.00 *soles* (approximately $180.00), or almost twice the salary received by the highest paid schoolteacher in Huaylas. Because of his success, this man has begun to play a very active role in district activities, and his occupational achievements are recognized and praised by Huaylinos generally. Although his family background is representative of the lower class in Huaylas, he now participates increasingly in upper-class social life, for example, and does not hesitate to invite members of this group to his new, elegant house in Santo Toribio.

His case is notable from several points of view. It illustrates the role that such a project as the hydroelectric plant can play in a small sierra community, both in the development of latent talents and in injecting more money into the local economy. The project provided avenues for talent mobility, which otherwise would not have existed. It not only rewarded workers financially for their skills and achievements but gave them local prestige as well. Thus, it has proved possible to change one's social status from the lowest to the highest local stratum in the course of two decades. The records of several other men similarly engaged in the construction and operation of the plant approximate this pattern. Even workers who did not have such striking success emphasize the experience they acquired with the corporation, and a great many middle- and lower-class men wear their construction helmets as symbolic testimony to this.

These persons, as well as others who have achieved some sort of specialization outside of Huaylas, often mention this as their primary occupation, even though they are not practicing their particular skills in Huaylas, for example, as mechanics or accountants. That such achievements are positively sanctioned was illustrated when the district government awarded *diplomas de honor* to thirty-nine individuals (thirty-five men and four women) and seven organizations on the basis of their work and character (see Table 18). Of the group of persons thus recognized, twenty-eight were of upper-class status and eleven were of middle-class status. Ten were from rural areas and twenty-nine from the town. Three of the organizations were Huaylas regional clubs, located in Lima; two were "sport clubs"—one in the town and one in Santo Toribio—and two were schools.

It can be stated, as a consequence, that relatively positive attitudes

Table 18. Individuals and groups honored for their achievements by the District of Huaylas government, 1957 *

Achievement	Individual citations †	Organization citations
Excellence in farming	8	
Excellence in teaching	3	2
Professional standing and technical skill	13	
Competence in their work	7	2
Exemplary dedication in their work	19	
Building modern houses	2	
Outstanding work on behalf of Huaylas	4	3
Their progressive attitudes	7	2

* Distrito de Huaylas, "Relación de ciudadanos que el Concejo Distrital de Huaylas ha premiado con un 'Diploma de Honor' a todos aquellos que se han destacado en las diferentes actividades desarrollados en el Distrito." Manuscript Document, 1957.

† Many were dual citations.

toward upwardly mobile individuals are held by Huaylinos and are important factors in the conduct of social relations. Moreover, it is evident that these attitudes are widely shared in Huaylas and affect all social groups, a situation contrasting markedly with that which obtains in many neighboring areas in the Callejón.

In Recuayhuanca, for example, the people are effectively blocked from local social mobility by the traditional controlling groups in Marcará, and their achievements go unrecognized.[30] These people must, therefore, look outside the local environment altogether if they are motivated by any desires to change their status. Since this is the case, as Snyder points out, the coastal style of life—*lo criollo*—becomes the point of reference and serves as the model from which the Recuay-huancaino patterns his new life. The people of Recuayhuanca appear to forsake their village, deny that it has a future, as such, and seek their place in the outside world without reference to it. Those who leave do not classify themselves in local terms, nor do they wish to, for the new roles have no place in the static, traditional system. Consequently, the fact that the people of Recuayhuanca are changing makes no impact worth mentioning on the Marcarino, and vice versa.

In Huaylas, the question of social change must be answered differently. Because there is intimate contact between social groups in Huay-las and strong functional unity, pressures on the society have been felt throughout the district society. In marked contrast to Recuayhuanca, the middle-and lower-class Huaylino who seeks to alter his status within the society finds that he can hold positions of relative importance and that his achievements are recognized. In contrast to many areas in the Callejón, then, Huaylas society allows for greater local social mobility. The relative openness in Huaylas' social stratification is of course sustained by the diminishing cultural visibility and by the fact that people are "permitted" to assimilate if they wish to do so.

The loss of the visible symbols of uniqueness is well illustrated by the history of the Chinese in Huaylas and their incorporation into the Huaylas upper class. In 1960 there were five families of Chinese descent in Huaylas, persons whose fathers and grandfathers had come from the coast or who themselves had come many years ago.[31] All are accorded

[30] Snyder, 1960:485–493.

[31] So far as I can discover, eight Chinese men, all reportedly born in Canton, came to live in Huayas between 1880 and 1920. If there were others, I have found no record of them. Most of the Chinese brought to Peru during the last century

the same respect and status in Huaylas as other members of the upper class. Nevertheless things are sometimes said about their Chinese ancestry behind their backs, a fact which is known to them and is a source of sensitivity to some.

Since all of them are of mixed descent (mestizo and Chinese) they have been given the name, *injerto*,[32] which refers to this particular biological heritage. It is a term that is never used in front of a person so classified, unless an insult is intended. In official usage, as in the registry of vital statistics, pure Chinese were referred to as *asiáticos*, while those of mixed descent were termed mestizos. According to some Huaylinos, Chinese-mestizos are supposed to be brutish in deportment but extremely clever businessmen, skilled in mathematics and science. A cartoon in a magazine published by the Huaylas colony in Lima in 1930 depicted the *asiático* smoking a pipe, wearing traditional Chinese garb, his hair in a queue. The caption read: "Oriental—native of Asia—a race, little desirable." [33] Others say that the Chinese are very loving, devoted to their families, and "don't run around" much.[34] During the early part of this century, there were at least eight native Chinese merchants in town whose efficient operations soon gave them a name, such as other Chinese had earned elsewhere in Peru, as clever businessmen and competitors.[35] Indeed, one merchant in Huaylas remarked in confidence that the older Chinese storekeepers were soon going to retire or die—"*Gracias a Dios*" (Thank God!).

Such attitudes have prompted the Chinese in Huaylas to lose their

---

were men who were "contracted" to work on the coastal plantations as "coolie" labor. Some, in fact, were brought from the United States after the construction of the transcontinental railroad was completed. For an account of this period in Peruvian history, see Watt Stewart, *Chinese Bondage in Peru*, 1951. A brief summary of the role and culture of the Chinese in contemporary Peru is to be found in Kwong, 1958:41–49.

[32] Used throughout Peru.

[33] *Huaylas*, 1930:35.

[34] Stewart (1951:225) quotes the following observations of the United States Ambassador to Peru in 1874: "They (the coolies) intermarry with the lower class of whites, mestizas, and cholas, and by these are looked upon as quite a catch, for they make good husbands—industrious, domestic, and fond of their children—while the *cholo* (Indian) husband is lazy, indolent, often a drunkard and brutal to his wife."

[35] In Lima, the best bargains and variety are considered to be at the shops of "*los chinos*," which are located around the main markets. This, like most other such stereotypes, is fallacious, but what merchant would wish to change that sort of image in the minds of his clients.

ethnic identity, so far as possible. Although one means to accomplish this was marriage to Peruvians, one of the Huaylas Chinese sent for his bride from China (in 1925). Of the other native Chinese (all of whom claim to have been born in Canton), three married daughters of the first Chinese who had come to Huaylas at the end of the nineteenth century, but two others (both born in Peru), who came to Huaylas later, married women who were not of Chinese descent. Four of the native Chinese retained their surnames, but the others sought to adopt Spanish names instead, for example, by assuming the surname of their *padrino* of baptism. Another means of obtaining a Spanish name was for the children of a Chinese father and a Peruvian mother to use their maternal Spanish name, as indeed some of the members of one Chinese-Peruvian family do in Huaylas today.[36]

In the old days, the Chinese remained Buddhists and so, when they died, were not buried in the municipal cemetery (which is reserved for Christians), but rather were interred at the top of San Cristobal, a small hill at the edge of town, in a spot which is still referred to as the "Chinese graveyard." [37] Many years have passed, however, since the last person was buried there, for now the Huaylas "Chinese" profess Catholicism and, like everyone else, are laid to rest in the proper place. The descendants of the original immigrants are now inextricably caught up in the web of kinship and *compadrazgo*. So far as I know, none of them learned to speak Chinese. They have become policemen, schoolteachers, farmers, and cattle breeders, thus departing from the stereotype that they are all merchants (five of them, indeed, are). By the next generation, they will have become almost indistinguishable from the rest of the population.

While the Chinese were striving to "disappear" from view by dropping their distinctive traits and to be absorbed into the local urban society, other outsiders from the region who have entered this setting, although required to make fewer adjustments, also found it necessary

[36] Of the members of one family of Chinese descent, one man uses his paternal name some of the time, but often signs documents using his maternal name. His other brothers and sisters generally use the mother's name all the time. This is a common custom elsewhere in Peru also and is regarded as an avenue of "cultural assimilation." See Stewart, 1951:224.

[37] Apparently it served for all persons of doubtful origin or religion, since an Englishman named José Berry was also buried there, in 1906, under somewhat mysterious circumstances (*Libro de Actas, Distrito de Huaylas*, entry dated May 16, 1906).

to conform to the norms of Huaylas life. Such adjustment, however, did not involve the drastic modification in behavior nor the psychological stress that must have weighed heavily upon the Chinese. At the present time, roughly 10 per cent of the upper class of Huaylas is composed of persons who have immigrated from other places in the region. This feature of the upper class suggests a pattern of regional social mobility. Many of the migrants to Huaylas came from middle-class (as in Huaylas) backgrounds and as entrepreneurs have entered the Huaylas upper class.

That the pathways of social mobility have been opened in Huaylas to these outsiders as well as to native Huaylinos is due in some extent to the departure of the upper-class "gatekeepers." Indeed, many of the old "good family" names are sparsely represented in Huaylas now. The exodus of the regional upper class apparently began during the second decade of the present century and increased as the roads were completed to the coast.

External influences have been strong in Huaylas, motivating the whole society to move toward something new in terms of social stratification and culture—a level which is not Indian, nor mestizo, nor coastal, but rather a synthesis of these. Although they appear willing to accept many things which are completely new, Huaylinos are not yet willing to discard all of their old habits and values. They continue to be proud of being *serranos*. They also continue to be proud of their independent work, and they see a future ahead for the district. Whereas the Marcará-Recuayhuanca-Vicos society remains thoroughly dichotomized, despite the changes affecting the individual there, Huaylas has moved toward greater sociocultural integration. There are marked tendencies in Huaylas to minimize social differences largely by removing the Indian stigma from the lower class, by placing value on achievements, and by emphasizing economic and occupational uniformity ("We are all farmers. There are no rich men here."), and by openly encouraging social unity—a "community of fate"—in promotion of the common welfare.

CHAPTER V

The Adobe World:
The Physical Setting

In many ways it is correct to say that the highland culture is an adobe culture. The classic mud brick of ancient origin shelters the family in the home, encircles the animals in the corral, and allows the dead to rest in security behind its walls. The adobe brick has no competition as a building material in Huaylas. Extremely durable when properly cared for, and remarkable for its adaptability, it lends itself to all kinds of construction designs. Adobe has still another virtue to recommend it: it is available to everyone and costs very little, about twenty centavos (eight-tenths of a cent, U.S.) per brick (1960).

While adobes can be easily made at any time during the year, the preferred time is the dry, or summer, season when a strong and constant sun dries the soft mud within a few days. This time falls during the slack periods in the agricultural cycle, the months of May and June and late August through early December. Then, throughout the countryside, men are to be seen making adobes in the fields, usually beside a partially completed house which had been started a year or so before. In urban as well as rural areas much construction is in progress, both in building new houses and in making repairs and additions to older structures. Few buildings, however, are ever completed in the same year in which they are begun, a fact which is true not only in Huaylas but elsewhere in the sierra as well. The roof tiles, which are made locally, are placed on the top of the walls to protect the unfinished adobe from the rain. Many builders, in lieu of tiles, cut sections of *penca* (agave leaf) and lay them over the adobes.

Before any construction is undertaken, the builder first must have sufficient adobes on hand, as well as other construction material which he had accumulated during the preceding months and years, whether by his own labor, hired labor, or purchase. Unless the builder considers himself to be a qualified mason, he usually consults or hires one to aid him in the construction. In the case of the urban upper class this is always done, since members of this class generally do not engage in such building trades as masonry, tilemaking, or plastering. In spite of the upper-class tendency to avoid this kind of physical labor, many do engage in it for short periods, working with the mason or plasterer and sometimes directly assisting in the work.

It is the rule, outside the upper-class group, that the owner of a house contributes a large share of the labor in its construction. To supplement his own efforts, a man may call upon his relatives, hire peons, or sponsor a *rantín* (or *minka*). Of the three methods, nowadays, the first two are the most common, but the labor-exchange "bee," or *rantín,* is by no means rare. It is quite clear, however, that when time and money are foremost in the thoughts of the builder, he will make use of hired help, since it is generally recognized that the *rantín* is not a particularly efficient means of getting a task done.

In all cases, the major task of the builder is to obtain as much work as possible from the others, particularly if they are being paid in some way for their labors. Thus, he cajoles, threatens, encourages, and plies his helpers with *chicha, alcohol,* meals, cigarettes, and *coca,* in various amounts, in accord with prior understandings and his financial capabilities. Depending upon what "extras" were included, a peon earned from S/6.50 to S/11.00 ($0.24 to $0.40) per day for his labors in 1961. The *maestro* or foreman (if there is one) who directs the activity received up to S/35.00 ($1.30) per day for his services.

Adobes are made in the following manner after a suitable piece of ground has been selected near the construction site. (So far as I could determine, there were no favorite sites for this in Huaylas, since the soil generally seems to lend itself to adobe manufacture.) The earth is loosened by means of crowbars (*barretas*), shovels, and hoes. Once a patch of some ten feet in diameter is thus prepared, water is poured into its center. The adobe-makers then proceed to tread on the loosened earth, mixing the water into it until a heavy, uniform mud is obtained. Wheat or barley straw, which has been saved from the threshing floors, is added to the mud and mixed into the preparation to provide the proper temper. When the *barro* (clay) is deemed ready, the *maestro* begins making the bricks, using a mold which is an open-sided, rectangular wooden frame, approximately eighteen inches in length, twelve inches in width, and six inches in depth.

Adobe-making is an all-day proposition, beginning at about 8:00 A.M. and often lasting till dark, that is, till about 6:30 P.M. This is the most arduous part of house building. Refreshments in the form of *chicha* and *alcohol* are invariably passed around to the hired men by the builder. When the work is performed by *rantín*, there is usually more eating, drinking, and horseplay, and the builder cannot demand a greater output from the workers. Houses may require from 4,000 to 10,000 adobes, or more. If the builder were to work constantly, with five or six men helping him, it would take from twenty to thirty days to prepare them. Because few men can devote so much consecutive time to the task, the preparation of sufficient adobes to build a substantial house may take two or three years.

Once adobes are on hand, however, construction proceeds rapidly. Even the walls of a large house may be erected within a week. They are erected over a foundation of stone which is laid in trenches roughly three feet deep. As in the adobe-making process, this phase of the work is frequently conducted with a great deal of enthusiasm, and a sort of competition may evolve between mason and adobe-and-mud carriers to see who can work the fastest. The hardest workers are considered the most *macho* or *guapo* (he-mannish). By late afternoon, when everyone has had a good deal to drink, there may be a great deal of joking and horseplay, and ear-splitting *guajes* (yells) ring through the air, signaling the close of the day's work. If another group of workers is in the vicinity, they will answer with louder *guajes*. Passersby are hailed in like fashion and may be invited over for some *chicha*, served in a gourd cup (*poto*) by the builder or his wife who circulate about with a large pitcher or bucket of the brew.

Lintels for the doorways and windows are prepared from eucalyptus trees, which are now grown by almost every householder. Eucalyptus beams are cut for the second floor and for the roof. All supporting timber is dressed by hand, using an adze. If the second-floor beams are not ready by the time the walls have reached the appropriate height, construction continues and space is allowed for their installation. Roofing requires somewhat more preparation. The beams are first closely covered with *carrizo*[1] or quartered *magueyes*.[2] These are tied crosswise to the beams with cord which may be either purchased or homemade from twisted *maguey* fiber. When this is done, the tiles are laid, being passed up to the men on the roof in bucket-brigade fashion. The roofing may proceed as the adobe work did, if a large party of men is involved.

Although tile roofs are the most common, many persons have used *calamina*, a corrugated and galvanized metal roofing material. At present, it is in use on some 51 out of 309 habitable houses in town. Although the *calamina* may be considered superior to tile (and, by implication, more prestigeful), it has not found universal acceptance because of such disadvantages as the greater initial cost, poorer insulating qualities, and the greater noise that rain makes on them. One frequently hears of another type of roofing material—*eternit*[3]—which is a corrugated, white cement composition board, used by the Santa Corporation for its employee housing in nearby Huallanca. Huaylinos consider this to be the superior roofing material, but do not buy it because of its cost.

Once roofed, the house, even though unfinished inside, will be put to use by its owner, if only for storage purposes. When the owner does not intend to finish the house immediately, adobes are piled in the doorways and windows to keep out stray animals and children.

The manner in which the house is designed and embellished is a matter of individual preference and affluence. Doors and window frames are quite uniform in style. If the house is of two stories, it invariably has a balcony or a place for installing one. These, too, are usually made of eucalyptus, and the better the house, the more elaborate the balcony. In the newest large houses in Huaylas, the balconies are elegantly trimmed with plaster in a style that could almost be described as baroque. Several houses also have wrought-iron grills for balcony railings.

If the owner can afford it, the house is finished on the outside with a

[1] A kind of bamboo grown in the eroded gorges.
[2] The long flower stalks of the *maguey* (agave).
[3] A brand name, but as in many other cases, the first or most famous product to reach acceptance lends its trade name as the generic term for *all* similar products. Thus, oatmeal is "Quaker," pressure kerosene stoves "Primus," and so on.

coat of locally mined plaster. Such a finish is almost never applied to the sides or rear of a building, if these do not face a street. This is true of the very best of houses and public buildings. Along the main streets, the lower portions of walls may be faced with concrete trim in various geometrical designs.

Someone who does not give his house a stucco finish may leave it as is, may apply a smooth mud coat over the adobe, or may whitewash all or part of it. A large number of houses in both urban and rural zones have a stucco finish, and most of the others are whitewashed in some part, for all the houses in Huaylas, by municipal order, are to be whitened for the celebration of Independence Day on July 28 each year. Accordingly, the plastered houses are brushed down to clean off the year's accumulation of dust, and many of the others are given a light, quick coat of whitewash, applied with a rag. The work is done for a few *soles* by numerous teenage boys and lower-class men, who hustle about advising the householders that they will be fined for not complying with the municipal order.

The cost of the house will, of course, depend upon the size and number of rooms which it contains. The present trend seems to be toward larger and more elegant houses, both in town and in the country. In 1961, for example, based on this consideration, the estimated minimal cost for a house of two stories and from four to six rooms (not including trim, doors, and so forth) was about $230.00. There are, however, many variations in design, as can be seen in Figure 4, and this, obviously, would affect the cost.

A common feature of virtually all the houses is that they are enclosed in some fashion and shut off from the outside. Homes that are not enclosed are to be found only among the poorest rural families. There is a patio in most houses, as well as a corral. In the poorer homes, the two may be combined. The corral has multiple uses: storage area, chicken and animal pen, and family latrine. The patio is, in most cases, an extension of the kitchen. In the poorest homes, this is its principal function. In the better homes, the patio may be cobbled and, as the center of much family activity, is frequently brightened by the presence of potted flowers, flower gardens, a scallion or herb patch, caged songbirds, pigeons, or, occasionally, a parrot.

For many families, the patio also serves as a *cuyero*. The shy *cuyes* (guinea pigs) scamper in and out along the edges of the wall, around the oven, or under the woodpile, which is their favorite hiding place much of the time. Many homes have a small, roofed area set aside for the *cuyes* in the patio or a reserved place for them in the kitchen. No home in Huaylas is without them, and their constant chortles and squeaks accompany all kitchen or patio activities. Large dome-shaped, adobe ovens also occupy prominent positions in the patios of almost 40 per cent of the homes in the district.

As indicated, new houses in Huaylas manifest a trend toward larger size and greater elegance in design and finish. The traditional home (now about 20 per cent of the houses), composed of two separate buildings divided by the patio, is apparently giving way to the large, single unit with multiple rooms. Houses under construction and recently completed in rural areas show a trend toward two-floor construction. Because the terrain is sloping, such buildings are often of "split-level" design. Balconies are also popular in the rural areas, apparently in imitation of prominent houses in town. Traditionally, as in other highland towns, even the best homes in Huaylas rarely have windows. When they do, their function is to provide ventilation through louvered openings rather than to admit light or the view. This is no longer true, for new houses invariably contain windows, often with glass panes. In addition, some of the best of these houses have windows, balconies, and second-floor porches so designed that they face the best views. Many of the most elaborate new houses belong to middle-class families.

These trends also point toward a quality of housing which indicates a notable improvement over the pattern shown in the rest of the Department in 1940. Whereas some 45 per cent of the families in the Department of Ancash lived in one-room houses in 1940, only 5 per cent of the families in Huaylas presently find themselves in this situation. In the district as a whole, the average number of rooms per house is 3.4, while in the urban areas it is almost four rooms per house. After seeing the ubiquitous *chozas* (tiny thatched huts) elsewhere in the sierra, one anticipates their presence and considers it normal. In Huaylas, they are rare and, for the most part, located in peripheral rural areas. Four out of five of these are converted *chullpas* (Inca burial houses), which are virtually the only stone houses in Huaylas. The persons occupying them are of lower-class status and the poorest in the district.

The houses of Huaylas also tell another story, that of movement and migration. While making the census maps, I was impressed by the large number of unoccupied houses and later, when conducting the census,

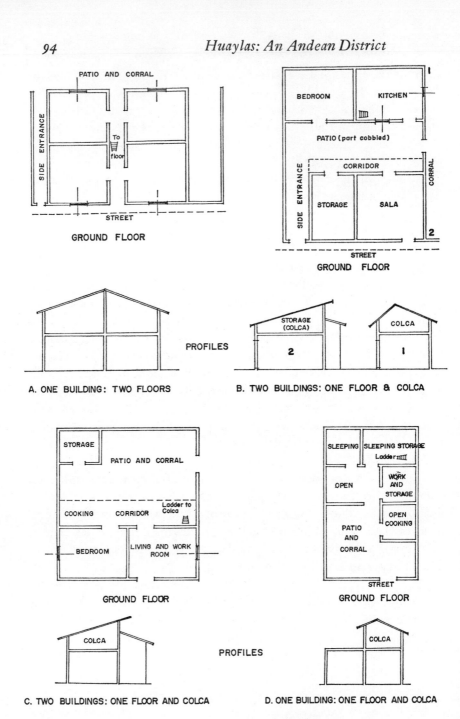

Figure 4. Huaylas house designs

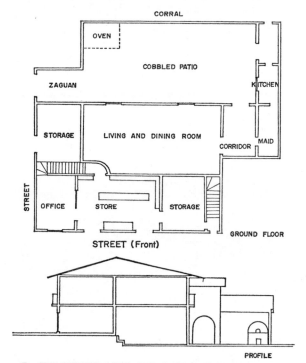

E. ONE BUILDING: TWO AND A HALF FLOORS

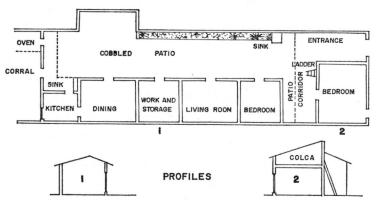

F. TWO BUILDINGS: ONE FLOOR AND COLCA

Figure 4 (cont.)

surveyed all of the unoccupied dwellings. The result gives yet another measure of the migration pattern (Table 19).

Table 19. Housing in the District of Huaylas by urban and rural areas and *barrios*, 1961

	Occupied houses	Unoccu-pied houses	Total habitable houses	Per cent unoccupied	Houses under construc-tion	Houses destroyed or abandoned
Urban Huaylas						
Delicados and						
Yacup	247	62	309	20.0	27	21
Rural						
Delicados	10	0	10	0.0	1	5
Yacup	88	29	117	24.3	9	4
Shuyo	154	44	198	22.1	14	15
Quecuas	201	68	269	25.2	28	19
Huayran	216	82	298	27.5	44	33
Iscap	129	33	162	20.4	33	20
Tambo	48	24	72	33.4	18	0
Total	1,093	342	1,435	24.1	174	117

The rate at which houses are being constructed in Huaylas is also interesting, 174 being in process at the time of the study. But why, with so many unoccupied houses, do people continue to build? Might it not be easier to rent or to use the empty home of a relative, for rents were very low, ranging from S/5.00 to S/100.00 per month for the best house in the district? [4] Many persons do live in the homes of relatives or have relatives living with them, but this is not the preferred residence pattern. This consists of not merely living away from one's parents, but, if possible, in a house on one's own land (or one's wife's land).

Interviews conducted with 22 per cent of the heads of households in the district revealed that 87.5 per cent (irrespective of social class) claimed to own their own homes. Those who rent do not form an isolated or distinct group but are to be found in all geographic and social sectors. For most Huaylinos it is a matter of great personal pride to be able to tell a visitor that their dwellings are indeed their own. It is a mark of adulthood and means that one is a responsible family head. Thus one young man remarked: "Our living quarters here with my

[4] We paid S/90 ($3.35) per month for the house, a price which Huaylinos claimed was very high.

mother are only temporary, but have you seen my new house in the next block?" Many others observed: "We may be poor here in Huaylas, but everyone, if you will, has his own house."

While there is agreement on the point that a family should own and live in its own dwelling, how a house is designed, finished, and maintained reflects socioeconomic differences in the population. Some of these differences are presented in Table 20. Upper-class families are at one pole and lower-class families at the other. The latter approach upper-class standards in areas where the presence of some dwelling feature represents individual effort rather than affluence. Thus, a majority of middle-class families live in well-kept houses, and almost half have living rooms (*sala*). This group likewise approximates the upper-class pattern in the kitchen, where the majority have a raised cooking platform and almost half have ovens.

It is where capital is expended that greater differences occur and where high-priority items can be singled out. Thus, the sewing machine, the watch, and the primus stove are demanded as the standard of living goes up, followed by other items, some of which are still beyond the financial reach of many or are not as yet appreciated as necessary. During the course of our stay in Huaylas, the pattern had begun to change, particularly with regard to electrical appliances. As a result of the rural electrification program begun in 1961 and the availability of current for eighteen to twenty-four hours a day, dozens of persons have purchased such items as blenders, hi-fi sets, radios, and electric irons. By 1964 a dozen electric sewing machines were in use. All of these items could be purchased from stock in Huaylas stores. In 1966, at least two families had large freezers and refrigerators.

The luxury paraphernalia and appliances, which symbolize modern life in the United States, Europe, and Lima, are therefore just beginning to infiltrate the homes of Huaylinos. Up to the present time, these things have not been symbols of status or prestige, but have, rather, been regarded almost as curiosities. Thus, it was not surprising to find that some members of the upper class had a few of these things and others did not. But this is no longer the case. Huaylinos have, increasingly, adopted Lima standards and styles. Middle- and lower-class families are not only building the living room but are also beginning to install the whole living-room complex: plastered walls and ceiling, a window perhaps, the six to twelve chairs that hug the walls, the center table with small knickknacks on it, a picture of the Sacred Heart of

Table 20. Selected dwelling characteristics of households by social class in the District of Huaylas, 1961 *

Dwelling characteristics	Percentage of households		
	Upper class	Middle class	Lower class
Owns own house	87.5	87.6	87.5
Condition of house			
Well-kept	97.5	92.0	54.4
Run-down	2.5	8.0	45.6
Number of floors			
One	48.8	74.4	95.4
Two	51.2	25.6	4.6
Exterior			
Stucco	89.9	19.4	3.8
Whitewash or adobe	10.1	80.6	96.2
Has living room			
Yes	97.5	46.0	17.8
No	2.5	54.0	82.2
Floor			
Cement, wood, tile	82.0	4.1	0.0
Earth	18.0	95.9	100.0
Interior			
Plastered	89.9	19.4	4.6
Unfinished	10.1	80.6	95.4
Cooking done on			
Cooking platform	69.2	66.4	47.2
Primus stove	61.6	33.7	13.4
Ground only	5.1	20.2	38.7
Oven			
Yes	56.5	47.0	31.8
No	43.5	53.0	68.2

* From a survey conducted by the writer with 268 (22 per cent) heads of households representing all *barrios* of the distinct.

Jesus, and a paved or wooden floor instead of an earthen one. This replicates the common pattern found in upper-class houses. Also popular as decoration are commercial color calendars featuring pretty girls.

One detects an increased tempo of social competition, as upholstered chairs and couches, side tables, and floor lamps make their appearance in the homes of some *notables* and even in the homes of some of the middle class. The kitchen, too, is an area for future change, at least in some homes. Several townspeople were speaking seriously of purchasing electric ranges. Doubtless, within a few years, this item, too, will find some acceptance.

Table 21. Ownership by social class of selected modern appliances in the District of Huaylas, 1961 *

Appliance	Percentage of households		
	Upper class	Middle class	Lower class
Radio	54.0	4.0	0.7
Phonograph	51.4	2.0	0.7
Electric iron	28.2	0.0	0.0
Typewriter	43.5	4.0	0.0
Sewing machine	82.0	40.7	13.9
Camera	23.1	2.0	0.0
Watch or clock	84.5	33.7	7.0

* Prior to the installation of the new electric current in the rural areas and the advent of transistor radios. Based on the survey of 268 (22 per cent) heads of household in the district.

For most townspeople, electricity has become a necessity. Its use increased noticeably with the new installation in 1961. By May of 1961, over 71 per cent of the houses in town had electricity, and forty home installations had been made in Santo Toribio. Rural electrification, just under way at that time, was proceeding much more rapidly than had been anticipated. By March 1963 over 40 per cent of *all* homes in the district had electricity and many more installations were scheduled. The current had been carried to the upper section of the *barrio* of Yacup and even to the more distant *barrio* of Iscap. It is quite probable that, within two or three more years, at least three-fourths of the homes in Huaylas will have the benefit of electricity. At this moment in history, Huaylas occupies a unique position in all of rural Peru in this respect.

CHAPTER VI

The Adobe World:
The People

Earning a Living in Huaylas

The household constitutes the basic economic and productive unit in Huaylas. While there is considerable specialization of labor by sex and age within the household, there are many tasks which are undertaken by almost every member. In all social classes, women not only engage in household tasks but often have specialties through which income is derived. Children, too, regardless of social class, are expected to perform such chores as pasturing the animals, cutting alfalfa, running errands, assisting in the family store, if there is one, and, at certain times, working in the fields. Despite the general similarity in the household activities of all social classes, there is a tendency in upper-class households for the roles of the different members to be somewhat more specialized. Thus, children of higher social status perform fewer subsistence tasks, and the women are seldom engaged directly in agriculture or in the pasturing of animals, these tasks being delegated to persons of middle- or lower-class standing who are hired for the purpose. Many, but by no means all, upper-class families have a servant to help in household tasks.

The daily routine in Huaylas is subject to relatively few variations. Most families begin the day between 6:00 and 7:00 A.M. and finish with the evening meal after 7:00 P.M. The events of the day unfold in unhurried fashion. Even among the many Huaylinos who have watches and clocks, there is relatively little effort to make activities conform to the mechanical measurement of time. For this reason, Huaylinos regard their life as being quite tranquil (*muy tranquilo*), in contrast to the "agitated" pace of city life, which they regard as being unsuited to them or, perhaps, a little unnatural. Although an hour is usually specified, few events begin on time. Indeed, one usually makes a liberal calculation as to how long after the scheduled time an event will begin. For meetings one may estimate an hour but for formal dances as much as two hours.

A light breakfast is usually eaten at about 8:00 A.M., often after various members of the family have completed some of their tasks, for example, drawing water, cutting alfalfa for the animals, or obtaining firewood. The midday meal is usually eaten at about 1:00 or 2:00 P.M. and is, for most families, the biggest meal of the day, unless the day's work has taken them to *chacras* which are often scattered and far from their houses. The evening meal is usually simple, often made up of leftovers.

The staple foods in the Huaylas diet are the cereals and other produce from the fields. Cereals and pulses are eaten in a number of ways. Jack beans (*habas*) and peas (*alberjas*) are ground into a flour from which a thick soup, called *shaqui*, is made. Thick soups and broths to which various combinations of eggs, vegetables, noodles, and meat are added constitute the first course of all meals other than breakfast. Barley and wheat are, of course, used extensively since these are major crops. Both are ground for flour and used in other ways as well. Huaylinos bake a great deal, producing a variety of excellent breads for both home consumption and sale. Despite the large quantities of bread baked in the district, several stores nevertheless sell bread that is imported from Caraz three times weekly.

Several varieties of maize are grown in Huaylas for use in *chicha* (maize beer), *cancha* (toasted maize kernels), *mote* (boiled kernels of yellow maize) or as *choclos* (maize on the cob). Huaylinos are especially proud, as mentioned in Chapter III, of the *terciopelo* variety of maize used exclusively for the *cancha* which is served at virtually all meals and at all festive occasions.

Huaylinos consume fairly large quantities of canned and other imported foods as well. Peruvian tuna fish is especially popular because it is inexpensive and plentiful—virtually all stores carry it in stock. Rice, many types of noodles, sugar, and canned Chilean peaches, Peruvian evaporated milk, Nescafe, Dutch lard, and vegetable oil are just a few of the items which are widely purchased by Huaylas families. Urban residents tend to consume more meat (mutton being preferred) than do the rural residents because the daily market usually has some for sale. Because there is usually but one sheep butchered daily and there are many persons who wish to purchase mutton, the councilman in charge of the market often has the butcher divide the meat equally, by weight, among all present and waiting their turns.[1]

All families in Huaylas own some animals that are regularly used for food, particularly *cuyes* (some households having as many as 100), chickens, turkeys, ducks, and sometimes rabbits. Larger animals of the "neolithic" barnyard most frequently found are sheep, goats, pigs, and cows. Many families also have the durable burro as a pack animal, but the horse, which is less common, is used in this capacity as well as for transportation, particularly by upper-class farmers. Because of the tremendous variation, it would be difficult to say just how many animals the average Huaylas family owns, but it can be stated, with some confidence, that almost all families have *cuyes*, chickens, hogs, and at least one dog or cat, although the latter are rarely seen, since they are primarily charged with defending the *colca* against rodent invaders. Herds of twenty cattle and as many as fifty or more sheep are not uncommon, although the average is much less. Since animals are frequently sold, the size of the herds tends to fluctuate considerably. Several persons of the middle and upper classes sell fattened cattle in the central slaughterhouse in Lima, speculating on market prices. Most men engaged in this business buy local cattle for this purpose, and some buy animals outside of the district as well.

First and foremost, Huaylinos are farmers, and the land is widely distributed. In many cases, both husband and wife own land, but seldom is property merged in joint ownership. At the death of a parent, the land is customarily inherited by the children in equal portions. There is a tendency then for the land to become more highly subdivided than it already is, although this situation is alleviated somewhat by emigration. Emigrants usually leave their land to be cultivated by their brothers or other relatives on a share basis. Because of this,

[1] This practice apparently depends upon the councilman's interest, for it was discontinued in 1963.

relatively little land is leased outright. Sharecropping is called *sembrar al partir* (to plant in order to divide) or *sembrar a medias* (to plant on halves) and cannot be said to distinguish any particular social group. Under the Huaylas sharecropping system, the landowner delegates responsibility for planting, plowing, irrigation, and harvest to the share-cropper (*partidario*), while he supplies the seed and the tools and, sometimes, meals for the sharecropper and the peons hired at the time of the harvest. The crop is invariably divided equally between *partidario* and owner, usually before, but sometimes after, the seed for the following year has been separated out, depending upon prior agreement.

Table 22. Percentage of population over twenty years of age according to land ownership and land-tenure arrangement in the District of Huaylas, 1961

	Nonland-owner	Land-owner	Renter	Owner and renter	Total	Share-cropper *
Urban men	33	57	4	6	100	16
Rural men	24	65	4	7	100	16
Total	25	64	4	7	100	
Urban women	44	53		3	100	1
Rural women	36	61	1	2	100	1
Total	37	60		2	100	
Heads of households						
Men	14	73	4	9	100	16
Women	11	85	1	3	100	3
Wives of male heads of household	32	65	1	2	100	

* Not included in total percentage. All other categories are mutually exclusive.

The best land in Huaylas is that which is irrigated and located in the main sections of the valley. Most unirrigated land, called *chuchín*, is located on the upper slopes, which rise to the *puna*. *Chuchín* lands are given over principally to the cultivation of wheat and barley and, in some zones, potatoes.

The simple farming techniques used in Huaylas are common throughout the entire region and have probably not been modified significantly since colonial times, although many farmers express a strong desire to improve their methods as well as their implements. The steel-tipped Egyptian plow pulled by bullocks is used for plowing. Crowbars and short-handled hoes are used for weeding and other farm tasks. Small sickles of European manufacture are used to harvest the grains which are threshed by horses on a packed earthen and dung floor. Winnowing is done by hand. All members of the family take part in farm tasks, with the men performing the heavier work.

Traditionally, fertilizers are rarely used and insecticides almost never, though some farmers attempt to use manure in certain fields by pasturing their sheep and cows on them after the harvest has been completed. Only a handful of farmers use the manure that collects in the corrals for this purpose. Household sweepings and refuse from the corrals are usually dumped into the *quebradas* (gullies) near town and in the rural areas, thus forming large, unplanned compost heaps. One townsman, at my suggestion, fertilized one of his small fields using the organic matter from a dump, but his action was not copied by others.

There is a general belief in Huaylas that the irrigated land, in particular, is extremely fertile and, therefore, does not require much fertilization. They point out that Huaylas has always been famous for its good harvests, noting that "harvest" is the nickname enjoyed by Huaylas throughout the Callejón. Despite this, a number of farmers comment that the harvests are "not like they used to be," a fact which they are inclined to blame more on various plant diseases, or on the scarcity of water, than on depletion of the soil.

One farmer from the town, however, felt that the declining productivity was due to the poor irrigation techniques employed by the Huaylas farmers. He pointed out that the basic system of irrigation was that of flooding the field, starting at the highest point and allowing the water to follow a natural course through the field rather than along the contour. This, he felt, tended to wash the topsoil toward the lower part of the field and, eventually, into one's neighbor's field or into a gully. The consequences of this were noted in several fields, where the wheat grown in the higher sections was smaller and sparser than that grown at the lower end of the field.

Because of the length of the dry season and the capriciousness of the weather, the water supply is of great concern to Huaylinos. Water is carefully husbanded in small tanks or reservoirs scattered throughout the district and is used by the farmers according to an elaborate and highly organized system, which is controlled by an irrigation council and persons known as *repartidores de aguas* (water distributors).[2] Because of the great demand and tight schedule, many farmers have to irrigate their plots in the evenings, particularly on moonlit nights. It is a rather frequent occurrence to see farmers leaving for their fields late in the evening or returning very early in the morning after spending the night irrigating their crops.

Few fields, however, are extensively irrigated during the course of the growing season, which lasts from February to July or August for the major crops of wheat, barley, maize, peas, and broad beans and from September to February for potatoes. Native Andean crops such as *oca, olluco, caijua,* and *quinoa* are grown by some farmers. Often, crops such as *quinoa* and *caijua* are grown in small quantities in the maize fields or around the borders of the fields.

Most of the crop is consumed by the farmer's household, although some upper-class farmers sell their surplus locally or in Caraz. Only a handful of farmers ship any of their produce outside of the region to be sold. Potatoes, which once were widely produced in Huaylas, suffer from a disease, locally known as *rancha,* that discolors and withers the plant. As a result, potato production over the last twenty years has declined to the point where many farmers do not plant potatoes at all. Potatoes are either grown in small quantities or purchased from the few farmers in Huaylas who manage to grow them successfully.

In addition to these crops, a large proportion of the irrigated land in Huaylas is devoted to the cultivation of alfalfa, which grows extremely well in the district and is rotated with other crops to replenish the soil. A small number of farmers have earned considerable local fame as producers of alfalfa seed which they sell both regionally and nationally. For the most part, the alfalfa is used for the animals, particularly for the cows and *cuyes,* which live almost exclusively on it. Stockmen fatten cattle in the alfalfa fields prior to shipping them to Lima. Pigs are allowed to graze and scavenge, often being sent off to pasture with the sheep, although prior to slaughter most pigs are fattened on alfalfa and barley. (Such pigs are called *cebones,* from *cebo,* the word for feed.) Some barley is grown on contract for a Lima brewery.

There appear to be relatively few insect pests that afflict the crops, but the maize is often severely damaged by the large numbers of

[2] See Chapter VII for a description of this system.

half-wild dogs that live in the rural areas. Thus, every year (as has been the case for the last seventy years, according to the municipal archives), the Concejo Distrital (the district council) is asked to obtain poison to put out in the fields to rid the district of the destructive animals.

Aside from farming, there are a large number of occupational specialties to be found in Huaylas, most of which are part-time activities. The following list includes most of the occupations through which money is earned by men and women in Huaylas.

Women's occupations

Baker	Merchant
Beautician	Midwife
Businesswoman	Municipal secretary
Chicha brewer	Restaurant operator
Clerk	Schoolteacher
Church cantor	Seamstress
Cook	Servant
Farmer	Shepherdess
Healer (*curandero*)	Stockwoman
Knitter	Vendor
Laundress	Woolspinner

Men's occupations

Accountant	Hotelkeeper
Baker	Hydroelectric plant employee
Barber	Laborer
Bartender	Livestock dealer
Blacksmith	Machinist
Brick- and tilemaker	Mason
Businessman	Merchant
Butcher	Miller
Cabinetmaker	Miner
Carpenter	Muleteer
Clerk	Municipal secretary
Dentist	Musician
Druggist	Painter
Electrician	Plasterer
Farmer	Poolroom operator
Healer (*curandero*)	Postman
Horse trainer	Practical nurse

Men's occupations—Cont.

Restaurant operator	Tailor
Schoolteacher	Tanner
Scribe	Telegrapher
Servant	Undertaker
Shepherd	Vendor
Shoemaker	Weaver
Stockman	Welder
Stonecutter and knapper	Woodcutter

The 135 men professing to be weavers, even though most work only part time at this task, demonstrate that Huaylas' self-sufficiency extends to areas other than food production. These weavers produce the common *bayeta* cloth used for clothing by the lower and middle classes. They also weave almost all of the blankets used by almost everyone and, in addition, the *ponchos* that most of the men, regardless of social class, own.

Although the final manufacture of woolen goods is in the hands of lower-class specialists, the preparation of wool for weaving is not. Most of the women are experts in the use of the weighted spindle whorl (*uso*) and are aware of the technicalities involved in preparing the proper wool for the desired fabric. Many upper-class women spin at home, while conversing with a neighbor or minding the family store. By contrast, the middle- or lower-class woman, who also spins at home, is often seen in the street, spinning as she goes about her errands. A number of the 270 women of middle- and lower-class status, particularly the latter, earn some income as professional spinners (*hilanderas*). The prevalence of homespun goods in Huaylas is also manifested by the daily presence of a vendor of manufactured dyes in the market. Most householders do their own dying, prior to weaving.

Among the men, carpentry is a very common occupation and one that is widely respected in the district. Many of the prominent citizens either have been or are carpenters. Most of the fifty-nine carpenters work at home in small shops with conventional hand tools, but six of them (two upper-class and four middle-class men) in 1961 operated diesel-powered, woodworking machinery (circular saw, planer, router, drill press, and band saw). Upon the installation of the new electrical system in Huaylas, one of these carpenters purchased two electric motors to power his machinery and began expanding his business both in Huaylas and outside of the district. Others followed his example, and by 1964 there were six shops using a variety of electrically powered tools. Several produced modern and traditional furniture for sale, not only in Huaylas but also in Chimbote and Huaraz.

Four of the five millers in Huaylas also used ten-horsepower diesel motors to drive their flour mills. The other one, in Tambo, operated his mill with water power. Anticipating events, an enterprising middle-class family from the *barrio* of Shuyo purchased a modern, electrically powered mill and put it into operation immediately upon the installation of the new electric current, thus lowering prices drastically and, for a while, virtually destroying the business formerly enjoyed by the other millers. This situation has since come into balance as several of the millers have purchased electrically powered machines, and three of the carpenters using electricity have added this as a sideline.

Of the other occupations, it is that of merchant (*comerciante*) which bestows a certain degree of prestige upon the practitioner. The owner-ship of a store is generally thought to provide the owner with eco-nomic security as well as respect in the community. When the workers returned to Huaylas after the termination of the hydroelectric plant in Huallanca with their separation pay (in some cases, almost $1,000.00), many used this capital to establish themselves as shopkeepers. This created much competition, and eventually many of the new stores failed. While the largest stores in the district are located in the town, along the principal streets leading from the plaza and around the small market, there were eighty-five stores of different sizes scattered throughout the district in 1961.

Only a few of the many stores in Huaylas can be said to specialize in a particular line of goods: one in stationery, school supplies, and a small selection of books, two in dry goods, and one in dry goods and novelty items. Another store has begun to carry a stock of electrical appliances. The rest are best described as general stores in which one can purchase anything from dried peppers and crowbars to clothing and champagne. At least five establishments in town would properly be considered bars, and in 1961 three restaurants and several boardinghouses were also in business. There were two drugstores in town in 1961, the Botiquín Popular, which is owned and staffed by the national government, and another, owned by a man from Santo Toribio who lived in Callao for over twenty years.

The stores in Huaylas open early—usually about 7:00 or 7:30

A.M.—and remain open for business until the early evening, closing only briefly at mealtimes or when the operator is otherwise occupied. Rural residents come to town on week ends and Mondays to meet the weekly truck that brings gifts from relatives and things ordered from Lima. Their purchases in the stores at these times quicken the pace of business which otherwise is slow. At slack times, the merchants often leave their stores to converse with one another in the warm sunshine along Commerce Street or in the plaza in the center of town. Others sometimes pass the time playing chess or checkers. Most transactions, accompanied at times by some haggling over price or credit arrangements, are in small units of merchandise. Each item is wrapped in newspaper and paid for individually by the buyer, who has confidence neither in his own nor in the merchant's ability to add up a long column of figures correctly.

Two large buses have provided daily service from Huaylas to Caraz and Huallanca. Leaving at 7:30 A.M. and usually returning by 4:00 P.M., the buses carry heavy loads, often including as many as sixty passengers and a ton or more of freight. With the arrival of the bus from Huallanca come twenty or thirty copies of a Lima daily newspaper, usually *La Prensa*, although copies of *El Comercio* and other papers are sometimes delivered. These are sold in town by a boy who receives a small commission from the bus driver for doing it. The local newspaper, *Atun Huaylas*, which deals with district and provincial news, is published by a Huaylino who lives in Caraz. *Atun Huaylas* appeared more or less regularly in a fortnightly edition.

The Tone of Social Life

The stores of Huaylas serve not only as the source of supply for things which are considered of first necessity (*primera necesidad*), but also as a vantage point from which one may obtain an introduction to the nature of social interaction and to the small subtleties that constitute the core of traditional behavior. The storekeeper greets his customer with the question: "What are you going to carry?" ("*¿Que va a llevar?*"), or, sometimes: "What do you want, little son?" ("*¿Que quiere hijito?*"), a phrase used with children or persons of very humble station. The customer replies with another question, asking if the storekeeper has a certain item in stock. Acquaintances are greeted by name, by some title such as *Señora* (Mrs.), *compadre* (godsib), or perhaps a nickname. If the customer is an acquaintance of the same sex, the purchasing process may be extended by a conversation of some duration. In the case of men, this often leads to the added purchase of some alcoholic beverage to accompany the pleasantries.

The stores constitute the principal place of informal relaxation, for they also serve as meeting places and bars. The principal male recreation in Huaylas is conversing with one's friends over a drink, and it is a rare store that is not the site of at least one lengthy social gathering each day. Several stores and bars offer their customers recreational facilities, the most common being *sapo* (toad) a game in which the participants try to toss brass disks through the mouth of a brass toad, mounted on a boxlike stand. Bets are usually made during the game, the losers generally agreeing to pay for the beer or soft drinks consumed by the winners. One bar, which is open only in the evenings, features a billiard table which attracts numerous enthusiastic players (all men). Several variations of the game are played and competition is usually between teams (chosen on the spot) rather than between individuals.

There are fewer such opportunities for women, outside of regularly organized fiestas and family gatherings. Most women find their principal recreation in conversing with neighbors as they knit, spin, or sew.

When going to and from work in the fields and pastures, Huaylinos are less inclined to spend time in light conversation. Salutations are brief and to the point: "Good morning" ("*Buenos dias*"), "Good afternoon" ("*Buenas tardes*"), "Good evening" ("*Buenas noches*"), or simply, "Good" ("*Buenos*"). Everyone is thus greeted along the road or trail, whether he is an acquaintance or not. Of course, with friends or relatives the greeting may be more elaborate: "Well, how are you?" ("*¿Que tal, pués?*"), or: "Where to that's good?" ("*¿Adonde bueno?*"). The common answer to the latter question illustrates, quite well, the frequent usage in Huaylas of diminutive forms: "Only to this little place" ("*Acacito no más*"). If people stop to converse, or if they enter someone's house, greetings are always accompanied by a handshake. It is customary to shake hands with everyone present. The normal handshake is light.

Taking one's leave in Huaylas follows a similar little ritual and has a corresponding set of pat expressions associated with saying goodbye. Again, one shakes hands with everyone on leaving, and individually says: "Until later" ("*Hasta luego*"), "Until tomorrow" ("*Hasta mañana*"), even though one may be leaving for Lima at that moment, or simply, "Goodbye" ("*Adiós*," or more often, "*Chau*"). The use of *chau*, a loan word from the Italian, is extremely widespread in Peru on the coast and in the urban centers in the highlands. Huaylinos often embroider it with the diminutive, saying, *chaucito*.

The family unit in Huaylas, despite being ravaged by migration and geographic mobility, remains the basic social unit. The nuclear family forms the basic element in the subsistence economy, and its various members have responsibilities to each other and to the group from rather early ages.

Due in part to Hispanic (and perhaps other) cultural traditions, and, because she is thought to be ultimately responsible for her children, Mother is idealized, indeed revered. The official celebration of Mother's Day (May 8) is taken with utmost gravity. Wayward sons return to their mothers' sides; migrants who can afford it even return to Huaylas for the day. Serenades are organized. Starting at midnight and fortified with pisco and vermouth, groups of men go forth singing and playing guitars, harps, and violins until dawn. The persons so honored are expected to invite the serenaders in for a drink and perhaps to dance for a short while, no matter what the hour. Finally, there is always a program in the schools. One announcement for this occasion in 1960 proclaimed:

Professors and students of the schools of this city, plethoric with the most real enthusiasm and love, have the honor of offering a simple 'LITER-ARY-MUSICAL MATINEE' with variety acts on this emotional MOTHER'S DAY, in homage to the Queen of all times. This performance, which is characterized by its fervour and filial pureness of heart, is dedicated with love to MOTHER on her day.

The "simple" matinee program contained thirty-two separate acts and performances, including songs such as: "Hymn to Mothers," "The Cradle Song," and "Dear Mother," and recitations entitled: "To my Mother," "Blessed Mother," and "A Mother's Advice."

The attachment to one's mother is as real as it is symbolic. Within the district, married children return to visit their parents, particularly mothers on a daily basis if they live in the neighborhood. Economic and social collaboration between children and parents continues throughout life. Emigrants who have made a permanent home on the coast invariably attempt to bring their elderly parents to live with them, although such moves are not always successful. The older people show a great reticence to leave their homes in Huaylas.

In talking or referring to one another, family members customarily employ the appropriate kin terms. Thus, the person is addressed as *primo* (cousin), *mamá* (mother), *tio* (uncle), or *abuelito* (grandfather). The given name is rarely used in combination with the kin term as a form of address, as in English, where one would say "Uncle John." It is also customary to use the diminutive form of address (for example, *mamá* or *mamita* instead of *madre*) in talking or referring to the individual, except in the case of collateral relatives. Not to use the diminutive form with the appropriate persons would imply a lack of affection. One's in-laws are not addressed using the kin terms except in the case of a brother-in-law (*cuñado*), but rather by their given names, preceded by the title of respect, Don or Doña, the same as when addressing any unrelated adult.

There are a variety of niceties connected with the usage of kin terms as forms of address. The use of the diminutive is one of them. The calculated misuse of a term is a common way in which one may poke fun at someone or insult or offend him. For example, a man could offend another by calling him "brother-in-law" even though they do not have this relationship with one another. The man alleging to be the brother-in-law is implying that the other man's sister is promiscuous and that he has slept with her. Similar use of the term for father- or mother-in-law (*suegro* or *suegra*) may achieve the same affect. On the other hand, the term "brother" (*hermano*) can be used with freedom, without derogatory connotations. Thus, a friend is hailed: "Listen, brother," or: "Brother, can you spare a *real*."

There is a certain fraternal air that accompanies many family gatherings, at the evening meal or on festive occasions, but still a certain formality is preserved. Age, experience, and particularly parenthood are respected, and parental authority can be asserted over the children even when they are adults. This is particularly true in the case of women who are protected through chaperonage at public events. In Huaylas, families do many things together in addition to functioning as an economic unit. Public events such as dances and fiestas are often attended by families as a group, and on these occasions family members genuinely (in most cases) enjoy each other's company.

Despite such displays of solidarity, men frequently undertake their pleasures independently. They may attend and participate fully in social events, such as dances, without other members of their immediate family being present. Men are often occupied in exclusively masculine activities such as playing billiards, drinking in one of the bars, or crashing a fiesta to which they have not specifically been invited.

The family, of course, remains the circle of closest confidence, although the relationships between one's peers of the same sex become especially important during adolescence and early adulthood. Because of the closeness of family characteristics, it has not been uncommon in Huaylas to give whole families a nickname, often with a derogatory connotation. In this area of the culture in all social classes, the Quechua influence (indicated in the list below by an asterisk) is especially noticeable as can be judged by the names.

los tutu *	the short ones
lechoncitos	piglets
los chucru *	the hardheads
huaripa *	chicken, e.g., coward

Derogatory terms (*apodos*) are carefully distinguished from nonoffensive nicknames (*pulidos*). In the case of individual names, the list of nicknames is very long, for almost everyone earns a nickname during his lifetime. In most cases the nickname is given by some member of one's own family, and, as above, the Quechua influence is great.

Tuti *	Shorty
Wisku *	One-eye
Kuchi *	Pig
Supepa llanquín*	Devil's shoe
Sakua *	Partridge
Alicates	Bowlegged, like a pair of pliers
Primer de Mayo	First of May, a holiday, implying that the person doesn't work much
Chongo	Mussel, e.g., one who eats mussels
La Crónica	*The Chronicle*, a Lima daily newspaper carrying lots of human-interest news. In this case, a gossip

The diminutive forms of the regular Spanish (and non-Spanish) given names are also greatly modified through the use of Quechuaized derivations in many cases. The following are typical Huaylas *pulidos*.

Antonio	Antuco*
Manuel	Mañuco*
David	Davicho*

Jacinto	Jashi*
Epifanio	Epichu*
Zósimo	Shoshi*
Jesús	Jeshu*
Cristobal	Kishtu*
Washington	Huashi*
Maria	Maruja*
Asunción	Ashu*

The great geographic mobility of Huaylinos, even nonemigrants, undoubtedly weakens the traditional family structure, though it is difficult to judge how much this has occurred, for Huaylinos have been participants in the migratory process since before the turn of the century. Nevertheless, many informants believed that the effects of migration are more widely felt now than before.

Despite the dispersion of the family, attempts are made to maintain as close contact as possible with emigrants, through correspondence and occasional visits. Taking advantage of the periods of agricultural inactivity, many Huaylinos journey to the coast to visit relatives and to find temporary work. At the time of Carnival and particularly for the Fiesta of Saint Elizabeth (July 6 to July 10) and the national holidays (July 28 to July 31) hundreds of people return to their homeland, and large family reunions take place. The various emigrant associations of Huaylinos in Lima, Callao, and Chimbote help maintain family contacts in those places as well.

The migrants who have been outside the district for many years, however, often do lose contact, particularly with their collateral and affinal relatives both in the city and in Huaylas. Families whose members have resided outside the district for more than one generation have still weaker ties with the emigrant members.

Child and adult alike are allied with others outside of the family through the elaborate system of fictive kin called *compadrazgo* (coparenthood) and *padrinazgo* (godparenthood or sponsorship). The network of social relations and obligations developed through this system serves to extend and strengthen the ties that one has both with consanguineal or affinal kin and with nonrelatives. Hence one of the most commonplace salutations is: "Good day, *compadre*," or: "How are you, *madrina?*" It has been shown that the complexity and varieties of fictive kinship, and the ways in which the relationships are structured in terms of social class, are reflections of openness, rigidity, or change in the social system.[3] Through a *compadrazgo* relationship mutually binding social ties are established with one's peers or with those of greater or lesser social prominence.

Although there are fourteen occasions or types of events at which one may acquire fictive kin in Huaylas, the ceremony of *padrinazgo* has the same basic form regardless of the occasion. The *padrinos* either hold or touch the individual who will become the godchild. If there is no godchild, and, instead, some object is to be blessed, ribbons attached to the object are held by the *padrinos* so as to establish the necessary contact. The person officiating at the ceremony then makes some appropriate remarks about the occasion and the role of the sponsors, and the ritual is concluded. In the case of church ceremonies, of course, the priest or bishop officiates in the prescribed manner.

Some of the relationships established are considered to be spiritual or holy in nature, while others are intended to cement friendships.

Because these ties imply a series of responsibilities and obligations (such as the exchange of gifts and the lending of money or other assistance) between the *compadres* or between the *padrinos* and the *ahijado*, many persons sometimes express reluctance to accept requests to serve in these capacities, particularly when the request comes from someone of limited acquaintance. Some prefer to limit their responsibilities of this kind to members of their own families or to close friends. This is especially true of the upper class, but not exclusively so by any means. One upper-class man said that when one becomes a *compadre* with a friend the relationship takes on a more formal tone; the *compadres* cease to address each other in the familiar form of address (*tú*), substituting the formal form (*usted*) because it implies greater respect. "For this reason," the man remarked, "I do not like the system because my relationships with my friends lose some of their warmth."

Other persons, however, particularly those of middle-class status or those desiring to use the system to obtain some specific advantage, often seek to establish *compadrazgo* relationships with persons of prestige or influence in the community. Yet persons of lower-class standing who do not have social ambitions may also choose *padrinos* from among their upper-class employers or the owners of the land on which they work as sharecroppers. Such relationships are intended merely to secure one's status in the existing system and do not represent an

[3] Mintz and Wolf, 1950:341–368.

Table 23. Types of ceremonial kinship and selected characteristics of each

Title of *compadrazgo* relationship	Pattern of relationship *	Occasion
Nacimiento or Parto	A†	At the birth of the child, the midwife (*comadrona* or *partera*) may become the *madrina*, her husband the *padrino*.
Agua de Socorro	A	Emergency baptism given a child who is ill.
Bautismo	A	Baptism. This is the most important form of *compadrazgo*. Priest officiates.
Corte de pelo	A	Ceremony at the first haircut given a boy. *Padrinos* usually the same as those of baptism.
Confirmación	A	Confirmation. *Padrino* must be of same sex as the child. Only one *padrino* chosen. Priest officiates.
Primera Comunión	A	First Communion. Same as above.
Escapulario or Hábito	A	A *madrina* is chosen to preside over the giving of a religious habit to another woman. (If married, the *madrina's* husband may be called *padrino*.)
Cambio de Aros	A	The exchange of engagement rings. The event is sponsored by both a *padrino* and a *madrina*.
Matrimonio or Boda	A	Marriage *padrinos*. Of great importance. Priest officiates.
Evangelio	A	Gospel. *Padrinos* sponsor the godchild in his request for improved health. The priest officiates at the ceremony at the church.
Manto	A	*Padrinos* sponsor the godchild seeking special aid from the Virgin, for health, success in school, etc.
Chasquiquí or Pila	A	*Padrinos* sometimes chosen to hold a child after baptism.
Carnival	B ‡	In recognition of friendship, two persons may select each other and call each other *compadre* after exchanging a gift during Carnival. At present, a rare custom.
Protectores	B	*Padrinos* selected to "protect" or sponsor the inauguration of some new, personal object.
Protectores	C §	*Padrinos* selected to sponsor the inauguration of something new that is acquired by some institution such as the school, a club. No interpersonal relationships established. Priest sometimes officiates.
Bendición	C	Same as above but for new additions to the church, for example an altar. Priest officiates.
Manto de la Virgen	C	*Padrinos* selected to preside at the blessing of a new robe for the image of the Virgin. Priest officiates.

* For the patterns of relationship, see Figure 5 on the following page.
† Spiritual relationship (*espiritual*) or honorary relationship (*de honor*).
‡ Relationship of honor or relationship of benediction (*bendición*).
§ Protector or trustee relationship.

Pattern for Type A: Spiritual or honorary godparents and godsibs

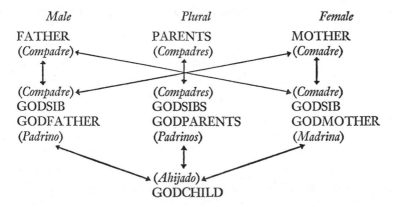

Pattern for Type B: Honorary and sponsoring godparents and godsibs

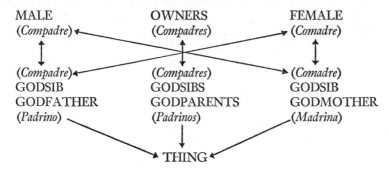

Pattern for Type C: Sponsoring or "trustee" godparents

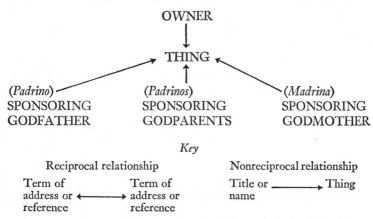

Figure 5. Patterns of ceremonial kinship

attempt to manipulate the social environment in order to facilitate the attainment of some new favor.

The basic configurations of the *compadrazgo* system as represented in Figure 5 are subject to some minor variations in particular cases. For example, in the case of a baptism, the *padrinos* are sometimes treated as *compadres* by the grandparents of the godchild. In other ceremonies, there may be only a single *padrino*, as in the case for the confirmation. Because of such modifications and because of the social motives behind the selection of *padrinos*, the number of relationships that may be acquired is truly astounding. One upper-class woman was able to name some 258 persons of all social backgrounds to whom she was related through the system. Although this number may be higher than the average, it is not unusual in Huaylas.

Since many *compadrazgo* relationships imply the exchange of gifts or the lending of assistance in various ways (for example, helping a godchild to obtain a scholarship or employment or making a loan or a gift of money to one's *compadre*), the system constitutes a form of social insurance through the creation of a "community of responsibility." Thus, if one finds it necessary to underwrite the cost of some fiesta as a *mayordomo*, he can always count upon the assistance of his *compadres*. During the Fiesta of the Discovery of the Holy Cross in May, one of the *mayordomos* (sponsors of a fiesta) was a woman who served the urban middle class as a midwife. Because of this, she had many *comadres* and *compadres*. (This is a common attribute of mid-wives, who are often called *comadronas*, implying that they are called *comadre* by many.) When I inquired about the expenses she was incurring, one man responded: "For her it is nothing because she has so many *compadres* to help her."

By extension and modification, the basic pattern (Figure 5, type *A*) is extended to situations and purposes beyond the original meaning and implication of the system. *Padrinos* are selected to sponsor the inauguration or the benediction of such personal belongings as a new house, a household shrine, a harp, or even a truck, thus establishing a personal relationship as shown in Figure 5, type *B*. By further extension, the system is utilized by the district government, the schools, the church, and other institutions for the purpose of honoring someone. The person so honored is obliged, by the ceremony, to make a cash contribution or a gift to the institution (Figure 5, type *C*). Such a ceremony accompanies virtually every new public acquisition and is thus a principal source of income for institutions. Used in this manner, ceremonial sponsorship constitutes a form of graduated taxation, since it is "levied" most often on the most wealthy. The financial purpose behind the selection of such *padrinos protectores* is openly acknowledged. When the new electric system was inaugurated, Huaylinos seriously contemplated naming prominent regional personages and well-to-do Huaylinos in Lima as *padrinos* for each of the 100 or more eucalyptus posts supporting the high-tension line. Each of the 200 persons to be so honored would have given S/100.00 ($3.70), resulting in a tidy addition to the municipal treasury. The idea was eventually abandoned as too crass.

In its various forms the system fulfills several functions. The most important is that of providing a means by which a sharing of wealth and responsibility is not only possible but obligatory. The establishment of kin-type relationships between nonkinsmen accomplishes this and at the same time binds the members of the community closer together, creating avenues of communication in both a horizontal and vertical sense through the social system. The fact that the selection of *padrinos* is still a one-way street, in that the upper class does not choose its *padrinos* from the middle or lower class, affirms the presence of a class hierarchy. Nevertheless, the great proliferation in the number and variety of *compadres* one may have suggests that this most plastic system has been adopted to fulfill the needs of a mobile society.

The basic set of acquaintances of every Huaylino includes the members of his nuclear family, other relatives who reside near him, his *compadres*, and his close friends, who are usually drawn into the circle of "kin" sooner or later. It is this group with which he associates throughout his life and which he thinks of as the group in which he may have "confidence." When one travels outside Huaylas, these are the first people with whom contact is made and from whom one is most likely to receive assistance. In like manner, if it becomes necessary to send a small package or to entrust someone to deliver a sum of money or an important letter to a friend outside the district, a person *de confianza* (of confidence) is sought, and no other is really acceptable. Full trust is not usually placed in anyone outside of this group, but if done and something goes awry, it is explicable in these terms.

Since most social activities revolve about these overlapping circles of relationship, immigrants to the district soon develop *compadrazgo* relations in the community. Not to do so would mean relative isolation, a situation that is uncomfortable for both immigrant and Huaylino. Only a transient is entitled to play the role of a complete outsider. The immigrants, engineers from the hydroelectric plant, and visiting anthropologists, are drawn into the system, and so into the life of Huaylas, by assigning to each one a status which then promotes further meaningful interaction.

Good Times and Bad

The routine of daily life is broken by small family fiestas which occur periodically throughout the year on the occasions of weddings, birthdays, baptisms, and other such events. In town, these take place with some frequency among members of the upper class. In both rural and urban areas the middle- and lower-class families have fewer such fiestas, usually organized around weddings or baptisms. This of course, depends upon family affluence. A family fiesta is often the occasion for a banquet of elaborate proportions. The menu and format vary little either with the event or the social class, although, as would be expected, upper-class functions are more elegant and formal. Middle- and lower-class families tend to follow the patterns of behavior established by the *notables*, at times somewhat self-consciously.

A tablecloth is usually spread (except in the poorest families), the best pieces of silverware selected, and small piles of tricolored *cancha* distributed across the table. Two or three bottles of wine or perhaps soft drinks are set out, and a pitcher or two of *chicha de jora* or *chicha morada* ⁴ complete the arrangements. Plates are prepared in the kitchen and then served to the guests. Bowls of food rarely are passed around the table for guests to serve themselves.

Meals are preceded by a *copita* or two of *pisco* or vermouth (or alcohol among the middle and lower class) and much conversation and joking. After the several courses have been served and the *picante de cuy* is finished, a dance is invariably held in the living room or in the

---

⁴ *Chicha de jora* is made of yellow maize which is moistened, allowed to sprout, ground, added to water and boiled. It is then allowed to ferment, with the help of brown sugar which is added for taste. The alcoholic content of Huaylas *chicha* is probably around 3 per cent. *Chicha morada* is made by boiling *maize morada* (purple maize) in water, then flavoring the purple liquid with lemon juice, cloves, and other spices, and, if desired, adding chopped pieces of fruit. The two types are served at room temperature.

patio. On such occasions, a *picup* ⁵ may be rented from one of several persons who make this their business, or some local musicians may be hired. Both young and old join in dancing the *vals criollo* and *huayno*. There are few fiestas not accompanied by dancing, which often lasts until very late in the evening or into the morning hours. At such affairs, only the invited guests are made welcome. Yet if there is some way to view the festivities from the outside a number of *mirones* (onlookers) soon collect in the doorway or some other vantage point to watch.

Among middle- and lower-class families fiestas follow this basic pattern but generally feature heavier drinking by both men and women, and the *huayno* with its lively rhythm and counterpoint is much favored over other kinds of music. In contrast to the upper class, the fiestas last much longer and on rare occasions end in arguments or even fisticuffs.

There are virtually no social events in Huaylas unaccompanied by drinking and conversation. Drinking is almost never done alone (this being considered odd) and always features the ritual of toasting one's companions. Thus one is *always* invited to drink *with* someone, each sip being prefaced by the toast—*salud* (health)—when alcoholic beverages are consumed, but less often with soft drinks.

Because all social occasions are accompanied by drinking and because everyone is expected to participate, the sale of alcoholic beverages and soft drinks probably accounts for a major portion of the income derived by many storekeepers. According to the records kept in the Caja de Depósitos (the tax collection office) 29,257 liters (7,682.4 gallons) of nationally manufactured alcoholic beverages of all types were purchased in Huaylas in 1958.⁶ The yearly rate of consumption, based on the population at the time of the census, is eleven liters (2.9 gallons) per capita for persons over twenty years of age.

Beer is by far the most popular beverage, particularly among the urban population and persons of middle- and upper-class status. Cane alcohol, which is second to beer in volume consumed, is drunk almost entirely by middle- and lower-class men, usually being mixed with water or a soft drink. Since the Caja de Depósitos does not take into account the *chicha* which is brewed from maize in almost every house-

⁵ A phonograph. *Picup* is derived from the English, pick-up, referring to the tone arm of the phonograph.

⁶ More recent figures were incomplete.

hold, the volume of consumption is unknown, but it almost certainly equals that of all the other beverages combined. *Chicha* is consumed at meals and often during work in the fields, where it is considered indispensable for quenching thirst. The rate of consumption of *chicha* as well as other beverages during fiestas is great.

There were three persons in town who appeared to be alcoholics and several others who might be so considered. Their condition was tolerated with sadness by Huaylinos who lamented the deterioration of these persons. Occasional drunkenness on the part of men, however, is considered a most natural occurrence. There is no stigma attached to this, and inebriated persons are tolerated with great patience and a certain kindness, unless, of course, they are too obnoxious.

A general characteristic of fiesta behavior in Huaylas (and among mestizos throughout the region) is that participation by all is demanded. Failure to eat and drink with the hosts or other guests is regarded at best, as poor manners, and at worst, as a deliberate insult. At family fiestas as elsewhere drinking is a ritual-like event, usually undertaken at the same moment when the host or one of the guests gives the customary toast, *salud* (health). The glasses are then collected on a tray, and those who may not have finished their drink are normally required to do so while the person waits to take the glass. Such demands are made less frequently on women however. In the same manner, everyone is urged to dance. If a male guest should prove reluctant to do so, the wife or daughter of the host may personally ask him to join as her partner.

Due to these customs, Huaylinos speak of themselves as being *muy exigentes* (very demanding). It proves difficult, for example, to leave while a party is in progress. The host or even another guest will insist that one remain and may even go so far as to bar the doorway with his person so as to prevent one's exit. Feeling ill, tired, or having some other obligation (*compromiso*) are usually rejected as legitimate excuses for leaving unless the host was aware of such contingencies from the onset of the party. Yet, even then, explanations of this kind may be skeptically received. Guests, therefore, seek to depart in ways which go unnoticed by the host or the others present. This is often done while the group is dancing or otherwise distracted, or on the pretext that one has to urinate.

People related through kinship ties (*compadrazgo*) continually reinforce these relationships through the exchange of gifts of food when special items become available during the course of the year. When a pig is butchered, a meal of *chicharrones*[7] is sent to the circle of relatives and selected *compadres*. A son, a daughter, or a servant delivers the plates of food in a basket, which is always carefully covered. Upon accepting the gift, the recipient returns the basket to the donor, usually with some small token of appreciation placed in it. Other articles often exchanged, when in season, are *choclos* (tender ears of maize), apples, peaches, and home-grown vegetables, and some-times flowers. It is assumed that these gifts will be reciprocated, as indeed they invariably are. Among the upper-class urban population particularly, birthday cards, invitations, Christmas and New Year's greetings, death notices, and notes of thanks are also exchanged.

Several social and sport clubs have functioned in Huaylas over the last fifty years, principally in the town and in Santo Toribio. At one time, during the height of the hydroelectric project work in Huallanca (1947 to 1955), there were at least six such clubs in the district. Most of these fraternal organizations have fallen victim to the emigration of their most prominent members. In 1947, three of the clubs registered at the municipal office for a soccer match, listing approximately 100 members each. The largest club, "Centro Sportivo Huaylas," listed 119 male members, whereas the others included both men and women. The three clubs based in the town of Huaylas included a large cross section of the middle and upper class and their families. There was some tendency for all of the members of a family to be associated with the same club, but this was never entirely true.

The club names themselves have a certain grandiose, romantic qual-ity that is difficult to convey without citing them. In addition to the Centro Sportivo Huaylas, there were others, such as the Club Sport Olympic, Club Audax ("bold"), Club Defensor Santo Toribio, and the Unión Juventud Huaylas. Of these, only the Centro Sportivo Huaylas (known as the Club Sportivo) remains more or less active at the present time. This is the oldest club, having been founded in 1919. Over the years, the Club Sportivo acquired some property until, at the present time, its members have constructed a large building on the plaza, complete with stage and dance floor. None of the other clubs have such a headquarters.

It is in the hall of the Sportivo that many public dances are held, and

[7] Cracklings and deep-fried tidbits of pork.

where, in fact, municipal government meetings are held if there are too many persons for the municipal office. Although there may have been considerable rivalry among the various clubs at one time, these feelings do not inhibit nonmembers from attending affairs held at the Sportivo. The auditoriums of the boys' school in town and of both boys' and girls' schools in Santo Toribio, are used mainly for school-sponsored activities. A former hotel located on the plaza of the town is also used for public dances. It and the Sportivo have been utilized as movie theaters on occasion, although movies are not shown regularly.

Public dances, usually for the purpose of raising money to support some local project, are enthusiastically attended by the urban upper and middle class in town and in Santo Toribio, although few persons participate in events in both areas. Dances are held during Carnival, the Fiesta of Saint Elizabeth, Independence Day, and on other special occasions at irregular intervals.

Despite the strength of traditional forms of behavior, which give substance to one's various roles in the community and family, such customs are not always sufficient to control all deviant behavior and all conflicts that emerge. As a result, the local authorities are called upon to discipline those who violate custom or law. Problems that cannot be solved or arbitrated by one's family and *padrinos*, or one's *compadres*, are invariably taken to the justice of the peace, the governor, or, in last resort, to the police, who often arrest the troublemakers and normally sentence them to a period of twenty-four hours in the municipal jail. In 1960, 4.4 per cent of the total population was arrested (see Table 24). With but one or two exceptions those arrested were of middle- or lower-class status.

Conflict and hostility also find their outlets in the gossip and the rumors that constantly circulate throughout the district. Cutting across class and family lines, voice is thus given to bitter discord and enmities that sometimes last for many years or even a lifetime. Persons who consider themselves as enemies avoid face-to-face contact if at all possible. Thus, if both are invited to a social or official gathering, one of the parties may well decline or simply not appear, depending upon the nature of the occasion and the intensity of the feelings. Just as one has his friends and circle of confidence, so also his enemies. Hostility is often provoked or maintained by rumors which enliven conversations in the doorways, along the paths, or over a drink or two at the store.

It is said that such malicious gossip and bad relations are provoked by

Table 24. Arrests in the District of Huaylas, January 1960 to April 1961 *

Reason for arrest	Men †		Women †	
	Number charged	Per cent charged	Number charged	Per cent charged
Intrafamily arguments and fights	29	14	4	8
Drunkenness	21	10	2	4
Fighting	33	16	5	10
Theft of money and material objects	27	13	7	15
Theft of food or animals	7	3	5	10
Slanderous gossip, abusive language	9	4	6	13
Morals charges	13	6	4	8
Cheating on transactions or default of contract	13	6	1	2
Failure to obey authorities	22	11	3	6
Disorderly conduct	9	4	2	4
Other charges	7	3	4	8
Charge not specified	19	9	5	10
Total	209	100	48	100

* Copied from local police records of arrests.

† Total number arrested: men, 198 and women, 45. Eleven men and three women were charged with two offenses each.

the envy (*envidia*) of those who are jealous. That persons will be envious of good fortune when this is not widely shared in the community is expected. A windfall, a particularly good harvest, or some other advantage which may be secured is expected to evoke some derogatory comments in the community. Such hearsay is usually accepted with a shrug and dismissed for what it is. If rumors continue for long, however, they can result in poor interpersonal relations.

Although such attitudes are constantly shifting and at times appear to be simple caprice, they often dampen enthusiasm for individual or cooperative enterprise. They also serve to monitor effectively those whose social or economic pretentions are unwarranted or disharmonious in the society. *Envidia*, then, is an important arm of social control.

This aspect of Huaylas personality has important implications for the process of change in the district. Innovations are often resisted until it is demonstrated that their benefits will be enjoyed by many and not by a clique or an individual. In one case, for example, a farmer who also was a storekeeper attempted to introduce a new variety of wheat. Having obtained excellent harvests with the new seed in his own fields, he purchased a 100-pound sack of it to sell in his store. Despite the man's personal popularity and his genuine interest in improving production, his customers refused to buy the seed, thinking it was a deceit. When I pressed him for an explanation, he remarked somewhat fatalistically that people refused to buy the seed because they were *envidiosos* (envious).

To act on the basis of *envidia*, however, may also lead to the imitation of practices and innovations begun by someone else. Thus, when a neighbor copies an idea, method of work, or a clothing style he may be accused of doing so out of *envidia*. The assumption, in this case, is that the neighbor has not been able to develop the innovation himself and must copy, that is, take advantage of someone else's initiative, having done none of the work himself. This is "resented" by the innovator, who, nevertheless, will evince some pride that people look to him for ideas and leadership. To say this openly, however, is regarded as pretentious.

A man may thus attempt to keep his affairs strictly to himself and prevent the neighbors from seeing or knowing of his actions. Secretive actions will, in turn, be resented if it is thought that someone possesses a bit of knowledge which could be of use but is deliberately not sharing it. A person acting in this manner, then, would be characterized as being *muy egoista* (very egotistic) in his comportment, acting only in his own selfish interest.

Envy and egoism cut through the fabric of social relationships, creating animosity and making some resentful (*resentido*) of others. This aspect of Huaylas personality poses a real barrier to innovation and change on a general plane in addition to its nagging personal implications. The extension of the *compadrazgo* system with its many responsibilities and obligations serves, somewhat, to facilitate conflict resolution. Despite such negative complexities and resulting factionalisms, it has nevertheless been possible to secure widespread collaboration for the execution of public works projects. How this has been accomplished will be considered in the following chapters.

The routine of daily life in Huaylas proceeds at a tranquil pace and involves many rewarding, though sometimes taxing, rituals and traditions, which, despite interpersonal rivalries or disagreements, make life pleasant, although not particularly exhilarating. Many Huaylinos rightly contend that there are no rich people in the district, but there is, nevertheless, a rather sizable disparity between the incomes of some of the upper-class families and those of the poorest families in the rural areas. Yet, the "rich" man in Huaylas is not affluent by either regional or national standards, and consequently a feeling of economic equality exists among the great majority of the population. This, coupled with the recognized self-sufficiency of the majority, tends to blur such social disparities and rigid structuralization along class lines as are attendant upon the prevailing sharp economic differences in neighboring areas of the Callejón.

Nevertheless, when one speaks specifically of the economic situation of the family in Huaylas, many complain, saying: "*Acá, no hay nada*" ("Here there is nothing"), or that there is a lack of "movement" and all is dead. The farmers are most vocal in expressing their needs, and they know them well: more water and better farming techniques. The pressure on the land, accentuated by population growth, stimulates and, indeed, in most instances, makes necessary the high outmigration. But just as the overcrowding on the land provides a "push" to leave Huaylas, so the cities, with their manifold and somewhat exaggerated promises of social and economic betterment, provide a strong pull. Yet, despite all of this, the complex of little traditions endures because of its plasticity and lends continuity and character to the social process.

CHAPTER VII

An Organized Community

District Government and Leadership

The District of Huaylas is organized politically along the lines of the constitution and the laws of the nation.[1] Heading the district political body is the *alcalde* (district mayor), who until 1963, was officially appointed by the *prefecto* (prefect) of the Department of Ancash.[2] The *alcalde* selected the members of the Concejo Distrital (district council) of which he is head. In addition to the *alcalde*, the council consists of four members who are known as the *concejales* (councilmen). Included in this group is a lieutenant mayor who serves as a councilman and replaces the *alcalde* when he is absent. Completing the list of personnel of the Concejo is the district secretary, who is in charge of the municipal office and the paper work.

The official duties of the Concejo concern the regulation and man-

[1] Fajardo, n.d. (a):71 and Fajardo, n.d. (b):39–43. An excellent, detailed study of departmental, provincial, and district government was made in the southern highlands and reported by the Plan Regional Para El Desarrollo del Sur del Perú, 1959:XXIII, 52. This report is partially reproduced in Allred, 1960:46–60. A more recent review of provincial and district government has been made by Austin, 1964. This study outlines many of the legal conditions and statutes which regulate local government and enumerates some of the problems.

[2] On December 15, 1963, municipal elections were reinstituted for the first time (officially) since 1919. Because the appointment system was in use at the time of my research, most of the chapter refers to this type of municipal government unless otherwise stated. The course of municipal government since elections is summarized in a section apart.

agement of all public activities and services. The basic responsibilities of the councilmen are of two classes: the first is concerned with the internal management of the Concejo funds and the second with community activity. With respect to the former, one councilman is appointed by the mayor to serve as *síndico de rentas* (trustee of income). He collects and accounts for Concejo income. A second councilman is given the position of *síndico de gastos* (trustee of expenses), and he accounts for all expenses.

The income derived from its various activities provides the municipality with only a modest amount of money during any given year. The funds derived from the rent charged for municipal land, issuance of licenses to merchants (particularly during the Fiesta of Saint Elizabeth), fines, and collection of fees for the use of electricity are normally augmented by private contributions made by the citizenry to support a specific public works project (see Chapter VIII). Occasionally the district receives a sum of money or materials from the national government to help finance public works. Excluding such donations, the municipal government can rarely anticipate receiving more than $1,500.00 during the year. For good reason then, Huaylinos state that the municipality is "poor."

With the installation of hydroelectric power (see Chapter IX) in Huaylas in 1961 the municipality has been able to augment its income considerably, as consumption of electricity has greatly increased. It became necessary to establish an office with two full-time employees to manage the installation and maintenance of the system and the collection of fees and accounting. Both men receive a modest salary from the Concejo Distrital.

As a result of this growth the mayor contracted a public accountant in Caraz in 1961 to assist in the balancing of the books. Bookkeeping methods and records had not kept pace with the times and were in a rather primitive state. The budget of the municipality was seldom planned in advance of a fiscal year, seldom accurately balanced at year's end, and almost never reported to any higher authority. This situation was not unusual or unique to Huaylas but, in fact, appears to be typical of the vast majority of provincial districts.[3] Thus the hiring of a public accountant was a significant innovation in Huaylas.

[3] Austin (1964:41) reports of the Bureau of Inspection and Accounting of Municipal Councils of the Ministry of Government and Police, that, "as of May, 1964, this department had copies of the budgets of only 85 of the 1,728 districts and provincial councils it is to supervise."

The management and supervision of district and especially urban activities is the duty of all members of the Concejo, whose responsibilities are divided into four *inspecciones* (inspectorships). The four councilmen who were in office during our residence in Huaylas divided the *inspecciones* among themselves as follows: (1) public lighting; water system (for the town); library; spectacles (parades, fiestas, and so forth); civil register; (2) education; public works; weights and measures; market and butcher shop; (3) transportation; park and plaza; damages to public property; public health; and (4) care of public buildings and their appearance; public announcements; bridges and roads; the cemetery.

The mayor supervises and directs the activities of the Concejo and must assume responsibility for his administration. The business of the Concejo is conducted in an informal manner from day to day. Formal meetings are held, on the average, twice a month, but this varies considerably.

The only member of the Concejo who receives remuneration for his work is the secretary, since he is expected to spend most of the day in the municipal office to serve the public in the registering of births and deaths, in answering questions, and in taking care of other paper work. The secretary received S/250.00 a month (about $10.00) during the time that we were in Huaylas. Prior to 1960, all the secretaries had been men, but because the job was a full-time one, and because the salary was so low, it was difficult for a man with family responsibilities to devote sufficient time to the work. Thus, there had been a rather rapid turnover of secretaries. The *alcalde*, recognizing the problem, appointed a young, single woman to fill the position, on the theory that she would have the time and would not object to the low salary. The innovation met with no opposition in the community, although some persons felt that young women were less serious-minded than men, and some of the older women thought that a woman might be "tempted" by the presence of so many men about her in the Concejo. Despite these reservations, it was generally felt that a young woman could fill the position adequately.

The frequent change in secretaries has taken its toll in the organization of the Concejo records. A general lack of concern for the historical value of such documents has also been a contributing factor, and this in turn is partly responsible for the shortage of adequate filing equipment and storage space.

The municipal office occupies the second floor of a large building, constructed by *repúblicas* (public work projects) in 1901, and faces the plaza. Despite its pleasant "colonial" appearance, it is much in need of repairs. The wooden floor of the main room, which serves as the office as well as meeting room, is thoroughly infested with termites (a common problem in Peru),[4] thus producing a "springy" sensation when one walks on it. The balcony suffers the same problem. The two rooms which comprise the office are plastered. Three large, glass-doored cedar cabinets hold about half of the archives, the remainder being stacked, without regard to any system, on open, unfinished wooden shelves in the small adjoining room.[5]

The back room fulfills a sort of "attic" function, for one finds pieces of miscellaneous equipment, such as hammers, wire, old signs, broken band instruments, and yellowed newspapers, tucked away in the corners. Under the table, there are often a few bottles of beer, champagne, or cola, which are kept on hand for refreshment and hospitality in case of surprise visits by regional authorities or distinguished persons. In the main room, business is conducted over a small table, usually covered with official papers and the current books of the civil registry. The secretary has the use of an R. C. Allen Company typewriter, which was purchased for about $200.00 in Lima. The other "modern" apparatus owned by the Concejo is a large prewar Philco radio with a short-wave band, a record player (78 r.p.m.), and a decrepit amplifier-loudspeaker system, which is sometimes used for public announcements and special programs. A surprisingly accurate pendulum clock (obtained in 1898) and sundry announcements and posters on the walls provide the decor, and four benches and some chairs complete the office furnishings.

The posts of *alcalde* and *concejal* were usually of one-year duration, although some administrations served for as long as four years (during the 1930's). While we were in Huaylas, there was no change for eighteen months; that particular Concejo served for a period of roughly two and a half years because of the popularity of its members. Prior to the reinitiation of local elections in 1963, the matter of who

---

[4] Another common insect pest is the *moscón*, a large flylike insect, which burrows into exposed beams.

[5] In order to make use of these materials, it was necessary to clean out the entire room, sort, label, and divide the various *legajos* (files) and papers by category and date. In doing this I was fortunate to have the assistance of two Huaylinos, Mr. Nilo Acosta R. and Mr. Libio Villar L., to whom I wish to express my gratitude.

would be mayor and who would serve on the district council was controlled by what was referred to as the junta of *notables* of the district, that is, the most vocal members of the upper class.

Under the authoritarian, highly centralized governmental system of Peru, one comes to the conclusion that the relative freedom of choice was due more to the inefficiencies of the governmental machinery than to official policy or design. Since the mayor had to be appointed by the prefect, the people generally called an assembly, in which a list (*terno*) of three names was drawn up of candidates for the office. Listed in order of preference, the *terno* was forwarded by the district *gobernador* to the prefect, who usually appointed the first man on the list. Since the prefect did not enter into Huaylas district politics (neither the prefect nor the subprefect visited Huaylas during the eighteen months we were there), he was forced, out of ignorance, to accept the choice of the people who submitted the list.[6]

If the people in the community disapproved of the policies or activities of the Concejo or any of its members, individuals would send letters of complaint (*denuncia*) to the prefect or subprefect asking that the personnel be changed. It was more usual, however, for the people to seek removal of an unpopular person from office simply by withholding their cooperation and conducting a "whispering" campaign against him. Such actions generally resulted in the voluntary, "irrevocable" resignation of the offending individual. The large number of persons who have held office in Huaylas and the fact that in several years as many as three different persons have been appointed and have resigned as mayor testify to the frequency with which this occurs. According to municipal records (1889 to 1962) 166 persons have held office, either as mayor or as councilman. Sixteen had acted as mayor, 130 as councilman, and 20 persons had held both positions. Unfortunately, there is no comparative data available for the area that would permit a judgment as to whether or not there is an unusual degree of participation in government in Huaylas. From other evidence, which will be presented later, and from casual observation elsewhere, it would appear that Huaylinos demonstrate a considerably more active interest

[6] During this time, the people of the nearby District of Corongo forcibly ejected a man from office whom the prefect had appointed *alcalde* without having had this sort of local approval. The people then submitted the name of another man to the prefect, who had no choice but to appoint him.

LEVEL OF GOVERNMENT

I. National	II. Departmental	III. Provincial	IV. District	V. Barrio
Ministerio de Gobierno (Ministro)	Prefectura (Prefecto)	Concejo Provincial (Alcalde and Concejales)	Concejo Distrital (Alcalde and Concejales)	Agente Municipal (Inspector and Brazos)
		Subprefectura (Subprefecto)	Gobernación (Gobernador)	Teniente Gobernador and Cívicos
	Comandante de Policia	Puesto	Puesto de la Guardia Civil (Comandante)	
Corte Suprema	Corte Superior (Juez)	Juzgado de la Primera Instancia (Juez)	Juzgado de Paz (Juez de Paz)	
Ministerio de Hacienda (Ministro)	Caja de Depósitos	Caja de Depósitos	Caja de Depósitos	
Ministerio de Agricultura (Ministro)	Servicio Regional de Agricultura		Administrador de Aguas and Junta de Regantes	Repartidor de Aguas
			Extension Service office (since 1966)	
Ministerio de Trabajo y Asuntos Indígenas (Comunidades)	Inspector Regional de Asuntos Indígenas (Inspector)		Comunidad de Indígenas (Personero)	
Ministerio de Educación		Inspección Provincial (Inspector)	Inspección Distrital (Inspector)	

Figure 6. Political and administrative structure of Huaylas as related to the national government of Peru

in the formal aspects of local organization than is shown in many other districts.

Another factor that has contributed to the high turnover and the large number of individuals who have held office is the high rate of migration to the coast, particularly among the upper-class men who have customarily filled the posts in the Concejo. The departure of qualified and acceptable persons has frequently created a vacuum of sorts, which allows young men, ambitious individuals, or outsiders to be drawn into administrative positions. This is evidenced by the large number of persons who have served but one term as councilman (87) or mayor (22) and by the surprisingly large number of non-Huaylinos who have acted in these capacities (Table 25). For example, of the five members of the Concejo who held office during the time of our research, only the mayor had had previous experience,[7] and in the group which succeeded to office in March of 1962, the only one with previous training was the new mayor who had served as a councilman during the previous administration. The average age of these new officeholders was just over twenty-seven years, and they comprised the youngest group ever to have held office.

Actually, the pattern of having promising young men serve on the Concejo is not a new one, as the community records indicate. It appears to have been a well-established pattern even at the turn of the century. Although not able to document it fully, I would estimate that the median age of members of the Concejo over the time for which I have records (1889 to 1962) is about thirty-five.[8]

The fact that young upper-class men, as well as some talented persons of middle-class status, are encouraged to assume administrative responsibility is certainly one of the key aspects of leadership development in Huaylas. The involvement of young people in the formal aspects of district life, as well as in other activities, has served to sustain community spirit and, at times, to rekindle it. Young adults are both rewarded and challenged—a situation which has resulted in the emergence of good leadership and a number of changes in Huaylas life.

---

[7] He had previously served as a *concejal* and also had been the *alcalde* of the District of Huallanca. Other Huaylinos have also held office in Huallanca.

[8] During the celebration of Peruvian Independence Day on July 28 each year, the key address in a *sesión solemne* (solemn session) before the *cabildo abierto* (public assembly) is always delivered by the youngest member of the Concejo. This is a widespread tradition in Peru.

Table 25. Number and percentage of persons according to place of birth who
have served as mayor or councilman, 1889–1962 *

	Mayors		Councilmen †	
Place of birth	Number	Per cent	Number	Per cent
Town of Huaylas	21	58.4	109	72.6
Santo Toribio	3	8.3	15	10.0
Non-Huaylinos ‡	10	27.8	23	15.4
Unknown	2	5.5	3	2.0
Total	36	100.0	150	100.0

* Distrito de Huaylas, *Libro de Actas*, 1889–1962
† Including secretaries
‡ Resident in Huaylas

Moreover, encouragement of the young has promoted their continued allegiance to the *terruño*. It was such a group of young men and women, for example, who were instrumental in 1940 in obtaining the diesel generator to supply the town with electricity for the first time.

The position of *alcalde* is the most important official post in the district, save perhaps that of parish priest. While the post of *concejal* is somewhat less prestigeful, it is, nevertheless, considered one of the most vital in the district. Consequently, persons selected to serve in these capacities have been chosen on the basis both of their status in the community and for their ability. Huaylinos, in specifying the qualifications a man should have for the position of *alcalde,* stress that he must be a person who will lend dignity to the office, for he is the person who represents Huaylas before visiting functionaries and to the outside world. Thus, he should be articulate and a person of "culture." Some Huaylinos expressed shame about a man who had served as mayor, stating how poorly qualified he was. "Imagine," they said, "Don Fulano doesn't even pronounce the words right, let alone know what to say. Can you picture him delivering an address before the North American ambassador? [9] What a disgrace!"

In spite of the desire to have experienced and cultured men serve, there have been times when qualified men were not disposed to accept the position either because of other commitments or because of the

[9] The United States Ambassador paid a three-hour visit to Huaylas on the invitation of the *alcalde* on July 8, 1961, while on his way to visit Vicos and was declared an "illustrious guest" of the District of Huaylas at a special meeting of the Concejo.

general political situation in the department or the nation. It is a recognized fact that the duties of *alcalde* or *concejal*, if seriously undertaken, require a fair investment of time and energy, and, without remuneration, these positions can prove as much a burden as an honor. Others have objected to serving because public officials are invariably subject to critical sniping and rumors that they may be abusing the powers of office or benefiting from them illegally, that is, dipping into the public till.

Despite such drawbacks, a great deal of respect and prestige accrues to the person who performs well in the post of *alcalde* and, to a lesser extent, as *concejal*. A good performance involves not only a satisfactory handling of the normal Concejo activities but also the initiation and, if possible, completion of projects viewed as enhancing the common welfare. Consequently, one of the attributes sought in a mayor is that he be "progressive," always working to accomplish such ends.

On December 15, 1963, the first municipal elections in forty-four years were held in Peru. Such a change had been promised by all the political parties during the presidential elections held in June 1963. The consequences of the prolonged campaigns and the results of the national presidential, congressional, and municipal elections have somewhat altered the power structure of the district. The elections have also served to factionalize the district more closely along party lines, a situation which did not obtain prior to 1962.

In the presidential and congressional elections scheduled for 1962, Huaylinos became personally involved in politics owing to old, or newly acquired, party affiliations and because a former popular district mayor was a candidate for congress from the province.[10] With the annulment of the elections and subsequent military *coup d'état* in July 1962, the presidential and congressional elections were rescheduled for June 1963. The resumption of the campaign renewed the bitter struggle of the preceding year and tended to deepen and perpetuate the animosities created at that time. The man who had been defeated for congress in 1962 remained neutral during these elections, not running

---

[10] He ran on a regional splinter-party ticket and lost, although he received the vast majority of Huaylas' votes. In 1962, the majority of Huaylinos supported ex-president Odria for president. In the rescheduled election in 1963 the APRA party won in Huaylas. In 1956 Huaylinos voted for Belaunde, who lost. Huaylinos have thus been fickle voters as well as on the losing side in each of the last three presidential elections.

for any office. Thus, when municipal elections were called for December 1963, he was asked by each of the three major parties to head its ticket as the candidate for *alcalde*.

The former mayor then attempted to form a single, multiparty list of candidates for the municipal offices in the hope that district unity might be salvaged. His plan failed when the Acción Popular group was forced to withdraw from the pact on orders from above. Largely as a result of the popularity of the former mayor, the APRA-Odria coalition which backed him was brought to power in the district, a fact which contradicted the pattern in the rest of the Callejón de Huaylas, where President Fernando Belaunde's party, Acción Popular, won most municipal offices.[11]

The elected Concejo then consisted of the popular, apolitical mayor, an upper-class woman as lieutenant mayor, and three councilmen, two of whom were residents of rural *barrios* and of middle-class status. The new composition of the Concejo thus represented a clear departure from the pattern which had prevailed under the appointive system prior to elections. It marked, for the first time, the emergence of the literate rural peasant as a power in local government.

In a district such as Huaylas, the continuation of local elections is certain to have a great impact on the political and social structure. Over 1,200 Huaylinos are registered voters, constituting one of the largest voting publics in the region. Because the middle class in Huaylas is, numerically, the largest element in the population, their voice will be heard as never before on the district level. Whether this will occur at the expense of the *barrio* organizations or whether it results in new power alignments and values remains to be seen. The increase in political factionalism has been already marked as formal party organizations have become established in the district.

The execution of "progressive" programs [12] depends upon the ability

[11] Again in 1966 an attempt was made to form a single list, composed of representatives of the two major political blocks, the "Coalition" (the Unión Nacional Odrista party and the APRA party) and the "Alliance" (the Acción Popular party and the Christian Democrat party). Both groups wanted the powerful incumbent mayor to head the ticket. At the last minute, however, the "Coalition" group withdrew because of strategy problems at the provincial level. Thus, the incumbent mayor "switched" parties and ran for the "Alliance" and won by an overwhelming majority, reversing the vote of the previous election and swinging the vote in favor of "Alliance" candidates at the provincial level.

[12] The opening of new roads, improvement of old ones, building of schools, and so on.

of the mayor to gain the cooperation of the nine *barrio* organizations in the district. The *barrios*, as indicated earlier, are headed by an *agente municipal* (municipal agent), or *inspector*, as he is called in Huaylas. The *inspector* is officially appointed by the mayor, after the family heads in the *barrio* have held a meeting to choose him. As was formerly the case with appointment of the mayor by the prefect, the decision of the *barrio* assembly is usually accepted by the mayor. The *inspector*, in turn, selects a group of assistants called *brazos* (arms) who are ranked in order of their importance to the *inspector* (first *brazo*, second *brazo*, and so on). Depending upon the *inspector*, the size of the *barrio*, and current activities, from three to six *brazos* are selected, usually from among the inspector's friends. There is no pattern of succession to the position of *inspector* through the ranks of the *brazos*, that is, becoming a *brazo* does not necessarily mean that one will become first *brazo* or *inspector* at some time in the future, nor is serving as *brazo* a requirement for becoming *inspector*.

In places such as Vicos and Hualcán, positions which roughly correspond to those of *inspector* and *brazo* in Huaylas are called *varayoq* or *alcaldes pedáneos* (petty mayors).[13] Carrying their silver-adorned staffs of office, the *varayoq* are a colorful vestige of the colonial period and today form part of the Indian politico-religious organization operative within the rigid and traditional dichotomized society of the highlands.[14] Because of certain structural similarities between Huaylas *barrio* officials and the *varayoq*, one concludes that the *barrio* organizations of Huaylas descend from the same colonial model. The evolution of the Huaylas *barrio* officialdom, however, has differed from the *varayoq*. No *barrio* official carries a staff of office, nor is there an air of sanctity attached to the status of *inspector* as there is with the *varayoq*. Perhaps most important, the *barrio* organizations are not considered as being Indian in character, but simply as the rural arm of official administrative and political authority. The *varayoq* are not accorded this status.

The position of *inspector* is one of considerable honor and prestige among the middle and lower classes. As in the case of the mayor, however, such honor will be withheld from any given individual who, as *inspector*, proves to be abusive, irresponsible, or lazy. *Barrio inspectores* are expected by everyone—the members of the upper class included—to be efficient organizers who command the respect of the

[13] Stein, 1961:182–199; Vázquez, 1964.
[14] Vázquez, 1961a; Holmberg *et al.*, 1965.

people of their *barrios*, thus making possible the success of the several activities in which the *barrios* customarily engage as units. A lack of cooperation between *inspector* and *barrio* residents results in a poor performance by the *barrio* in the lively competition between the *barrios*— particularly in *repúblicas* and in the Fiesta of Saint Elizabeth—and, consequently, in a loss of *barrio* prestige in the district and ridicule from the other *barrios*.

Thus there is considerable pressure on the *inspector* to perform well, and those *inspectores* who do not fulfill the expectations of the *barrio* residents are forced to resign. One of the common entries in Concejo records is a complaint to the mayor that the *inspector* of a given *barrio* is no good and that the people wish him removed in favor of someone new. The mayor, in such cases, asks for the resignation of the *inspector* and requests that an assembly of the *barrio* select another. Because of this, there may be a high turnover in *barrio* officeholders. But if all goes well, the *inspectores* (and *brazos*) are changed yearly. Prior to 1963 this occurred after a new mayor had established his Concejo.

The *gobernador* (governor) of the district is an appointee of the prefect of the Department of Ancash. He is charged with law enforcement,[15] particularly in rural areas, and he issues orders for arrests and fines and mediates disputes of various types. The governor, on appointment, selects a man to serve as his *teniente* (lieutenant) in each *barrio*. They are officially confirmed in office by the subprefect of the province. As in the case of the *inspectores*, the *tenientes* choose a group of assistants, called *cívicos*. In Huaylas, the power of the governor is limited by the strength of the Concejo and the *barrio* organizations, which, historically, have been the most important bodies in the district.

Elsewhere in the Callejón area, this is not always the case, and one usually hears that in the *caserios* and *estancias* (outlying areas), it is the *teniente* who represents the "authorities" there. The *teniente* in this traditional setting, according to Stein:

. . . is usually selected because the provincial authorities know that they can depend upon him for information or other help in the village. His fellow villagers know this and are likely to consider him an opportunist. . . . His favor in the eyes of mestizos is resented by fellow villagers.[16]

[15] Beltrán, n.d.:50–53.
[16] Stein, 1961:193.

The *teniente*, then, is the representative of the local mestizo upper class in the *caserios*, or rural hamlets, and is often despised, while the *varayoq*, whose formal legal status is dubious, are the leaders of the closed Indian community.

The contrast with Huaylas is striking because the *inspectores* of the *barrios* are closely bound to the Concejo, while they are, at the same time, freely selected by the middle and lower classes. While the *teniente* is not considered a leader in either case, in Huaylas he is not looked upon with the disrespect described by Stein in Hualcán. The political and administrative integration of the district, one of the most significant features of life in Huaylas, stands in sharp contrast to the situation in other districts of the Callejón, for in Huaylas individuals, regardless of status, enter into and are part of a single system of government.

Until the organization of a national police force (*guardia civil*) the municipality of Huaylas developed, paid, and controlled its own modest force. The Concejo is still entitled to maintain a municipal force, but only for the purpose of policing the market place and for similar activity which is closely related to the specific functions of the Concejo. There is no such police unit in Huaylas now.

The national police organization, however, maintains a post (*puesto*) in Huaylas, which is usually manned by three persons: a sergeant and two members of the *guardia civil* (civil guard) who are often changed.[17] These men are usually not Huaylinos but may be from anywhere in the country. During our residence, however, one *guardia* (with the rank of corporal) who was stationed there was a Huaylino, and another Huaylino had been in charge of the *puesto* a few months prior to our arrival. The relationship of the police with the town and the district is generally one of cooperation. They did not abuse their authority while we were there nor usurp the power of local authorities. Indeed, they could not, for Huaylinos, at the slightest provocation from the police, set out to check any irregularity, using whatever influence they are able to muster, usually in order to effect a change in personnel.

An example of this is recounted concerning a Huaylino who died several years ago. An influential man in Huaylas and the region, he had been insulted and threatened with arrest when he had protested the police sergeant's illegal behavior. He reacted by going to Huaraz and

[17] There were five different sergeants in charge of the *puesto* during our stay there. The *guardias* were changed less often.

obtaining an order for the sergeant's transfer from Huaylas, which he delivered to the sergeant personally. A somewhat similar instance occurred during our stay in Huaylas when the people and the parish priest objected to the fact that the sergeant in charge of the *puesto* was a Protestant (and had refused to attend the official Holy Week Masses) and requested his transfer on that basis.

The *puesto* is located on the first floor of the same building that houses the Concejo office. The post consists of a one-room office in which all the records are meticulously stored, a dormitory with three beds, and, behind the building in a patio surrounded by a fifteen-foot adobe wall, a three-room jail, which seldom houses more than one offender at any given time.

Police activity in Huaylas is limited to such things as registry and control of commercial vehicles (and foreigners) [18]; handling cases of petty theft, drunkenness, fighting, and other misdemeanors; and occasionally conducting investigations (see Table 24). None of these duties was particularly time-consuming or difficult, and the police were generally to be seen sitting on a park bench, chatting with someone. As one sergeant expressed it, "Huaylas is a good place to 'work'—it's like a vacation." The police detachment voluntarily accepted the responsibility of caring for one quarter of the garden in the plaza. As gardeners, they always kept their portion well watered, clipped, and weeded.

In spite of their relative inactivity, the police are considered important, for the presence of the *puesto* lends some prestige to the district, since not all districts have police detachments. The personnel of the *puesto*, particularly the sergeant, can expect to participate in many social functions at the upper-class level.[19] Indeed, failure to participate properly (as in the case of the Protestant sergeant) is almost sure to bring unpopularity and difficulty. Thus, one sergeant in performing his duty of enforcing a general municipal ordinance prohibiting nighttime serenades in urban areas, placed four youths in jail. The mayor and others exerted considerable pressure on him to release the offenders, saying that it was not the custom to observe the ordinance in Huaylas. Thereafter, there were no more arrests for this reason.

There are two Justices of the Peace in Huaylas, both residing in the

[18] We had to check in at the *puesto* every time we left the district or arrived from outside.

[19] While they may be invited to attend dances and the like, there were many occasions when it appeared that the sergeant had "crashed the party." At such times, his presence would be tolerated, but not encouraged.

town. Appointed by the provincial court for a period of one year, the Justices of the Peace handle simple litigation, registry of legal documents, wills, and so forth, as required by the laws.[20] The two Justices of the Peace in Huaylas, while serving an important legal function, nevertheless do not exercise the kind of influence on district life that the mayor does, for they deal with individual, not collective, problems. It is with the Justice of the Peace that such problems may be aired and decided as inheritance disputes, support for children by deserting husbands, and adoptions. While the Justice of the Peace is not allowed to charge for his services, he is entitled to a small salary (paid by the provincial court) and is, consequently, expected to attend his office daily. For the most part, the Justices have little to do, in an official sense, with the rest of the formal administrative officeholders, although, theoretically, the Concejo has the right to review their records. So far as I know, this was not done in Huaylas during the time we were there.

Because of its size and location, the district also has a branch office of the revenue division of the Ministry of the Exchequer (Hacienda). The office is staffed by one man, charged with collecting property and inheritance taxes and sales taxes, controlling the sale of alcoholic beverages, tobacco, playing cards, salt, matches, and *coca*, and serving as paymaster for all government employees in the district (himself, all forty-five schoolteachers, several persons on government retirement pensions, and the two employees of the national drugstore). Despite the formal list of taxes to be collected, the office was too understaffed and underequipped to attempt seriously the collection of what was owed.

The tax collector's job is further complicated by an almost universal lack of sincere cooperation with him in the performance of his duties. Sales of land are almost never registered (although the sale is not legal unless recorded) in order to avoid payment of tax, and storekeepers fail to record as many as half of their transactions in order to evade the sales tax.[21] One storekeeper confided, with some pride, that because he was a trained accountant he knew how to keep two sets of books—one for the tax collector and one for himself. Compounding the problem of falsification of accounts is the fact that most of the small storekeepers

---

[20] Martinez G., n.d.

[21] The sales tax is infinitesimal, amounting to one *centavo* for every ten *soles* in sales. The tax is paid by the purchase of tax stamps which are affixed to the official accounts of the business, periodically reviewed by the tax collector.

do not even bother to keep records. The tax collector in Huaylas lamented that he was unable to control this or to review all of the business accounts in the district. It must be said that the task of auditing these accounts is one of considerable proportion, since there are over eighty stores in the district; some, being located far from the town, would require almost a day's travel to reach.[22] He said that because he did not have an assistant, he was unable to leave the office to do this. He also claimed that there were a number of stores that were not even registered and licensed.

This inefficiency of perhaps the most important aspect of national government in Huaylas is a case study in microcosm of one of the great national problems, that of taxation reform. It also provides an interesting contrast with the effective collection of funds for the Fiesta of Saint Elizabeth (Chapter XI). The situation in Huaylas, it should be noted, is not unique, but rather one which is common throughout the country.

Comunidad Indígena

Also present in the district of Huaylas is an officially constituted Comunidad Indígena (Indigenous Community), one of some 1,662 such legally recognized organizations in the country.[23] While it is not necessary to discuss in detail the complex history and development of the Comunidad Indígena in Perú, it should be noted that they enjoy a special legal status, established by the Peruvian constitution.[24] Each Comunidad consists of a group of Indian members and their families who own land for their common use. The Comunidades are subject to the control of the Bureau of Indian Affairs of the Ministry of Labor and Communities (formerly, Indian Affairs), which, through its regional inspectors, supervises, counsels, and assists in various ways.

As an organization, the Comunidad Indígena until 1963, was the only official administrative unit of government in which the local election of officers was sanctioned and permitted. Such elections in the Comunidades can be conducted in theory only under the supervision (presence) of the regional inspector or delegate assigned by the national

[22] In the *barrios* of Tambo and San Lorenzo.
[23] Perú, Ministerio de Trabajo y Asuntos Indígenas, Dirección de Asuntos Indígenas, 1964.
[24] Articles 207–212 of the Constitution of 1933, in force at the present time (Velasco, n.d.:8–13).

ministry for this purpose. Although originally abolished at the outset of the Republican period of Peruvian history, the Comunidades were returned to legal status in 1919 and, again, in 1933 (under new constitutions) for the purpose of protecting the organizational integrity of those Indians who still maintained some semblance of their Incan communal organization and held land in common.

Under the law, the lands of the communities are inviolate and not subject to sale or mortgage by individual members or by the group as a whole. The law does not, however, prohibit members from holding private lands for their own use, apart from those of the Comunidad. Thus constituted, a Comunidad Indígena may require its members to work on behalf of the common good, pay fines for noncompliance with the norms of conduct, and collect funds with which to meet financial obligations or other expenses incurred in the operation of the organization. Each Comunidad Indígena elects a *personero* (manager or chairman), who manages the financial and legal business of the body; a president, who presides at meetings; and several lesser officers, such as a treasurer and a secretary. In theory, the Comunidad also selects one of its number to serve as their representative to the Concejo Distrital.[25]

The Comunidad Indígena de Huaylas was organized in January 1937 in the Campiña of Santo Toribio, where it continues to maintain its headquarters, and was officially recognized by the government in 1940.[26] It was conceived, in part, with the notion of retaining for public use the extensive grazing lands in the *puna* on the Cordillera Negra, and elsewhere in the district, particularly in the fringe areas, which are not cultivated.

The request for official recognition of the community and the survey of the lands by the Ministry of Labor and Indian Affairs was not begun until October 1938.[27] It is interesting to note that the original request

[25] In actuality this practice seems to have fallen into abeyance in many—perhaps most—areas, if indeed it was ever followed. The assumption by Austin (1964:15) that "the principal advantage in becoming a recognized community is the ensuing right of representation on the local district council," is misleading. The chief rationale for the Comunidad Indígena both historically and at present is to preserve communal land rights and the subsistence economy of Indian peasants (Velasco, n.d.:7-13 [Articles 203-212]).

[26] To obtain legal status, a Comunidad must be officially recognized by the Ministry of Labor. There are many groups, however, which function as Comunidades but are not officially recognized.

[27] Perú, Ministerio de Trabajo y Asuntos Indígenas, Dirección General de Asuntos Indígenas, n.d.: 1-13.

which was submitted by the president of the Comunidad, was accompanied by other letters, seconding the request, from a person residing in Callao (Lima's seaport). With this was launched a long series of letters, reports, and other correspondence, which now form a voluminous file, several inches thick, in the Bureau of Indian Affairs.

It is clear that, from the very outset, there was not only strong official opposition from the governor to the formation of the Comunidad but that there was opposition also from individuals in various *barrios*, who alleged that their lands were being usurped. For these reasons, as well as others to be discussed, the Comunidad has not prospered.

Because the story of the Comunidad in Huaylas illustrates a number of problems that are characteristic of Huaylas life in general as well as life in many other communidades elsewhere in Peru,[28] I shall treat it in somewhat greater detail than the organization perhaps merits in relation to its importance to Huaylas life as a whole.

The problem of conflicts over land, which began with the establishment of the Comunidad, has persisted without interruption to the present.[29] In fact, the lands to which title was originally contested by the Comunidad were still in litigation twenty-four years later. In 1939 the civil engineer filed his report on the survey of the lands claimed by the Comunidad and noted that the ownership of almost half was disputed.[30]

In 1961, according to an official of the organization, the Comunidad was engaged in seven lawsuits over land, five of which were initiated when the Comunidad was first organized. These suits are with an hacienda in the neighboring district of Huallanca, the Parish of Huaylas, two of the largest landholding families in Huaylas (each of which claims the land), and other smaller landholders. All of this litigation has been before the courts for many years without final resolution. Indeed,

[28] See Dobyns, 1964, for a comparative analysis of selected characteristics of Comunidades Indígenas. An economic analysis of Comunidades is presented in Ritter, 1965.

[29] Dobyns (1964:38) reports that over 73 per cent of 640 Comunidades surveyed were involved in such territorial disputes in 1961.

[30] Perú, Ministerio de Trabajo y Asuntos Indígenas (Comunidades), Dirección General de Asuntos Indígenas, n.d.:20–29. This report noted that of the 5,253.1 hectares claimed by the Comunidad Indígena of Huaylas, 2,367.3 hectares or 45 per cent were disputed. For a review of this problem in other Comunidades, see Dobyns, 1964:20–29, and Ritter, 1965:28–34.

the president of the Comunidad could recall only two suits which had been resolved during the history of the Comunidad.

Apparently, it is the pattern for the cases to lie "dormant" in the courts until one or the other of the parties, having collected enough money and wishing some action, presses for a decision. The loss of the suit in a lower court brings the inevitable appeal at a higher level, and so on. Litigation may be temporarily ended, but usually the losing party will make new claims so as to continue the process ad infinitum. The reluctance to accept a verdict is indicative of the general attitude that people of all classes have toward the legal process. An unfavorable decision is generally laid to *"mala suerte"* (bad luck), a poor lawyer, a technical faux pas, or, perhaps most commonly, the lack of *vara* (influence, or more accurately, "pull") in the right circles. Thus one member of the Comunidad explained that the only reason the Comunidad had not been able to win one of the lawsuits was that one of the families involved had a great deal of *vara* in Lima.

If there is one thing that epitomizes the popular attitude toward legal proceedings, as well as toward many other official acts, it is the belief that something was lacking in the presentation of one's case, if one loses, or that the right things were done, if one wins. Few appear willing to accept a decision in terms of the fundamental validity or error in the positions taken by the litigants. Thus, as one person put it: "It depends upon who arrives first, with the most chickens, at the judge's house." [31]

Nevertheless, persons who have knowledge of legal proceedings and the law are generally powerful figures in any community. Lawyers and judges command the respect of the populace. In the district, ranking below them in personal status are the various official personnel of the judicial and governmental hierarchy. Low-level officials and other persons outside the government apparatus without specific legal training often set themselves up as scribes, referred to in a derogatory manner as "ink dippers" (*tintorillos*). These people are of middle- and upper-class status in Huaylas. Equipped with straight pens, ink, desk, and, nowadays, a typewriter, the scribes will, for a fee, impart advice or compose official-looking documents for presentation to the appropriate authori-

[31] There are a multitude of stories and jokes about judges, courts, and lawyers working in collusion to prolong and complicate the legal process so as to make more money.

Table 26. Adult membership in the Comunidad Indígena according to *barrio* residence in the District of Huaylas, 1942 and 1958 *

	1942		1958	
	Number	Per cent	Number	Per cent
Santo Toribio †	153	59.5	108	57.6
Iscap	71	27.5	18	9.7
Yacup	14	5.4	19	10.2
Delicados	2	.7	21	11.3
Shuyo	14	5.4	13	6.9
Others	4	1.5	1	
Lima	0	0.0	7	3.8
Total	258	100.0	187	99.5

* Comunidad Indígena de Huaylas, Padrón General, 1942 and 1958. Includes adults only. According to the *Atlas Comunal* (Ministerio de Trabajo y Asuntos Indígenas, 1964), there are 979 members enrolled in the Comunidad. This figure includes 219 men, 228 women, and 532 children, grouped in 195 families. In the introduction to the *Atlas* (no pages are numbered in it) it is stated that: "In 1962 the survey of Comunidades Indígenas was sponsored in which the population of each Comunidad differentiated by age and sex was noted. In the preparation of the data, the questionnaires corresponding to 1961 that the Comunidades sent for the fifteen-year (census) updating were taken into account. These data were meticulously reviewed and their exactness proven, so that it can be affirmed that the 1962 Survey contains not one error." Despite this emphatic statement, the data contained in the *Atlas* are the same as those presented in a previous listing in 1961 (Perú, Ministerio de Trabajo y Asuntos Indígenas, 1961). These materials, however, represent the population of the Comunidades at the time they were officially recognized and are *not* based on any recent census. Thus, in the case of Huaylas, the membership figures correspond to the year 1940 and not 1962. Also included in the *Atlas* are estimates of communal land ownership, ownership of animals, and the "economic potential" of the Comunidades. Land that is attributed to the Comunidad Indígena of Huaylas includes only undisputed land. The list of animals recorded in the *Atlas* is apparently those owned by Comunidad members in 1940. The "economic potential" of the Comunidad Indígena de Huaylas is estimated at 1,641,774 *soles* ($61,260.00). What this represents or how the figure was obtained is not revealed.

† Includes the *barrios* of Quecuas and Huayrán.

ties or to intimidate someone. For this purpose, official paper (called *papel sellado*), bearing a number and document seal, is purchased from the Caja de Depósitos at the cost of nine cents (U.S.) per sheet. The role of the "ink dipper" in district and personal affairs is much debated, since many feel that such persons tend to encourage disputes rather than resolve them, for the purpose of making money or gaining power.

Just as other persons and organizations, the Comunidad Indígena in Huaylas has fallen victim on occasion to such individuals, both in and outside of the district.

The consequence of all this has been a constant outflow of time, effort, and money on the part of the officials and members of the Comunidad. While I was unable to obtain exact figures for their expenses, there is no question that they have been considerable. One of the most frequent entries in the *Libro de Actas* of the Comunidad is that of members being asked to donate money in order to finance a trip of the *personero* to Caraz, Huaraz, or Lima to see a lawyer or to present a case either before the Ministry or the court. This expense, of course, is not unique to the Comunidad in Huaylas, for squabbles over land are one of the most common phenomena of social life in the district. It is perhaps because so many persons are involved in their own legal problems that they quickly tire of supporting an organization with the same difficulties and expenses.

The second reason cited by the *comuneros* (members of the Comunidad) for its failure to develop is that not enough people understand the purposes of the organization or how the Comunidad is supposed to function. Many townspeople quietly confide to the listener that one must be wary of the *comuneros* because they are *"media comunista"* (half-communist) [32] and that the institution has "subversive" designs on the lives and property of other Huaylinos. The fact that the Comunidad is officially sponsored by the government of Peru and has legal status carries no weight at all with most townspeople and other opponents of the Comunidad. Hence, the Comunidad receives almost no support from the authorities in the district. The Comunidad is supposed to name one of its members to represent it before the Concejo Distrital, but, at the time I inquired, the president of the Comunidad said that this was useless, because the Concejo has never paid any attention to the representatives. He couldn't remember if the Comunidad had such an agent at the time.

In addition, the *personero* of the Comunidad stated that the governor of the district seldom aided the Comunidad in enforcing attendance at work projects that were undertaken or in collecting dues and fines on recalcitrant members, as he is legally supposed to do. Members of the

[32] Whether the communist accusation has been prompted by recent events is hard to say. Several men told me that there were many "communists" among the founders of the Comunidad. This is conceivable, but unconfirmed and dubious.

Comunidad felt that their requests or complaints were ignored by district officials, who reflected the negative attitudes of most townspeople and many others toward the Comunidad. It is safe to say that a large number of persons of all social classes consider the Comunidad a definite threat to their well-being, because of the fear that they might lose their land to it. Then, too, the concept of communal property in Huaylas is not appreciated; indeed, it is considered by many to be a dangerous thing, foreign to the ways of Huaylas.

Nonmembers flatly state that there is no such thing as a Comunidad in Huaylas because there has been neither common property nor communal organization since Bolivar abolished them by decree at the time of Independence. While the members of the Comunidad deny this and say that there has always been communal land, they do not maintain that there has always been a communal organization. They do, however, say that others, particularly the bigger landholders, continue to usurp the communal land, and for this reason affirm that it was necessary to form an official community. Be this as it may, the fact that there was no tradition of communal ownership or economic action has important consequences for the operation of the Comunidad.

Despite its organization, official purpose, and the law, the Comunidad engages in no significant communal economic activities. One of the reasons for this, as already mentioned, is that there is no tradition of it in Huaylas. This is not to say that the people do not undertake some enterprises in common, for they frequently do, as will be discussed. But these activities have for the most part been confined to public works projects with which the majority of the people could identify and in which they could participate, feeling that such work would yield direct benefits for them and their families. Because this kind of work is carried out under the auspices of the Concejo, it is accepted on that basis as well. The only other cooperative work carried on is the *rantín* or *minka*, which are systems of mutual aid used for house construction, harvesting, and other farming activities. The *rantín* usually involves one's relatives, *compadres*, and, sometimes, neighbors and friends.

Most of the land of the Comunidad lies in the highest regions of the district, stretching over the treeless *puna* for many miles at an average altitude of over 14,000 feet. Since this is too high for agricultural purposes, cattle and sheep are grazed over the grassy, unfenced pampas. Individual members of the Comunidad turn their cattle out there, rounding them up only for the purpose of selling them, if an occasion to do so presents itself. The Comunidad has no communal herd. During most of the year, the *comuneros* simply allow their animals to roam freely over the pasture, and then, usually once a year, the Comunidad holds a rodeo or roundup. This takes place on June 24 each year, that being the Feast of Saint John, patron of ranchers and shepherds. When the individual owners have identified their animals, they are charged twenty-four *soles* per head for the year's grazing privileges. This is considered to be a small charge and most reasonable when compared with the cost of grazing the same animals on private lands.

The president of the Comunidad said that several attempts have been made to form a communal herd by having each member contribute one calf to start it, but this proposal, he said, was never accepted. The reluctance of the *comuneros* to enter into a common economic venture has prevented the permanent assignment of one of them to serve as a year-round herdsman. The president said of the members:

They prefer to continue to lose some of their cattle to rustlers or condors instead of hiring one of their number to watch the herds. They used to have a man and wife doing this, but the other members of the Comunidad, who had agreed to take care of the man's *chacras* in his absence, did not fulfill their obligations with the result that the man had to return from the *puna*. The last time there was a cattle herder was in 1950. This indicates that the people are not really acquainted with the purposes of the Comunidad and are only interested in themselves; they are "muy egoistas." [33]

Thus, individualism, or egoism, as they put it, serves to inhibit the economic growth of the Comunidad. The individual ownership of animals is extremely variable. Some of the *comuneros* have as many as thirty head of cattle and sixty head of sheep, while others at any given time may have none. Consequently, many cannot even share in what small economic advantage the Comunidad has to offer, and they are, therefore, little interested in the problem of managing the pasture lands. It is thus perfectly understandable that they should drop out, or remain members in name only, when they cease maintaining a sufficient number of cattle to make membership worthwhile.

Officials of the Comunidad are quick to admit the need for some expert guidance to help the organization out of the dilemma in which it finds itself. They feel that the Ministry of Labor and Communities should have personnel available to consult with them on these problems

[33] Doughty, Field Notes, May 18, 1961:6–7.

Table 27. Number and types of animals owned by members of the Comunidad Indígena of Huaylas, 1954 *

Animals	Number
Cattle	438
Sheep	1,047
Horses	91
Donkeys	208
Goats	7
Hogs	304

* Comunidad Indígena de Huaylas, Padrón General, 1954.

and to help inculcate in the members the ideas of cooperative enterprise and the duties and responsibilities of membership, as well as to lend assistance in land management and other technical problems. It was often remarked that if the Comunidad had one or two blooded bulls available for breeding, the members might be more willing to work together on the problem of range management and might become interested in establishing a communal herd.

Such help has not been forthcoming, although, during our residence in Huaylas, the Regional Inspector of Indian Affairs on two occasions assisted in settling minor legal disputes. One of these was a dispute with the Concejo over the right to auction off some stray, unclaimed cattle found on the lands of the Comunidad. Both entities claimed jurisdiction over the animals, and at a hearing conducted by the Regional Inspector of Indian Affairs the case was decided in favor of the Comunidad, much to the consternation of the mayor and the *concejales,* who felt the decision to be lacking legal precedence. Neither the incident nor the decision contributed much toward greater cooperation between the two bodies.[34]

The position of the Comunidad in Huaylas is further complicated by the fact that, as an organization, it competes for the loyalty of its members with the *barrios.* Because of the strength of the *barrios* and their internal cohesion, the Comunidad has had to deal with the problem of *barrio* rivalry, through seeking official representation in each of

[34] I was told later that the inspector was convicted and sentenced to a short jail term for abuse of authority and for illegal actions he had taken in another case elsewhere. This certainly did not help the image of the Comunidades in the region.

them. Thus, there are representatives of the Comunidad in Yacup, Delicados, Shuyo, Iscap, and Quecuas and Huayrán. The purpose is to gain support through the recognition of the importance of the *barrios*. It would appear, however, that in spite of the fact that prestigeful persons in the different *barrios* were selected, the move has not been particularly successful in recruiting new members or in creating positive attitudes toward the Comunidad.

The preponderance of members from Quecuas and Huayrán (see Table 26), furthermore, has served to create the impression that the Comunidad is, for the most part, allied with the political and social aspirations of the people of these *barrios* and, consequently, does not represent the views of persons from other areas. Indeed, the Comunidad has made several gifts to the primary schools in Santo Toribio and conducts *faenas* (or *repúblicas*) only in that area. Members living outside these *barrios* then, have little to gain by support of such actitivies, since they are also asked to work in their own *barrios* and irrigation sectors and to make donations to the *barrio* or town schools that their children attend.

The fifth problem and another reason for the lack of vitality in the organization derives from conflicts between individual members and between individuals and the organization. This is perhaps best illustrated by the following example. The president of the Comunidad noted that of the forty-seven persons who had signed the minutes of the first session of the Comunidad in 1937, twenty-one were deceased, eleven were still active, and fifteen had resigned their membership either because of fights and conflicts of interest or because they were "tired." He explained that most of the conflicts were over the policy and course of action pursued by the Comunidad in its legal entanglements or arose because members could not get along with the Comunidad's leaders. In the several cases, however, the Comunidad had entered into litigation with members or their families over land, a fact which caused them to resign from the organization. The president cited these men as "traitors" to the Comunidad.

Finally, there is the fact that being a member of the Comunidad may imply that one is an *indígena*—an Indian. One of the older members said that this was one of the major reasons for the lack of interest expressed in the Comunidad by the youth, whom he called very "pretentious." He said that this was particularly true of the sons of members who had worked or gone to school in Lima. It is interesting to note that the criteria for judging whether or not one is an Indian for the purposes of the census of the Comunidad reflect, to some extent, the strength of a person's relationship to the organization, particularly if he is an officer. Thus, as noted in Chapter IV, one of the officials who is very Caucasoid in appearance, was usually classified as an Indian because he felt that he should be an "Indian" in order to justify his position. Nevertheless, many persons (both members and nonmembers of the Comunidad) declare their strong support in favor of Indian causes and the Comunidades elsewhere in their fight to gain social dignity and justice, but exempt the Comunidad in Huaylas and its membership on the ground that there are no "real" Indians in Huaylas.

By way of summary, then, the problems faced by the Comunidad in Huaylas are, in part, the same ones that all Huaylinos face: the lack of technical aid and guidance; litigation over land, complicated by an inefficient system for resolving such disputes; conservative attitudes toward cooperative economic ventures; and a tendency toward personal and political factionalism. In addition to these difficulties, which also beset other Comunidades, the implication that one is an "Indian" if one is a member (and, therefore, of the lowest social status) fosters a tendency to disassociate one's self from "Indian" organizations.[35]

Water Administration

Agriculture is the basis of Huaylas economy. Like a great majority of districts throughout Peru, successful agricultural production in Huaylas depends upon a system of irrigation that, beyond doubt, was established long before Pizarro set foot in the country. Reference has already been made to the pre-Columbian ruins to be found in Huaylas and to the fact that there are many terraced fields. In the ruins of Pueblo Viejo the irrigation canals can still be discerned in places and the techniques employed by the *gentiles*[36] appreciated. It is apparent that much of the pre-Conquest system of irrigation in Huaylas fell into disuse after the arrival of the Spanish because of the enormous decrease in the population and the introduction of Iberian techniques, which, in

[35] It should be noted that there are many Comunidades in the coastal regions, as, for example, in the city of Chimbote, which probably have no members who would ever be classified or think of themselves as Indians.

[36] *Gentiles* is the word often used by Huaylinos to refer to the pre-Columbian peoples. In this parlance, it means heathens, or non-Christians.

many cases, were inferior to those of the Incas and their predecessors.[37]
Moreover, the fact that the Spanish were primarily concerned with the
exploitation of raw materials for ready sale, rather than in developing
the agricultural basis of the economy, undoubtedly contributed to its
decline in Huaylas just as it did elsewhere in Peru.

Despite this loss, Huaylinos continued to cultivate their fields, although they were greatly reduced in area. Antonio Raimondi, the
Italian geographer described their use of water, in the decade following
1860, in this manner:

In few places in Peru have they known to take advantage of water and land
as they do in Huaylas, and due to this practical knowledge of agriculture,
Huaylas produced abundant harvests that validate its nickname
(harvest). . . .[38]

The system of irrigation, at the time that Raimondi observed it, was
managed by the municipal government, as it continued to be well into
the twentieth century. The present laws governing the use of irrigation
waters in the sierra were enacted in 1936.[39] At the head of the Water
Administration is a council called the Junta de Regantes and a water
administrator, all of whom are appointed by the Bureau of Waters and
Irrigation of the Ministry of Agriculture (see Figure 6). The Junta is
changed every two years and the administrator yearly, although this
may vary, since the same situation obtains here as formerly obtained in
the case of district officials who served shorter or longer terms, depending upon the mood of the people and the desires of the individuals
holding the positions. Some resign before the expiration of their terms.

In selecting the administrator and the president of the Junta, the
people using the irrigation waters make their preference known to the
governor of the district, sometimes through an election. The governor
then forwards a list of the men nominated to the Bureau of Waters and
Irrigation, which appoints men to fill the two positions. The president
of the Junta then selects four others to serve on the council with him,
and the administrator chooses an assistant, called the subadministrator.
The Junta selects from their number a vice-president and a treasurer.
According to the law, if there is a Comunidad Indígena in the district,

---

[37] Many terraces were, and still are, torn down to permit the more efficient use
of the plow. This, however, leads to greater erosion on the slopes.
[38] Raimondi, 1873:105 (my translation).
[39] Fajardo, n.d. (c):64–123.

there should be a representative of that body on the Junta, as was the case in Huaylas.

The district of Huaylas is divided into irrigation sectors, called *tomas*, within each *barrio*. The *tomas* each have several small tanks or reservoirs (from three to ten) in which water is collected for distribution.

The use of the water for agriculture is directly supervised by a man called a *repartidor de aguas* (water distributor), who is selected by the farmers who hold irrigated land in each *toma*. The *repartidor* is selected at a meeting of the farmers and is officially appointed through the office of the administrator. He is then responsible to the administrator for the management of his sector. It is the *repartidor* who, in a meeting with the users of the water, determines at which times each can expect to have water for his fields. All of the farmers in each *toma*, being aware of the schedule of use, plan their agricultural activities accordingly.

The irrigation system in Huaylas depends on the storage of rain water in the many small dams or tanks scattered throughout the district and on the water found in the twenty-eight or more small lakes in the *puna* regions of the district. The irrigation of the *chacras* is accomplished through a complicated, though somewhat primitive, canal system (*acéquias*), which must be maintained at the cost of many days of labor each year. The members of each *toma* and the *repartidor*, as well as the administrator and Junta, are responsible for the maintenance of the canal system and the dams and tanks upon which agricultural production depends. The administrator, as well as the Junta de Regantes, may order *faenas* or *repúblicas* (communal work) whenever they are deemed necessary, which is quite often, particularly after the rainy season when the heavy run-off from the steep Andean slopes plays havoc with the simple earthen canals and fills the tanks with eroded soil. One administrator estimated that during his time in office (approximately one year), there were about one hundred *faenas* conducted in various parts of the district under his auspices. These *faenas* did not involve all of the farmers on each occasion, but rather the members of the *toma* in which the canals required repair or improvement.

One cannot reside in Huaylas for long without hearing something about water-supply problems. Because Huaylinos must rely upon the rains, not having the benefit of the glacial melt as the people dwelling on the east bank of the Santa river do, they are at the mercy of a climate that, at times, can be rather capricious. The rainy season, when most crops are planted, normally begins in December in Huaylas and lasts until April. In the 1960 to 1961 season, however, there was very little rain during this period, with the result that the planting was late, and the water that was collected was carefully husbanded, each farmer being restricted to a smaller quantity of irrigation water than normal.

This situation aggravated the problems that exist in a year when there is a normal rainfall, since even then there is not quite enough water for everyone. There are, consequently, many violations of the irrigation schedule, the most common one being the "stealing" of water, that is, the diverting of water from the canal into one's field in clandestine fashion when someone else is supposed to be receiving it. Since the demand is very great, irrigation continues throughout the night, a time that lends itself to such misconduct for obvious reasons. Other persons attempt to "buy" more water by offering bribes to the *repartidor* of their *toma* to alter the irrigation schedule to favor them. Because such acts are frequent, hundreds of *denuncias* (complaints) are filed with the administrator and his assistant who try to discover who the offenders are and fine them accordingly—a never-ending task, which is rarely, if ever, performed to the satisfaction of everyone.

Because this is coupled with the responsibility for maintaining the system and improving it, the job of water administrator is one of the most difficult in the district, with the result that few men actively seek the office. It is, as they say, *mucho compromiso* (very compromising). The work is also very time-consuming. Were he to do all that is required of him, the administrator would have full-time employment. Since no one in the Water Administration receives a salary, this is impossible because the personnel must, of course, also pursue their normal occupations.

Due to the pressure placed on the administrator and his assistant, as well as on the *repartidores*, it is not uncommon to find them accepting the *pequeñas gratificaciones* (small tips), which may be offered them. It is because of this, in fact, that the position of *repartidor* is often sought by persons eager to exploit the situation for financial reasons, as well as for reasons of prestige because of the importance attached to the work. The position of *repartidor* is held exclusively by lower- and middle-class persons in each of the *tomas*, despite the fact that it is a key position in the society. Thus, the upper-class farmer is inclined to express his resentment of the *cholos vivos*,[40] as he sometimes refers to the *repartidores*, when he finds it necessary to offer them "tips." This aspect of the management of the irrigation system is lamented by most Huaylinos, who readily admit that it constitutes a problem, since the poorer farmers often do not have sufficient funds to compete for water in this manner. Yet it is felt that such corruption is inevitable because of the nature of the situation and because none of the administrative personnel is paid for his work.

The Water Administration finances its operations mainly through the collection of fines for usurping the water rights of others, for causing damage to the canals or dams, or for failure to attend a *faena* and work with the other members of the *toma*. Fines range from S/10.00 to S/50.00, ($0.37 to $1.90) depending on the violation, and are collected by the administrator or his assistant. In the event that someone refuses to pay his fine, the case is referred to the governor, who collects what is due, threatening the offender with a day in jail. Occasionally the administration receives some financial or material aid from the government, but to date this has been of a minor nature and not sufficient to resolve the major problem facing agriculture in the district, namely, how to increase the water supply.

The problem of the water supply is one which has occupied the attention of Huaylinos for many decades, and one cannot talk about agriculture without the subject coming up. Moreover, there is universal agreement on how the situation could be remedied. The hope, Huaylinos feel, lies in creating large reservoirs by damming several lakes in the *puna* regions. Some attempts have been made to do this, and small dams have been built to increase the capacity of at least two of the lakes. Huaylinos feel that with an increased water supply, there could be a more intensive cultivation of the land already in production and the opening of some new land to agriculture, which at present is not farmed for lack of water. An increased supply of water not only would lessen the conflicts arising over irrigation but also would lessen, to some extent, the tide of emigration by creating more employment opportunities in the district.

The people of Huaylas and their representative organizations in Lima, such as the Huaylas District Association, have, on numerous occasions, sought government aid in undertaking this water project,

[40] The word *vivo* has many slang meanings. Here the implication is knavishness or taking advantage of a compromising situation.

which would require expert engineering advice. In response to these requests, the Ministry of Development conducted a brief survey in the 1930's and another in 1958. The conclusion of the engineer who made the last study was that, despite the fact that the damming of the lakes would indeed have the results suggested by Huaylinos, the project would be "uneconomical" and thus not worthwhile. Notwithstanding the lack of government interest in providing assistance, Huaylinos have continued to maintain an interest in this project. A Huaylino living in Lima published a pamphlet urging all Huaylinos to give their full support to the development of such a project so that Huaylas would improve its own economic condition and at the same time lead the way for the whole Callejón.[41]

[41] Acosta, 1959. A Peace Corps volunteer stationed in Huaylas from 1963 to 1965 worked on this problem, making studies of the water resources and terrain. As this book went to press, Huaylinos were working to dam three of the mountain ponds and had received some aid from the Ministry of Agriculture.

CHAPTER VIII

The Community at Work

The formal Huaylas administrative bodies discussed in the preceding chapter are supplemented by traditional institutions that provide a broad base for general participation in public affairs. Among these institutions are the *república*,[1] or public, collective work, and the civic committees, which are officially sanctioned by the Concejo and made up of persons interested in some special public activity.

The República

The history of the *república* in Huaylas is a very long one and, although documentation of it is sketchy at best, it is safe to conclude that the present system of public work has its origins in pre-Conquest times. The monumental structures, roads, bridges, and terraces, for which the Incas are justifiably renowned, were built and maintained through a highly efficient system of draft labor, called the *mita*, which obliged able-bodied men (called *mitayos*) to perform such public service when called upon. In effect, it was a system of taxation, the burden of which was distributed more or less equally among the working population. Judging from the number of ancient agricultural terraces that exist in Huaylas, the fact that the Incan road passed through the district, and the fact that two large suspension bridges

[1] Also called *acción cívica, acción popular, faena,* and other similar names. The term *república*, some say, stems from the decade from 1920 to 1930 when such work was mandatory, that is, defined as "work for the republic (nation)."

crossed the Santa river to the town, it seems probable that the ancient inhabitants of Atun Huaylas spent considerable time in their construction and maintenance through the *mita* system.

Given this firmly established organization and the predatory nature of the conquerors, it is not surprising that the Spaniards incorporated the *mita* into the colonial system—albeit in an extralegal manner, since forced labor was supposedly outlawed. In his succinct discussion of the Incas during the colonial era in Peru, Rowe describes the *mita* as follows:

When the Spanish Control was first extended to the provinces of the Inca Empire, governors, encomenderos and doctrineros made their demands for native labor in the form of orders to the caciques to furnish a specified number of men for a stated project. The caciques equated these demands with the ones formerly emanating from Cuzco, and they raised their quotas by the traditional method. Thus, any sort of forced labor done for the Spaniards came to be called *mita,* and the word retained this general meaning throughout the Colonial Period. The word is sometimes understood to refer specifically to service in the mines, a particularly burdensome form of forced labor, but this is properly designated as *mita de minas. . . . Mita* labor was also applied by the Spaniards to building and road construction, service to travelers in the tambos, labor in privately owned *obrajes* (factories), the cultivation of Spanish farms, the care of cattle, and in short, to all types of manual labor.

At first the colonial *mita* system was simply an abuse, for the private profit of the conquerors, of the Inca system of service to the state. Since *mita* labor had not received any direct wages under the Inca emperors, the conquerors saw no reason why they should pay any. It was only with the greatest difficulty, and after the failure of the armed rebellion of encomenderos led by Hernandez Giron (1553–1554), that the Spanish government succeeded in introducing the principle that native labor should be paid. The legal wage for *mita* labor, however, was never as high as that paid to native laborers in the free market and during much of the Colonial Period it was less than the minimum which the laborer needed for his own food. Furthermore, the *mitayo* was not excused from paying his regular tribute assessment just because he was called away to put in several weeks' work in the encomendero's wheat fields. Naturally, the natives showed no inclination to hire themselves out for Spanish projects on such terms. The Spanish settlers thereupon enunciated the doctrine that "Indians are lazy by nature and must be forced to work for their own good." The government accepted this verdict and used it to justify continuation of the system of forced labor throughout the Colonial Period. The regulations which governed the *mita* gave first consideration to the wishes of the Spanish settlers for cheap and submissive labor and then added a multitude of ineffectual restrictions designed to protect the natives from the abuses the system invited.[2]

History records the participation of Huaylinos in this system. It is known, for example, that in 1594, 137 Indians from "Atunguaylas" worked in the mines at Carhuas and Sihuas and in the *obrajes* or textile mills of the *encomenderos* who held Huaylas during colonial times.[3] The *mita* was officially abolished by the Spanish Crown in 1812. Despite the fact that the royal decision was supported in 1821 by San Martin, at the time of Peruvian independence, the strength of the custom was such that it has persisted to the present day.

In 1921, President Augusto B. Leguia decreed the "Ley de Conscripción Viál." [4] The "Road Law," as it was called, obliged all able-bodied men between the ages of twenty-one and fifty to work for twelve days a year on road construction, able-bodied men of eighteen to twenty years of age and fifty-one to sixty years of age were required to work for six days a year on such projects. Under this law, farmers were not required to work at times of harvest or planting, army veterans were excluded from work, and food and drink were to be provided, if this were the local custom. In addition, laborers were to be paid by the day according to the local standard for such work.

Conceived with the idea of giving legal status to the old custom of public labor for the purpose of developing the provinces through the extension of the highway system, the law in and of itself had considerable merit. Nevertheless, it was abused in many areas of the country, with the result that it came to be a symbol of repression in the minds of many, a fact that led to its abolition as one of the first official acts of Colonel Sanchez Cerro, who deposed Leguia in a coup d'état in 1930.

In order to protect the public from such abuses, the new constitution, instituted in 1933, contained in Article 55, a specific statement concerning forced labor:

No one can be obliged to lend his personal labor without his free consent and without due remuneration.[5]

---

[2] Rowe, 1957:170–171.   [3] Varallanos, 1959:242–243, 253–254.
[4] Perú, 1922:7–8.   [5] Fajardo, n.d. (a):33 (my translation).

Despite this constitutional provision, there is continuing conflict in the law, as well as in practice, over this point. For example, the Organic Law of Municipalities, Article 135, states:

In case of a lack of special or municipal funds, for the maintenance of roads and bridges, all the capable inhabitants will contribute to maintain them in good state, with their personal work or with that of peons from their funds.[6]

Elsewhere, in the Code of Waters and Irrigation, we find that the local administrators are empowered to order the cleaning and maintenance of irrigation ditches by all interested parties, who must cooperate in such work, provided that they have been given five days' advance notice.[7] Although this conflict in the law is confusing, wherever such a discrepancy occurs, the Constitution theoretically takes precedence over other ordinances and regulations.[8] Despite the fact, therefore, that the district or provincial governments or water administrations are given the "power" to exact labor from residents of their areas in the specific instances stated (namely, for the repair of roads, ditches, and so on), the people appear to be within their rights to refuse to work if they so wish.

Thus, regardless of colonial and nineteenth-century abuses of public labor, regardless of the recent unsuccessful attempt to legalize it (by Leguia), and, finally, regardless of constitutional prohibitions, the *faena* or *república* survives in an apparently large number of Peruvian Andean communities.[9] It was not unusual to see such communal activities in progress, even as a casual traveler, and the provincial sections of the Lima newspapers carry constant reports of such work. Because of this longstanding and still virile tradition, the present government of Peru under the leadership of Fernando Belaunde Terry has made a major commitment to supporting such community initiatives through his "Popular Cooperation" program.[10]

[6] Fajardo, n.d. (b):40 (my translation).

[7] Fajardo, n.d. (c).

[8] Dr. Pelegrín Román U., personal communication.

[9] This type of labor has been reported for the Callejón de Huaylas by Stein (1962:188–91). Richard N. Adams (1959:177–83) found public labor common in the Mantaro Valley community of Muquiyauyo, as have others in different towns of that region. Dobyns (1964) reports the many and varied activities of Comunidades Indígenas in this regard.

[10] Belaunde, 1965:380–400.

The *república* in Huaylas has persisted over the years and is still one of the most viable of local institutions. A review of the municipal archives from 1889 to 1960 shows that there have been approximately ten work projects per year sponsored by the municipal government.[11] Judging by the character of most of the entries, this would appear to be a minimum estimate of the number of projects undertaken and not an estimate of the number of *repúblicas,* since the work orders recorded in the *Libro de Actas* mention only the fact that work was done at a given place or on a given project, but do not mention the total number of days on which residents of the different *barrios* worked.[12]

From this record, however, it is evident that one of the principal concerns has been the repair and maintenance of the avenues of communication in and out of Huaylas. Until 1942, for example, although there were no vehicular roads, there was a marked preoccupation over the condition of the *caminos de herradura* (trails) by which mule trains and people on horseback traveled, particularly to the coast or to Caraz. These roads were cleaned every two or three months. They required particular attention in the rainy season, when frequent slides along the steep slopes of the Cordillera blocked travel. The concern over transportation, however, has probably been present since pre-Conquest times. The chronicles written at the time of the Conquest report that there were at least three bridges crossing the Santa river at or near the district of Huaylas, and it is more than probable that at least two of these were maintained by Huaylinos through the *mita* system. The most important of these was the bridge at Yuramarca, which, until fairly recently, was within the boundaries of the District of Huaylas. In the municipal archives, we find almost yearly entries about Huaylinos working on this particular bridge, keeping it in good repair.

The management of the bridge was much the same as that described by Adams for Muquiyauyo in the Mantaro valley.[13] The bridge was owned and maintained by the District of Huaylas, which rented the concession for its operation to the highest bidder or *rematista.* The *rematista* was then allowed to charge tolls for the use of the bridge. The amount of the toll, however, was controlled by the Concejo Municipal. The almost yearly task of repairing the bridge continued to be reported in the *Libro de Actas* in Huaylas until the second decade

[11] Distrito de Huaylas, *Libro de Actas,* 1889–1960.
[12] Each day's work is counted as one *república* or *faena.*
[13] Adams, 1959:183.

of the twentieth century, at which time the government of Peru constructed a large steel bridge to replace the old one.

The public works projects listed in Table 28 do not include the work spent in the maintenance of the facilities already in existence, but only new facilities built or introduced into the community through the medium of *repúblicas*. It is probable that as much work has been expended in maintenance as in the creation of new facilities.

Relatively few of the public works projects undertaken through the course of the years, however, have actually been finished in the same year in which they were begun. For example, three years were re-

Table 28. Major public works projects undertaken since 1890 in the District of Huaylas *

Date	Project
1899–1901	Municipal office
1899	Telegraph
1905	Telephone
1919–1967	Market (with additions and improvements)
1922, 1946–1947 1957, 1961–1967	Road to Huallanca
1927–1942	Road to Mato
1929–1934	Water system for the town
1932–1966	Three complete primary schools: Santo Toribio, 2; town, 1; and eight other rural schools in the *barrios:* Yacup, 1; Quecuas, 1; Iscap, 2; San Lorenzo, 1; Huaromapuquio, 1; Tambo, 2
1934–1957	Building for the library
1934–1957	Plaza improvement: paving and park
1940	First electricity installed in town
1945	New road to Santo Toribio
1946–	New plaza and roads in Santo Toribio
1955	Road to Iscap
1959	Reconstruction of the church and parish house
1960–	Electrification project in six *barrios*
1960	Reconstruction of cemetery wall
1961	Road to Yacup school
1961	Addition to Yacup school
1962	Post Office building in Santo Toribio
1962–1963	Concrete bridge over Huaylas creek
1963	New lighting in town plaza
1964	Two bridges, in Shuyo and in Quecuas
1964–	Primary school in Shuyo
1965–	Construction of dams for water storage on puna
1966–1967	Potable water system in town
1966–1967	Construction of Medical clinic and Doctor's house

* Distrito de Huaylas, *Libro de Actas*, 1889–1960.

quired to build the municipal office on the plaza, that is, from 1899 to 1901. The market place presently in use in Huaylas was begun in 1919, but over the course of the years it has been enlarged several times, with work continuing to the present time. Perhaps the most outstanding of the many work projects undertaken by the people of the District of Huaylas was the construction of the seventeen-kilometer road connecting the district with the rest of the Callejón de Huaylas. Work on this road began in 1927 under the auspices of the Ley de Conscripción Viál but was only partially completed by 1930, when the law was rescinded. Work continued on the road until it was completed in 1942. The road to Huallanca, begun in 1922, is now being completed. Because of the lag in the completion of projects, it is not uncommon to find several projects at different stages of completion at any given time.

There are six different institutions or organizations in Huaylas which, by tradition, institute public works projects. These are: the Concejo Distrital; the office of the governor; the Patronato Escolar, which attends to the maintenance and construction of schools at the various locations in the district; [14] the district Administration of Waters and Irrigation; the Comunidad Indígena, which may order *repúblicas* on its lands; and the individual *barrios,* which, if their members so desire, may conduct independent work projects within their boundaries. The *repúblicas* sponsored by the Patronato Escolar, the Administration of Waters and Irrigation, and the Comunidad Indígena are all supervised by the officials of these organizations, with the consent and agreement of their members. The same is true of work sponsored by the *alcalde* and Concejo, the governor, and the *barrios.*

Since the mayor is officially charged with the maintenance of the public roadways, and so forth, he may, from time to time, instruct the *barrios* to repair them. He does this by contacting each of the *barrio inspectores,* who, with their *brazos,* advise the members of their *barrios* of the work announcement. On the specified day, the eligible male residents of each *barrio* gather at the house of the *barrio inspector* who leads them to the work site. Usually, the *barrio inspectores* keep a register of all the eligible men in their *barrios* and check attendance on

---

[14] A Patronato Escolar is organized by the teachers of each school. All the parents who have children attending a particular school are members of that Patronato. Roughly equivalent to the Parent-Teachers Association in this country, the Patronato has periodic meetings to discuss school problems with the teachers, in particular the raising of funds for school improvements.

such occasions. Those who have served in the armed forces or are under nineteen or over sixty years of age are exempt from such work. For the rest, acceptable excuses are sickness, absence from the district, and such obligations as the irrigation of one's fields when the water is available.

If a person simply refuses to attend, the *barrio* authorities attempt to obtain some such contribution from him as a gift of *chicha, alcohol, coca,* or a cash gift of between S/5.00 and S/10.00.[15] Storekeepers and upper-class men often participate in this way, although many of them also work. One elderly member of the upper class said that it was traditional for everyone to work on the *repúblicas* without distinction "*de rango*" (of class). "Even at the turn of the century," he continued, "even the *caballeros* (gentlemen) had to go and work like everyone else." Those who neither work nor give a donation are called *morosos* (delinquents). Because of social pressure and the importance attached to public works projects by Huaylinos, a very high percentage of eligible men participate in these activities through the course of the year, although on any given day participation is seldom higher than 50 per cent. The *morosos* are reported to the mayor, who, through the governor, exerts additional pressure on them to cooperate. If this fails, fines of five or ten *soles* may be levied on the delinquents.

Although the *barrio* authorities maintain a register of the *republicanos*, these records are not always up to date nor are they very accurate. I was, however, able to obtain rather complete work records from the *barrio* of Delicados for the months of October 1959 through July 1961 (Table 29) as well as some from the other *barrios*. The average number of *repúblicas* held each year is probably eleven or twelve for each *barrio,* not including the many days spent in repairing the irrigation system, although for the period considered (1959 to 1960) it may well have been higher. The president of the Junta de Regantes said that almost fifty *repúblicas* were held in 1960 on the irrigation system. Thirteen *repúblicas* were conducted over a ten-month period by the *barrio* of Delicados in which there were a total of 619 participants, 442 of whom actually worked (see Table 29). During this period, there were only five men in the *barrio* who did not contribute in some way to the projects. Although records from the other eight *barrios* of

---

[15] One *sol* was equal to $0.04 U.S. Thus contributions were approximately $0.20 to $0.40.

Table 29. Number of *repùblicas* held by the *barrio* of Delicados from October 1960 to July 1961, with number of participants and donations

Date repúb-licas held	Number of workers	Donations of money	Gifts of food and drink	Total number of participants	Per cent of eligible participants (N = 146)
		Cemetery wall project			
October 8	Public col-lection	S/410.50		40	27
October 11	42	104.00	8	63	43
October 12	21	5.00	1	22	15
October 18	20			20	13
October 22	12	2.50	1	14	9.5
Total	95	S/522.00	10	159	21
		Electrification project			
January 30	28	119.00	7	53	36
January 31	40	10.00	2	44	30
May 2	48	190.00	6	73	50
May 3	50	90.00	6	71	49
May 9	48	30.00	4	58	39
May 10	48	40.00	1	54	37
May 31	51	45.00	9	65	44.5
July 4	34	25.00	6	42	29
Total	347	S/549.00	41	460	39

Huaylas were not complete, it would appear from observation that the level of participation in the others is as high as it is in the *barrio* of Delicados. Furthermore, there is an organization of army veterans (*licenciados*) which also participates in work projects when called upon to do so, in spite of the fact that veterans are, by custom, exempt from such work.

On the day designated for a *república* the mayor or the *concejal* in charge of public works, along with the *barrio* officials, supervises the activities of the *republicanos*. If some aspect of the work calls for particular skills, those residents of the *barrio* who possess them are usually put in charge of it. Finally, a wage of S/1.00 is paid to each individual who actually participates in the work. This, according to the officials, is a symbolic gesture, since neither the district government nor any other official agency could afford to pay the regular S/10.00 wage of a day laborer (*jornalero*). If it accomplishes nothing else, the symbolic wage lends an air of legality to the proceedings and emphasizes the sacrifice made by the participants. Finally, no large scale *república* is conducted without music being provided by one or two *caja* and *roncadora* players, who sometimes donate their services but often are paid by the *barrio*.

Repúblicas concerned with the maintenance of district facilities are ordered directly through the office of the mayor. Work such as the electrification project, however, entails consultation by the mayor with various local authorities, *notables,* and the *barrio inspectores.* On such occasions, the work schedule is usually arranged so that it will not conflict with seasonal labor or other special events. The results of the consultative meetings are reported to the residents of each *barrio* by the *inspectores.* In the town, however, it was the custom to make the results public by having a "town crier" read an announcement of the *república* at the main street corners. This custom had been abandoned for a number of years but was revived during the time that we were in Huaylas, and the *inspector* of the *barrio* of Delicados went through the streets of the town making the announcements to the accompaniment of the local brass band.

In 1960 and 1961 the district undertook an ambitious electrification program through the system of *repúblicas,* with the cooperation and help of the Corporación Peruana del Santa.[16] The town has had the use of electricity since the year 1940, when the first diesel generator was installed.[17] The electrical service in Huaylas since that time had been relatively good, though limited to the hours of 6:30 to 10:30 P.M. each evening. About 40 per cent of the houses in town had electricity installed. But, with the exception of a few houses in Shuyo, no houses in the outlying areas of Huaylas enjoyed electrical service. By 1959 the generator was in constant need of repairs and did not have the capacity necessary to allow extension of the service to those who wanted it.

The desire for more electricity in Huaylas was stimulated in part by the presence of the Santa Corporation (Corporación Peruana del Santa), which had been at work in the District of Huaylas since 1943 on the hydroelectric plant in the Cañon de Pato at Huallanca. The

[16] For a detailed discussion of the project, see Doughty, 1961:3–6. Background information concerning the Corporación Peruana del Santa is available in Corporación del Santa, 1958.

[17] This particular generator was replaced in 1946 by a newer model, which the government purchased for the district.

original purpose of the hydroelectric development was twofold: to industrialize the Callejón de Huaylas and to provide power for some of the coastal cities. In the course of its construction, the hydroelectric plant excited the imagination of many in the area, including, of course, the 600 or more Huaylinos who had worked on it. In all, some 14,000 workers from many areas of Peru and from foreign countries as well were employed in the construction of the plant between the time of its inception until the inauguration of service in 1958. The project provided a new source of income for Huaylinos and wages considerably higher than those to which they had been accustomed. Moreover, many were trained in such fields as electricity, pipe fitting and plumbing, mechanics, and other technical and construction trades, which had previously not been common in the area.

Together with the benefits which accrued to the Huaylinos from the development, there were some grievances. The power from the hydroelectric plant was first carried in 1957 to the city of Chimbote, on the coast, via a high-tension line that passed through the *barrio* of Iscap in the District of Huaylas. The high-tension line and the road built to service it passed through many of Huaylas' irrigated fields, and the property owners had never been compensated by the company for the land so used. This was cause for considerable resentment on the part of many Huaylinos. Furthermore, the company had used the roads built and maintained by Huaylinos as their main supply routes and had never contributed very much to their maintenance.

It was also claimed that many Huaylinos had lost their lives or were permanently injured during the construction of the plant, and Huaylinos strongly felt that the company owed the district something for these sacrifices. The work in the Cañon del Pato and in the rest of the Canyon of the Santa river was particularly dangerous because of the topography as well as because it involved much blasting (at which Huaylinos are quite proficient). One disaster occurred (in 1950 or 1951) during the reconstruction of the railroad (also the property of the Santa Corporation) at a place called Condor Cerro, and many Huaylinos were killed. The tragedy is recalled in the *huayno,* "3 de Enero." [18]

En la fecha del 3 de enero	The third of January is the date
Les voy hacer recordar	I'm going to make you remember

[18] El Jilguero del Huascarán, *Serranía,* phonograph record (my translation).

La dolorosa tragedia	when the grievous tradegy came
De Condor Cerro sucedió	to pass on Condor Mountain
La Represa del Malpaso	The dam of Malpaso took away
Muchas vidas arrastró	many lives with the price of
Con el precio de la muerte	death Condor Mountain brought
Condor Cerro los compró	them
En luto cubieron los pueblos	The towns went into mourning:
Macate en primer lugar	Macate in first place;
Bambas, Huaylas y Chimbote	Bambas, Huaylas, and Chimbote
Maldicen con tentación	curse with feeling
Condor Cerro, Condor Cerro	Condor Mountain, Condor Moun-
Víl traidor sin compasión	tain, vile traitor without com-
Regaste el dolor sangriento	passion; you watered the bloody
Dando la muerte a traición	sorrow, adding death to betrayal
(Fuga) [19]	(Fugue)
Así es la vida cholita	Such is life, cholita,[20] and such is
Y así es la vida zambita	life, zambita; [21] for two miserable
Por dos reales miserables	reales [22] the poor man loses his
El pobre pierde su vida	life

Some compensation had been paid to the families of the deceased workers and to the injured, but this was not felt to be commensurate with the losses incurred. The people considered the deaths and injuries a loss to the district as a whole and not merely to the particular families involved. Consequently, there was considerable feeling on the part of Huaylinos that the company should take steps to rectify some of the abuses they felt had been committed in the district, by helping to ameliorate conditions in the district, particularly with regard to the electrical service.

In 1957 the mayor of Huaylas first went to the administration of the Santa Corporation and requested support of an electrification program

---

[19] The *fuga* is the last verse of the *huayno* and is played at a faster tempo than the rest.

[20] Little Indian girl.

[21] Little Negro girl.

[22] A *real* is an old Spanish coin. Today the term is used to mean a ten-cent piece. Thus, two *reales* are worth S/.20 or about $0.0075 U.S. and symbolize the low wages paid laborers. Actual daily wages ranged between S/2.00 and S/10.00 ($0.07 and $0.74 U.S.) at that time.

for Huaylas. Although the request was not favorably received at that time, the desire for the program lingered with the Huaylinos, and in 1959 a new mayor reopened the question. As one of the Huaylinos working at the hydroelectric plant (approximately 40 per cent of the personnel employed in the operation of the hydroelectric plant were Huaylinos), the mayor had many friends among the supervisory personnel who became interested in the project. One of the engineers voluntarily surveyed the route of the proposed power line and consulted with the mayor. By December of 1959 the company had agreed to see what could be done about the Huaylas request.

Meanwhile, the mayor and councilmen contacted the 100 or more property owners involved in the dispute with the Corporation over the land taken by the right-of-way. Through persuasion and explanation, the mayor succeeded in having the disputed land donated to the Concejo Distrital of Huaylas so that the Concejo could present a unified claim to the company. Then, instead of demanding payment for the land, the Concejo requested that the company help Huaylas install modern electric power from the hydroelectric plant by assisting in the technical aspects and by providing wire and heavy equipment, such as transformers, which Huaylinos could not afford to buy themselves. The people of Huaylas agreed to perform all the labor necessary for the installation of the system and to donate all the posts necessary for the 10-kilometer power line. While there were no formal agreements signed, the company accepted the proposal, and, in January of 1960, the *barrios,* under the direction of the mayor, had begun work on the project.

The *barrios* not directly involved in the electrification project were not asked to participate in the work, but each of the five principal *barrios* affected—Delicados, Yacup, Shuyo, Quecuas, and Huayrán, and later, Iscap—donated approximately 25 posts each and carried them to the plaza, which was to be the central distribution point. Later, the posts were distributed to the proper places along the line, which had been surveyed by a Corporation engineer and qualified members of the Huaylas community. The work of carrying the posts was going on when we first arrived in Huaylas. The following excerpt from my field notes describes a *república* held on April 24, 1960.

The barrio of Shuyo held a *faena* today (and) carried 11 posts for the electric line to the plaza. . . . The work is voluntary and one does not have to participate, but, according to Don Ricardo, the social pressure is strong so most of the men cooperate in one form or another. He said that if a man does not want to work, he may hire someone to go in his stead, or buy a bottle or two of pisco for the workers. Those persons who have eucalyptus trees which are big enough have been asked to donate them. The mayor, who has property in Shuyo, has donated several. Two storekeepers did not work, instead providing beer and pisco for the workers. Some of the eucalyptus poles are dry but many are freshly cut and weigh a great deal. Most of the poles are from 10 to 14 meters long. The *faena* carried six poles up the hill from Shuyo on their first trip late in the morning. On the second trip, which I also observed, they brought five more. The poles are carried by anywhere from eight to thirty men, depending upon the weight and length. In the second round, the last pole was extremely heavy, and the 25 men were staggering under its weight. The pole is carried by means of stout cross-poles, about four feet long which are lashed, crosswise to the post across the top. Two men, one on each side, rest the ends of the cross-poles on their shoulders which are padded with ponchos or other suitable padding. In this fashion, the pole is hoisted to the shoulders and carried. The procession of workers is accompanied by a pair of *cajeros* (drummers), playing their *roncadoras* (flutes). *Huaynos* predominate. The musicians also donate their services instead of helping to carry the poles. They keep up a steady rhythmic beat on the drums and a spirited tune with the *roncadora*. The workers shout encouragements to each other and let out with wild *guajes* (shouts) particularly when the going gets tough, as when they climb the steep hill on the street leading to the plaza. The *cajeros* accompanied the last pole which was very heavy. The workers who had finished carrying their poles, i.e., arrived first, ran back to help with the last pole, shouting encouragements to the carriers as they did so. In spite of the additional help, those carrying the last pole fell as they reached the crest of the hill and the pole almost went to the ground. When this occurred, many of the other workers came over and helped carry the pole the remaining distance. When the posts were set down in front of the Club Sportivo, the men let out whoops. . . . The music continued and bottles of pisco were brought out and passed around, each man drinking his share from the bottle, then passing it on to the next man. . . . For "show," they walked around the block (one block over from the church), whooping and shouting as they went. . . .

After about an hour, we heard the music again and went out to watch the workers bring up the rest of the posts. They only carried one, but it was huge, a good 14 to 15 meters long and very heavy. There were 30 men carrying it and they staggered under its weight, shouting and giving *gritos* (shouts). The musicians were either tired or a bit drunk for they had a difficult time staying on the same tune. The drum beats remained constant and in unison however. When they dropped the pole with the others, one of the men hurt his knee and he limped to the side of the road and sat down, wincing with pain. Three or four men went with him and when he sat down, one rolled up the man's pant leg and began to massage and pull vigorously on the injured part. One man said to me with a big grin, "Sabemos como curar, pues. Acá no hay doctores!" ("We know how to cure, anyhow. Here there are no doctors!") He laughed. The injured man did not seem to be benefiting from the treatment, however, for he continued to wince. He then got up and limped about without aid, although it was offered to him. The gang then went over to the plaza on the suggestion of one of the workers, to whoop it up. They stopped by the fountain, where the musicians began to play vigorously. About eight to ten men began to dance; two of them carried the cross-poles used in carrying the post over their shoulders like rifles. Others stopped periodically to take draughts from the bottles of pisco which were handed to them. One man danced, drinking from the bottle. Others stood about, drinking and talking. . . . Afterwards, pairs and trios of men began to drift away and finally the remaining group of about 20 men "marched" down the street accompanied by the musicians, going back to Shuyo.[23]

As the project continued it seemed to gather momentum, and more and more Huaylinos began to take an active interest in the course of events. At first, it was suspected by those in the Campiña that electrification would benefit primarily those living in the town. On the mayor's insistence that it would benefit all Huaylinos, the people from Quecuas and Huayrán, who traditionally have been opposed or suspicious of town authorities, began to show considerably more interest. By the middle of May, the posts had all been collected and distributed along the route to be followed by the high-tension line from the hydroelectric plant to the town and the Campiña.

With men from each of the five *barrios* working approximately five days (in total) during the months of May and June, the high-tension line was finished. The enthusiasm was such that during this time men over sixty, who on other occasions would not have worked, volunteered to dig the postholes for the line posts all along the route, and the veterans' organization also contributed three days of labor. On two of the important workdays on the week end, when most of the posts were erected along the line, there were more than 150 men working each day, including some of the storekeepers, who actually shut down their

[23] Doughty, Field Notes, April 24, 1960:2–3.

stores—a rare event—so that they would be able to participate in the work. During this period of great excitement many persons who were visiting the district (Huaylinos who reside in Lima and elsewhere) were also drawn into the activities. Many women participated by providing meals for the workers. On one of the days, a Sunday, meals were provided at the site where I was for well over 100 workers.

Throughout the course of the work, the men who took leadership roles were those who had worked in the construction of the hydro-electric plant or who currently were working at the plant. The man who supervised the technical installations was the chief electrician under the plant manager in Huallanca. The mayor, together with other members of the Concejo, the governor, and the *barrio* officers partici-pated actively in the work, their efforts and interest having the very noticeable effect of helping to keep morale high and community spirit in a jubilant state. I asked some Huaylinos about this as they returned from a day's work on the project.

We loaded the car and the mayor and several others climbed in the car. We rolled off to town, driving behind the body of workers who walked in front of us. Contentment ran high. Shouts . . . filled the air. Julio com-mented that there was certainly a good deal of enthusiasm, something he felt exceptional for Peru; the mayor agreed. Someone in the back of the car said that the whole Callejón and particularly Caraz were jealous of Huaylas because Huaylinos could and had done so much for themselves and they couldn't. All agreed. I asked the mayor why he thought that the Huaylinos had so much spirit and willingness to work like this. He said that he didn't know but that he had always known, from seeing such projects as a boy, that Huaylinos had "the spirit." Julio said the same thing, noting that he remembers (as a small boy) when they were working on the road (to Mato).[24]

Also reflected was a feeling of competition between the *barrios*, which was mentioned in an earlier chapter and which is manifested in other inter-*barrio* activities. *Republicanos* boasted of their day's work, the number of posts contributed or carried, the holes dug, the wire strung, and so on—always letting everyone know what had been done by their *barrio*.

Later the wire was strung over the posts, and transformer stations were erected and completed under the direction of Huaylinos who

[24] Doughty, Field Notes, April 24, 1960:2–3.

were employed at the hydroelectric plant in Huallanca. Electric power was installed not only in the town of Huaylas but in the Campiña, and shortly after that installation was made the people of the *barrio* of Iscap began to erect power poles so that electricity could be carried to their more distant *barrio*. Electricity has also been carried to the upper sectors of the *barrio* of Yacup and to the *barrio* of Shuyo. The new service began on November 15, 1960, and was inaugurated officially on January 6, 1961, with the president of the Santa Corporation acting as *padrino* in the ceremony, the celebration of Epiphany being postponed a day.

It is apparent that the *república*, in many of its facets, is very similar to the *rantín*, or *minka*, described earlier. Even though the work may be intensive and rather heavy, there is often a festive mood. It is a time when one can enjoy the company of one's friends while gaining public recognition for supporting the progress of one's community. During the day's work, refreshments are provided by the *barrio* organization from donations. Upon finishing a day's labor, the workers often pass by the mayor's house to be treated to a glass or two of *chicha* in his living room.[25] Such times are occasions for prolonged and noisy adulation— one's participation in the work and one's *barrio* are held up to praise before all present. The music of the *roncadoras* in the streets when the workers pass also calls attention to the fact that the men of such and such *barrios* have been performing their public duty in good faith, and the workers do not hesitate to bring this to the attention of the various storekeepers along the way who are invariably asked to make contributions to support them in the work.

Civic Committees

While the *repúblicas* give important concrete expression to public concerns, there is another important aspect of public life in Huaylas, one that involves voluntary organizations of the type that I call civic committees. A civic committee is organized with the approval of the mayor and the Concejo Distrital in response to some need or desire expressed by the populace, usually at the session of the Concejo or *cabildo abierto*.[26] Members are either appointed to the committee by

---

[25] So many *repúblicas* were held during the electrification project that this custom resulted in a rather heavy expenditure for the mayor.

[26] Committees may be formed by an interest group, of course, and this is often done. All such committees, however, report their existence and the names of their

the mayor or volunteer at his request. Depending on its purpose, the committee normally has between five and fifteen members.

This group meets and selects officers, a president, a secretary, a treasurer, and whatever others may be desired, for example, *vocales* (trustees) or secretaries to take care of particular facets of committee activity. Persons need not be present in order to be chosen for service on such committees. For example, my wife was appointed a member of the reception committee for the inauguration of the electric service and was notified of her appointment through an *oficio* (official announcement) delivered the following day. Others were similarly advised of their appointments. This is standard procedure, and those who do not wish to serve may resign. Once appointed to the committee, however, a person rarely resigns without having a number of compelling reasons for doing so.

The committees hold meetings as needed to handle the matters for which they were selected. Since most committees are concerned with the handling of money, either the raising or the spending of funds, a public accounting is made to the mayor, Concejo, or *cabildo abierto*, and elaborate reports are frequently posted about the town. When its job is completed the committee resigns, and, if there is a treasury balance, the money is turned over to the Concejo.

The following are excerpts from field notes taken at a session of the *cabildo abierto* in November 1960 at which plans for the inauguration of the electric system were discussed by the various committees meeting together.

The mayor opened the discussion (of) the various problems and possibilities for the celebration and then opened the meeting for discussion. The main room of the Club Sportivo [27] was ringed with chairs and benches which had been brought over from the Concejo office to supplement those in the Club. All the chairs were taken and many persons were standing in the back of the room, behind the mayor and at the doorway. There were about 120 persons present, including many of the notables, all members of the Concejo, and many persons from the Campiña and the other barrios, including all the inspectors. . . . The inspector of Quecuas asked if it would be possible to have part of the ceremony in the Campiña to inaugurate the transformer station there also. The mayor said he thought

---

officers to the Concejo. It appears that the majority of committees are of the type sponsored directly by, or through, the Concejo.

[27] The large hall of this private club is often used for town meetings.

that it would be inconvenient because the padrino and Bishop (of the Huaraz Diocese) could only stay a short while and that transportation might be a problem. The point was discussed at length, with the people from the Campiña holding out for their point. After a few minutes a man from the hydroelectric plant stepped forward and delivered an emotional plea for unity: "We're all Huaylinos and it doesn't matter where the ceremony is." This was followed by much applause from the townspeople but few of the Campiñeros applauded. He continued on this theme, noting that: "Huaylinos, we should be very happy at what we have done—as you see unity is everything and division is nothing. The important thing is that the current is here and we did it together." More applause, this time by more people. He was very emotional at the end of his discourse. This was followed by a supporting statement by a man from Iscap and then the inspectors followed with acceptances and little speeches. . . . The motion seemed to be carried. . . . A man from town suggested that a High Mass be held giving thanks for the successful completion of the project, but no action was taken on the motion. . . . More discussion of other details and then a prominent man from the Campiña suggested that Mass be held on the second day. This was immediately accepted by all. A storekeeper from town asked who was going to pay for the rockets [28] and almost in unison the people said that the barrios would cover this cost. . . . The inspector of Quecuas was very active in the discussion, generally giving much support to the comments of the mayor and adding other suggestions. An upperclass farmer from town then thanked the barrios and others for the spirit of unity expressed and suggested that, in order to cut banquet costs, the people bring their own box lunches to the affair, since it would be held outside. This was agreed upon at once. A woman schoolteacher offered a minor suggestion. The mayor's mother then suggested that the Mass be held prior to the arrival of the padrinos, opening this topic up for discussion again. The man who made the plea for unity then thought that it would be a nice idea if Mass could be said up at the substation,[29] but this was talked down on the basis that so few people could attend it were it to be held there. They agreed to let the matter rest as before. The inspector of Quecuas requested that the mayor order the *repartidores de aguas* to assist the inspectors in collecting food for the banquet.[30] A storekeeper from town seconded the motion and asked for additional help in handling the finances (he was finance chairman). The mayor agreed to do this and then called for committee reports. The wife of one of the town school-

[28] Rockets are used as part of religious celebrations and are considered essential on such occasions.

[29] Where the transformers are located.

[30] As they do for the Fiesta of Saint Elizabeth. See Chapter X.

teachers stood up, list in hand and discussed the banquet menu in detail, giving the estimated costs for everything and asked where the money would come from. Many persons said that they were sure that there would be many donations in kind. The mayor then said that some people had not had good harvests and might not be so willing to give food, so it would be hard to ask that they give. After more discussion it was decided that S/4,000 would have to be allotted for the menu as it stood. The upper-class farmer who was chairman of the "Bar" *comité* said that beverage costs would run to S/4,250. The mayor then spoke for a while saying that he thought the costs should be much lower and that the plans would have to be less fancy. Don Victor, who is in charge of making the cocktails, was planning something that no one had ever heard of which required all kinds of high-priced liquors to be purchased in Chimbote. The mayor said that this was all very well, that everyone wanted to impress the visitors in the best way possible, but that he thought that Huaylas would do best by being typically Huaylas. "When they come here," he said, "they won't expect to find things like they have in a Lima restaurant." He continued, saying that the menu should be more characteristic of Huaylas, like *picante de cuy*, *shaqui*, etc.; it would be more *típico*, especially with lots of *cancha*, more *chicha*, and less beer and wine. This idea went over very well, since many persons were beginning to react adversely to the mounting costs. . . . The mayor then called for an accounting of the gifts to date for the banquet and general expenses. A woman schoolteacher from town (who was treasurer of the *comité*) stood up with her list and read as follows: S/3,845 were already collected from the town and surrounding area and some S/1,300 more were promised. Everyone chimed in that the *comité* should be sure to follow up on the promises. The gifts in kind were read and much discussion followed with the inspectors and nonofficials taking part. The *comités* were requested to continue their work in making the preparations and the Lieutenant Mayor commented that although the date was still uncertain (for the celebration) it was good that everyone was getting prepared so that things would be ready, just in case the ceremony came earlier than anticipated.[31] General agreement, much individual talk among the people, a lot of excitement in the air. The mayor then asked that those present sign the Libro de Actas. The brother of the lieutenant mayor who was recording the discussion, reread the notes and then people began to sign. The book was first taken around to the women (about 25 were

---

[31] The president of the Santa Corporation wasn't sure when he could come and the date had to be changed about three times. He finally set the date, giving the Huaylinos about four days to prepare. Fortunately, they were well organized and most of the basic things had already been done.

present, all from town) and then the men came forward to sign. There was no special order, except that the mayor and councilmen went first. Everyone signed. The meeting lasted from 3:00 P.M. to about 8:00 P.M.[32]

It is important to note that the community conducted its business in an orderly way, attempting to follow certain rules of order, and, although most of the participants were townspeople, all the major areas of the district were represented. It is also noteworthy that participation was by no means passive; rather, disagreements and conflicts were openly discussed before decisions were reached. Frequently, persons whose ideas were disputed or rejected by the group withdrew their suggestions in favor of better ones and did not insist on their own ideas. Thus, decisions in this case were usually unanimous, arrived at by consensus rather than by vote. On other occasions, however, a vote is usually taken. The great interest shown in reports of committee activities, in accounts, and in the smallest details, which were faithfully reported, are also typical. Much later, after the celebration, a final report listing all the persons and their specific contributions to the inaugural events was prepared and signed by the president and the treasurer of the committee. This was posted on all of the main street corners in Huaylas.

Selected from the district archives, the following list of civic committees (Table 30) illustrates the range and variety of the concerns handled by these groups. Committees are organized not only in the district but also in Lima. The committees in Lima are usually sponsored by one of the several district associations and related to some parent committee in the home district. For example, in 1940, there was a Comité Pro Radio-Luz[33] in Huaylas and in Lima. A subcommittee, which was organized to collect funds for the project from the Huaylas "colony" in Lima, even published a mimeographed bulletin which ran to several numbers before the project was over. By the establishment of dual committees in Huaylas and Lima continued relations are fostered between the emigrants and those in Huaylas. Moreover, the expression of interest in the problems "back home" by those residing elsewhere encourages the people in the district in their efforts. It was proclaimed of the Huaylas District Association (in Lima):

[32] Doughty, Field Notes, November, 1960:1–5.
[33] Committee for Radio and Lights (that is, for electricity).

Table 30. Representative civic committees and their activities in the District of Huaylas
1895–1961

Year	Committee and function
1895	Committee for the collection of funds for the telegraph
1896	Comité Pro-Banda (for collecting money for band instruments)
1899	Hijos de Huaylas (for collecting funds for a fountain in plaza)
1916	Comité Pro-Templo (for collecting funds for church improvements)
1929	Comité de Construcción de Locales Escolares (for the construction of schools)
1931	Comité Pro-Apertura de la Avenida Unión (for the opening of Union Avenue)
1931	Comité Pro-construcción de Locales Escolares Santo Toribio (for school construction in Santo Toribio)
1933	Comité Pro-Ornato Barrio de Yacup (for raising funds for the water system)
1933	Unión Feminina Huaylas (for raising funds for the water system)
1936	Comité Pro-Parque Huaylas (to promote improvements in the plaza)
1940	Comité Pro-Radio-Luz (to promote the installation of electricity)
1946	Comité Pro-piscina (for raising funds for the construction of a swimming pool)
1946	Comité Pro-Restauración Capilla Pallpó (for the restoration of the Pallpó Chapel)
1946	Comité Pro-Radio-Luz Huayrán (for electricity in the *barrio* of Huayrán)
1946	Comité Pro-Banda Quecuas (for the Quecuas band)
1946	Comité Pro-Bancas (for park benches)
1946	Sub-comité Beatita de Humay (for the Beatified Virgin of Humay)
1946	Comité Pro-Biblioteca (for the library)
1953	Comité Pro-Integridad Distrito de Huaylas (for the preservation of the political unity of the District of Huaylas) *
1957	Comité Pro-Reconstrucción del Templo (for the reconstruction of the church)
1958	Comité Pro-Damnificados del Sismo de Arequipa (for the victims of the Arequipa earthquake)
1960	Comité Pro-Luz (for supporting the electrification project)
1960	Comité Pro-Agua-Desague (for water and sewerage)
1961	Comité Pro-Celebración de la Fiesta Inaugural del Nuevo Servicio Eléctrico (for the celebration of the inaugural fiesta of the new electrical service)

* At the time when Santo Toribio was attempting to become a separate district.

This regionist entity, located in Lima, has the purpose of uniting the
Huaylinos resident in the Capitol in order to resolve questions that
directly concern their native land.

Its members show their affection to the homeland when they project,
initiate, or perform some task: they actively seek out a Deputy, go to the
ministries or influential persons until they obtain their objective. When it
came to obtaining electric light for Huaylas they gave money and work.
. . . The social and cultural activities undertaken are a complete success
because they spring from the spirit of Huaylas. On occasion they have
made visits as a group to the district, especially for the popular fiesta of
Saint Elizabeth.

In this institution, political discussions never occur: the only policy established is that of the WELFARE OF HUAYLAS.[34]

While the statement should be regarded as embodying the ideal and not what is invariably attained, this kind of motivation and spirit usually underlies Association activities, whether or not they are rewarded by success.

While many of the civic committees are short lived, others last for many years, some expanding into semipermanent organizations with long and involved histories. One such committee was the Comité Pro-Biblioteca Acosta (Committee for the Acosta Library), which was organized first in the early 1940's, became active again in 1946, and once more, finally, in 1951, and which had several subcommittees. It had a history of arguments and conflicts between the committeemen in Huaylas and those in Lima, of resignations, lack of interest, inertia, and other problems peculiar to such activities, even the most successful of them. Finally, we may note that while some of the committees are very specific in their stated goals, such as the Comité Pro-Bancas (Committee for Park Benches), others have purposes which are more diffuse, such as the Comité Pro-Progreso Huaylas (Committee for Huaylas Progress).

The material results of committee work are the money and material goods channeled into the district coffers for public use. Through various committees Huaylinos have donated thousands of *soles* for such things as the purchase of dynamite, plaster, and tools, while other contributions have secured band instruments, flags, clocks, prizes, and books.

To earn money the committees sponsor dances, raffles, box lunches, and other similar events. During the week of the Fiesta of Saint Elizabeth in 1960, for example, the Comité Pro-Luz was active in soliciting money for the electrification project in typical fashion. Two dances were held in the evening at the Club Sportivo, and the proceeds from ticket, food, and beverage sales went to the project. A *kermés* (dinner) was sponsored by the committee at noon on the principal day of the fiesta in the center of the plaza. With tables and chairs arranged under a temporary roof for shade, meals were sold to those taking part in the fiesta, particularly visitors from outside Huaylas and members of the upper class. The food was contributed by many women who

[34] *Atun Huaylas*, 1948:32 (my translation).

prepared special dishes, and several young women volunteered to serve as waitresses. Formal invitations, such as the one below, are often sent to the more affluent local citizens and to all prominent persons. The intent of such announcements is clear.

COMMITTEE
For the Construction of the
Building for School No. 3272
Shuyo

Mr. . . . . :

The Committee for the Construction of the Building for the Co-ed School No. 3272 of the *barrio* of Shuyo-Huaylas, has the honor of inviting you and your family to the *kermés* that will be held on the 7th of July at noon in Raimondi Park of this city; whose goal is to increase the funds of the Committee.

Convinced that your presence will contribute to the success of our program, we anticipate your presence with profound gratitude.

THE COMMISSION
Huaylas, 3 of July, 1964

Raffles and chance games were also held at this time. Small cards (*escapularios*) with the committee name printed on them were pinned on passers-by by young, female members of the committee, and, in exchange for the cards, the persons "pinned" were asked to make a cash contribution to the cause.[35] In this fashion, a considerable amount of money was earned for the project.

The Fiesta of Saint Elizabeth is a favorite time for fund-raising activities. Many school and church committees vie for time during this fiesta because there are many visitors, and the public is in a "spending mood." The Concejo gives permission to hold these fund-raising activities, thus regulating them to some extent and often intervening to prevent conflicts. In 1960, with the electrification project in full sway, other committees were asked not to compete with the Comité Pro-Luz so that most of the money could be collected for the electrification project. This request was, for the most part, respected.

Community Enterprise and the Concept of Progress

Community work, both through *repúblicas* and civic committees, is of obvious importance to life in Huaylas. The complementary labors of

[35] This method of soliciting money is common in most urban centers, particularly in Lima, where large cloth banners are sold at S/10.00 each.

the two traditions are invariably concerned with civic improvement of some kind, religious or secular, educational or decorative. The support of Huaylinos of all social classes is required for the success of such enterprises, and frequently the financial collaboration of emigrant Huaylinos is actively sought. There is ample opportunity to participate in community affairs. The prestige gained by the individual who engages in the collective work of the community, particularly as a leader at the formal level of government (Concejo, *barrio,* and so on), as a member of a committee, or as a work leader in a *república,* is considerable. An issue of the local newspaper, which published a list of all the mayors of the district since 1890, evaluating them in terms of the things they had done for Huaylas during their administration, is illustrative of this.[36]

Underlying the high value placed on community work is the almost ideological appeal of the concept of "progress." As defined in Huaylas, the idea of progress is intimately associated with youth, education, and the notion that it is good to do something for one's homeland. The words progressive and progressivist (*progresista*) and youth (*juventud*) are usually employed when referring to those considered to be good leaders and workers. The names of organizations and institutions in all social classes bristle with these terms. The nickname of the *barrio* of Delicados is the "*Barrio* of Progress."

Apparently, the popularity of the concept has its origins in the latter half of the nineteenth century, for one of the earliest schools in Huaylas was called the "Institute of Progress." The relative age of the concept, its propagation through and identification with formal education, and the comparatively open nature of Huaylas society would seem to account for its widespread appeal.

The fascination with "progress" is well illustrated by the Unión Juventud Huaylas (Huaylas Youth Union), which declared in its organizational announcement:

> This institution of Huaylinos at the Hydro-
> electric plant has opened the inscription of
> members, whether they be Huaylinos or sympathi-
> zers with the progress of the district, for
> which each member will pay the following dues:
> Membership fee   S/5.00
> Local progress   2.00 (monthly)
> Mutual fund   1.00 (monthly)

[36] *Atun Huaylas,* July 1, 1957:2.

Social welfare   1.00 (monthly)
Burial fund   5.00 (in case of a member's
                        death) [37]

The Unión Juventud Huaylas is quite active. The majority of the members are men who are employed, or have been employed, at the Santa Corporation in Huallanca. Its members come from different *barrios* and, for the most part, represent the most affluent sector of the middle class in Huaylas. As a group, they are notable for their aggressive social mobility. Just as for similar Huaylas organizations, the institutional hierarchy of the Unión Juventud Huaylas is amazingly complex and formal. The "identity" needs of its members are met through the creation of numerous official statuses and the distribution of responsibilities. In 1957 there were some twenty-nine offices or positions in the organization with the following titles: Advisor-Trustee, President, Vice-President, Secretary General, Sub-Secretary General, Secretary of Local Progress, Treasurer, Assistant Treasurer, Welfare Secretary, Social Assistance Secretary, Organization Secretary, Culture Secretary, Discipline Secretary, Spectacles Secretary, Inspector, Recording Secretary, Interior Secretary, Propaganda Secretary, and Sports Secretary, and also: *barrio* delegates from Delicados, Shuyo, Quecuas, Iscap, San Lorenzo, Yacup, Nahuinyaco, Huayrán, Tambo, and Huaromapuquio.

It is a noteworthy testimonial to the value Huaylinos place on doing things for the collectivity and to the social acclaim one may derive therefrom, that the most socially mobile group in the district chooses to identify itself and, indeed, base its whole prestige as an organization on a platform of "progress for Huaylas." [38]

The value placed on being "progressive," coupled with a genuine, widespread desire for material improvement, is an irresistible combination supporting community activity. The ability to enlist enthusiastic support for collective activities at different social levels implies the existence of a common core of values to which such appeals can be made and indicates, furthermore, that there is some agreement as to felt community needs. The success of such community projects as district

[37] *Atun Huaylas*, March 2, 1958:1 (my transation).

[38] In addition to working many days on the electrification project, the organization (at considerable cost) paid for a band to come and play for two days during the inauguration fiesta, gave money to the schools, and offered to buy a metal flagpole for the boys' school in town.

electrification has depended upon the degree to which the people have identified with these projects and the extent to which they have thrown the weight of their own organizations behind the efforts.[39]

The degree of social integration manifest in Huaylas is one of the features that distinguishes the district from others in the Callejón. Although the diminishing cultural and social differences between the urban and rural and the Indian and mestizo elements of the population are most evident in such visible characteristics as the style of dress, of even greater significance is the degree to which persons of all social classes participate in the same formal social and political system and tradition (which is representative of the national society). The relatively discrete social systems of rural Indians and urban mestizos in the district of Marcará and in Hualcán, for example, preclude the kind of cooperation between social classes found in Huaylas and inhibit the emergence of expressions of unity and common desires.

The history, organization, and spirit of community enterprise in Huaylas have shown that the people themselves are capable of managing their own affairs and guiding their own destiny without authoritarian leadership or undue dependence on outside agencies. "Dependent" communities, whose members speak only of their problems and demand aid from the government or outside agencies without indicating any willingness to attack their problems themselves, are a common phenomenon in Peru. They constitute some 59.8 per cent of a preliminary sample of ninety-seven Comunidades Indígenas throughout the country.[40]

Government aid is widely sought by Peruvian communities, and many of them consider it indispensable if there is to be any progress or improvement. The members of the Chamber of Deputies and the Senate are besieged by delegations asking for aid. In actuality, the dispensing of small sums of money is one means by which congressional representatives pay for political favors and attempt to win votes. Promises of such aid are also part of the politician's standard speech to his constituents and are regarded, for the most part, with extreme skepticism by the people. Huaylinos feel that they have been neglected rather badly by the government, and they often register complaints to

[39] This point is always stressed by students of community development (Ross, 1955:35; Goodenough, 1963) but often forgotten by planners and developers in the field.

[40] Dobyns and Carrasco, 1962.

this effect.[41] Yet Huaylas has received government aid from time to time in its projects, both in the form of direct cash grants, ranging from a few hundred *soles* to as much as S/100,000, and in the form of such materials and equipment as roofing, cement, dynamite, tools, a diesel generator, doors and windows for the school, and furniture for the library.

Notwithstanding, aid is accepted with considerable discontent in many cases for reasons illustrated below. In 1930, the government gave the district eighty barrels of cement for the installation of the piped water system in the town. By 1934, only half of them had arrived in Huaylas, and the project was, by then, finished. In 1956, the Callejón de Huaylas Sanitation Unit of the Ministry of Public Health initiated efforts to install a new water and sewerage system in Huaylas and later had some pipe delivered to be used for this purpose. The pipe was still piled in the plaza at the time of our stay in Huaylas for lack of technical help to make the installation. Representatives of the Ministry came to Huaylas from Huaraz in 1961 to take the pipe back, but the mayor successfully persuaded them not to do so. In 1957 a congressman, visiting Huaylas for the inauguration of the library, declared that he would obtain the necessary funds to build a new primary school for girls in the town, but this promise went unfulfilled.

The first truck to operate in the district was one sent by the government to help transport workers and materials for the work on the road to Mato in 1929. The vehicle had to be pulled up the mountain from the rail depot in Huallanca, since there were no roads to Huaylas at that time. While this, among other government contributions to Huaylas, was gratefully acknowledged, more often than not the people tend to remember the errors, inefficiencies, and lack of interest. Government agencies and their representatives are considered to be *muy incumplido* (very unreliable). Huaylinos are quick to say that if anything is to be accomplished at all, they themselves will have to do it. "We can at least rely upon ourselves," they say, underlining their role in whatever is done.

The mistrust of government actions and motives, as mentioned here and in the preceding chapter, marks a common pattern throughout Peru. It has been noted that Huaylinos are extremely reluctant to pay national taxes and, in fact, make special, sometimes elaborate, efforts to

[41] Dobyns (1964:44) reports that 70 per cent of the Comunidades Indígenas reported feeling neglected by the government.

evade them. In the light of this and the desire for progress, it is, I think, quite understandable that Huaylinos should be more than willing to tax themselves through endless days of voluntary labor and donations of all kinds, amounting to many thousands of *soles*. On the completion of the electrification project, I estimated that Huaylinos had contributed money, gifts in kind, and work with a cash value of over $7,400 (S/200,000) in a year's time. This, moreover, did not include what was expended during the year on community projects other than electrification.

There are two other salient, though less obvious, consequences of the vitality of the *república* and the civic committee. The first is that, because large numbers of persons are able to hold positions of responsibility through these activities, a training ground is provided in which experience in leadership roles may be acquired. Participants are able to familiarize themselves with the local government process and often to work directly with district authorities and more experienced persons. Young people are encouraged to engage in community activities, and thus the tradition is passed on. Individuals who are skilled in certain fields are rewarded by being chosen for positions of responsibility that cannot be handled by others. Many persons, particularly in the middle-class sector of the population, are drawn into these activities and encouraged to play important roles in this way.

Finally, the pattern of collective activity bolsters community pride and the sentiment that Huaylas has a special individuality which distinguishes it from the neighboring districts and towns. This feeling emerges in the quotations from my field notes and in the ways indicated in Chapter III. The almost patriotic interest in public affairs and the enlightened self-interest demonstrated by the people is often sufficient to override the strong undercurrents of factionalism and personal enmity which also characterize interpersonal behavior in the district. The strength of the values that underlie participation in public affairs is a significant indication that, despite the high rate of emigration and urban influences, Huaylinos continue to view the future of the district optimistically and are not abandoning the district's traditions and organizations. Public life in the district is, in fact, greatly stimulated by the migrants acting individually and through the regional associations, and, ultimately, by Western civilization as represented in Lima.

While the *república* falls within a certain mode of community activity which equates Huaylas with rural communities throughout the world, the civic committees and regional associations are, at times, almost the epitome of what is sophisticated and urban. Their coexistence indicates a way in which tradition may not only blend into contemporary life but may play an active role in it in harmony with institutions of more recent origin.

CHAPTER IX

Formal Education

The Educational System

The role of formal education in Huaylas has been important for many years. Although the archives in the municipal office did not yield much historical material from the last century, occasional references indicate that there were a number of small schools in Huaylas during the middle of the nineteenth century. In 1874 there was a municipal school operated by the district government, and in 1884 a small private high school with the name "Instituto El Progreso" was established by several university students who had returned to Huaylas from Lima during the Chilean War. This school, like many others of the period, was short-lived, lasting only two years. Another municipal school (for boys) was established in the town in 1886, again with the name "Instituto El Progreso." In 1892, a second municipal school, called the "Instituto Santa Rosa" (for girls), was established.

From that time on, numerous schools functioned for short periods in various parts of the district. By the end of the first decade of the twentieth century, there were schools functioning in all the *barrios* of the district. Several were private schools, established by someone equipped to teach, and operated by permission of the Concejo. Gradually, however, all of these were taken over by the municipality or ceased to function.

Municipal records in 1896 showed that the boys' school had an average daily attendance of 150 pupils out of a total of 257 matriculated students. The girls' school, at the same time, had an average attendance of 90 students each day out of the 106 girls matriculated. In 1902, the boys' school in the town had an average daily attendance of 120, while the girls' school had 84 pupils attending daily. Between 1895 and 1905, the idea of education and the need for educated persons was promulgated and stressed to the Huaylas public by the mayor and others. At that time, the district government was empowered to collect school taxes and to fine parents who did not send their children to school. Fifty centavos was the usual fine, a substantial amount of money, since the Peruvian *sol* at that time was quite strong.

Another feature of the education movement at the turn of the century was that most of its proponents were prominent members of the local upper class. Throughout the municipal school system, augmented by the private schools, this group spread the acceptance of formal education to all sectors of the district and to all levels of society.

By the end of the second decade of the twentieth century, most of the municipal schools had passed under the control of the federal school system, thus ending an era in which the municipal government and the people of the district had direct responsibility for the development of their schools as well as for the selection, supervision, and payment of their teachers. The national government assumed these responsibilities, theoretically providing for the care, construction, and maintenance of the schools as well, but, with few exceptions, this is still done by the parents and residents of the district. Eleven of the fourteen schools now in use in the district have been built by the populace (the other three schools occupy rented space).

The advent of the nationalized school system also spelled the end of such locally inspired school names as "El Progreso," "Instituto Santa Rosa," and "Instituto Huaylas." These were replaced by the official school numbers in the national system, and the schools were classified according to their category.

Currently, there are schools of several different official categories in Huaylas with an attendance of 1,333 pupils (Table 31). The largest schools, found in the town and in Santo Toribio, are of a type called "second-grade" schools, meaning that they offer the full six years of primary school. The schools in the *barrios* of Tambo and Iscap, called "elemental" schools, have instruction through the third year and operate on a noncoeducational basis. The schools in the other *barrios* are called *escuelas mixtas* or "mixed" schools, indicating that they are coeducational and offer education through the second year. A coeducational kindergarten is also operated in the town of Huaylas.

The initial year in all primary schools, regardless of official category, is called "transition" and is intermediate between kindergarten and the first year. After "transition," the grades proceed numerically to the fifth year at which time the student graduates from the primary school and is ready to continue his education at the secondary level. Those students, attending the elemental or the mixed schools in the *barrios*, who are desirous of furthering their education transfer to the schools in Santo Toribio or in the town of Huaylas. Students from the distant *barrios* of Tambo and San Lorenzo find it difficult to complete their primary school education, since it requires them to live away from home, an economic and social hardship for most families. It is not unusual for a child to work his way through the primary-school years as the servant or errand boy of someone (often a *padrino*) living in the town who has agreed to accept the responsibility for him during the school year.

On completion of primary school, those wishing to continue their education must leave Huaylas and board at a school or at the home of a relative in Caraz, Huaraz, or Lima. This, of course, requires a considerable emotional and economic sacrifice by parents. While many families cannot manage it, others spend years planning for it. Often an entire family will move to Caraz or Lima and make a new life there so that the children may attend high school and university.

The schoolteachers of Huaylas, considered as a group or as individuals, are a powerful element in the society now, as in the past, since most of the early teachers came from local upper-class families. This is not to say that others who are qualified do not achieve the social respect accorded those of upper-class backgrounds, for being a teacher is one of the surest routes to social mobility as well as to a certain degree of economic well-being. Consequently, many Huaylinos have aspired to the teaching profession. The district, in fact, has exported teachers for many decades.

Huaylinos work as schoolteachers not only in neighboring Caraz, Macate, Yuramarca, Huaraz, and Mato, but also in the cities of Chimbote, Lima, and Ica, among others. Many Huaylinos are graduates of teachers' colleges, and some have taken doctorates in pedagogy. One Huaylino, resident in Lima, was a principal organizer and president of the Primary School Teachers' Association of Peru, a national organization with considerable influence and power.

With this model of success before them, it is not surprising that many children in the Huaylas schools express a desire to become schoolteachers. Of the forty-three teachers, all but nine were Huaylinos, and almost half had attended or graduated from teachers' colleges. There were, however, twelve teachers with primary-school training only, and the fact that some teachers have not received appropriate training undoubtedly contributes, in large measure, to the failure of many students to finish their primary-school education.

Nevertheless, in comparison with most other districts in rural Peru, particularly in the Andean region, the district of Huaylas enjoys a most favorable position with regard to its teachers and schools. This is, of course, partially due to the impulse given to education at the turn of the century. There have usually been enough teachers in Huaylas to meet the minimal demand of the populace for elementary education, although the teacher-pupil ratio leaves a great deal to be desired in some cases (Table 31). Moreover, because most of the teachers are Huaylinos, it is possible to maintain schools in areas that might otherwise have difficulty in finding persons willing to make the sacrifices to work there, far from their families and friends (a common problem in the Andean areas). Further, there is less temptation for the teachers to cut classes or absent themselves for long week ends and vacations.

As a group, the teachers esteem their position and role in the community very highly, and their view of themselves is supported by the public, judging from comments. The number of articles that appear in local publications lauding the activities of teachers and eulogizing the efforts of particular individuals would seem to support this.[1] A majority of the teachers in Huaylas also exhibit a great deal of professional pride, as evidenced by the expressed desires to perfect their skills and improve their standing in the school system. Almost every issue of the local fortnightly newspaper, *Atun Huaylas*, carries an article devoted to the teacher or to some aspect of the teaching profession, treating

[1] This impression is biased by the fact that most of the contributors to the local newspaper happen to be schoolteachers who, it seems, are not reluctant to praise the work of their colleagues or of the profession in general. Indeed, the teachers association of Huaylas erected a large concrete monument to education in the plaza of Huaylas in July 1966.

Table 31. Primary schools according to the number of teachers and the number of pupils enrolled in each, 1959

Location of school	Official school number	Number of pupils	Number of teachers	Number of pupils per teacher
Town of Huaylas				
Boys'	323	239	7	34
Girls'	324	209	7½ *	27.8
Kindergarten	128	70	2 †	35
Santo Toribio				
Boys'	329	245	7	35
Girls'	330	162	6½ *	24.9
Quenti (in Quecuas)	3280	51	2	25.5
Yacup	3269	49	2	24.4
Shuyo	3272	37	2	18.5
Huaromapuquio	3213	35	1	35
Iscap				
Boys'	3247	51	2	25.5
Girls'	3227	38	1 †	38
Tambo				
Boys'	3258	45	1	45
Girls'	3228	46	1	46
San Lorenzo	3260	56	1	56
Total		1,333	43	31

* One craft and sewing teacher alternates between these schools.

† These teachers had paid, nonteacher assistants.

such matters as the educational theories of John Dewey and the responsibility of the teacher vis-à-vis the community.

The enrollment in the fourteen schools of the District of Huaylas (Table 31) includes approximately 88 per cent of all the children between the ages of six and fifteen years, the period when education is mandatory. This percentage is very high when compared to such nearby areas as Vicos, which had about 35 per cent of its school-age children enrolled (over 90 per cent of whom were boys).[2] The level of schooling in Huaylas stands out more clearly, perhaps, when compared with the situation which obtains in the rest of the Department of Ancash and in the country as a whole (Tables 32–34). Although the 1961 national census provides an estimate of the degree of literacy in Peru, it has not reported data which is comparable to that found in the

[2] Vázquez, 1961c:34.

Table 32. Percentage of the population over six years of age in the District of Huaylas Department of Ancash, and Peru, having attended school, 1940 and 1961 *

	Per cent of men			Per cent of women		
	Has attended	Has not attended	Total	Has attended	Has not attended	Total
Peru, 1940	50	50	(100)	38	82	(100)
Ancash, 1940	44	56	(100)	20	80	(100)
Huaylas, 1940	72	28	(100)	41	59	(100)
Huaylas, 1961	89	11	(100)	68	32	(100)

* Based in part on Perú, Ministerio de Hacienda y Comercio (1944, I and III). Comparative data for 1961 were not available.

Table 33. Percentage of literacy in the population over seventeen years of age in the District of Huaylas by sex, and urban and rural residence, 1961 *

	Urban		Rural		Total		Total
	Literate	Illiterate	Literate	Illiterate	Literate	Illiterate	Total population
Men							
Number	292	21	827	154	1119	175	1294
Per cent	9.7	.7	27.5	5.1	37.2	5.8	43.0
Women							
Number	255	118	679	665	934	783	1717
Per cent	8.5	3.9	22.5	22.1	31.0	26.0	57.0
Total							
Number	547	139	1506	819	2053	958	3011
Per cent	18.2	4.6	50.0	27.2	68.2	31.8	100.0

* Based on the data in Perú, Instituto Nacional de Planificación, 1964. The 1961 national census asked the question, "Do you know how to read and write?" Although this is by no means an accurate measure of literacy, it does give the only estimate of this characteristic available.

1940 census. The tables cited, nevertheless, indicate the rather sharp divergence of Huaylas from the regional and national pattern especially with respect to the rural population. The degree of literacy in the rural areas of Huaylas is almost double that found in the rest of the Callejón de Huaylas and four times the rate of literacy in the Province of Huaraz in which the Departmental capital is located. In contrast to the other areas cited in the tables where literacy and urban residence are highly correlated, this pattern is less well defined in Huaylas.

The political implications of literacy are considerable, since it is an electoral requirement. Fifty per cent of the Huaylas adults (population

Table 34. Percentage of literacy in the population over seventeen years of age in the Districts of Huaylas and Caraz, Provinces of Huaylas and Huaraz, Department of Ancash, and Peru, by urban and rural residence, 1961 *

| | Distribution by residence | | | | | |
| | Per cent of urban population | | Per cent of rural population | | Per cent of total population | |
Place	Literate	Illiterate	Literate	Illiterate	Literate	Illiterate
Huaylas District	18.2	4.6	50.0	27.2	68.2	31.8
Caraz District	27.1	7.8	22.9	42.2	50.0	50.0
Province of Huaylas	15.7	5.8	30.3	48.2	46.0	54.0
Province of Huaraz	26.3	9.2	21.8	42.6	48.1	51.8
Ancash Department	24.9	8.8	23.1	43.2	48.0	52.0
Peru	40.0	8.8	20.5	30.7	60.5	39.7

* Based on statistics from Instituto Nacional de Planificación, Dirección Nacional de Estadística y Censos, 1964.

Table 35. Percentage of urban and rural population over seventeen years of age declared literate in the Districts of Huaylas and Caraz, Provinces of Huaylas and Huaraz, Department of Ancash, and Peru, 1961 *

| | Per cent of urban population | | Per cent of rural population | |
Place	Literate	Illiterate	Literate	Illiterate
Huaylas District	79.7	20.3	64.7	35.3
Caraz District	77.8	22.2	35.2	64.8
Province of Huaylas	73.0	27.0	38.6	61.4
Province of Huaraz	73.9	26.1	14.3	85.7
Ancash Department	73.8	26.2	34.6	65.4
Peru	81.6	18.4	39.4	60.6

* Based on statistics from Instituto Nacional de Planificación, Dirección Nacional de Estadística y Censos, 1964.

over seventeen years of age) are both rural and literate, whereas only 18.2 per cent of the literate population is found in the town. Because the rural areas have been under-represented in municipal government under the appointment system which prevailed until December 1963, municipal elections would be predicted to bring about some important sociopolitical changes in the district. As of 1964 in Huaylas there were approximately 1,300 registered electors (minimum age is twenty-one) or 59 per cent out of a possible total of 2,200 persons of this age group.[3]

[3] Electors are given a brief, functional reading test before they are permitted to register, and this, therefore, constitutes a rough way in which the national census

The phenomenon of higher school attendance by men than women is marked to an extreme degree in the case of Vicos, as it is in most other Indian and rural communities. In Huaylas, the pattern still persists, but to a much lesser extent, and in the two decades since 1940 the gap between male and female school attendance has closed considerably (Table 32). A more or less equal school attendance rate in Huaylas indicates a change in the androcentric nature of rural society to meet the needs of modern urban-oriented life. This, of course, greatly enhances the opportunity for women to migrate successfully to coastal cities.

In theory at least, education is free. There are, however, a number of expenses incurred by the students and their families if they are to follow local and national custom. Parents are urged to become members of the Patronato Escolar (School Patrons Association) and contribute money for various school needs. Members of the Patronato Escolar often contribute their labor as well in constructing or repairing the school buildings. The Patronato Escolar of each school elects its own officers representing both teachers and parents, and the activities of these associations are supervised by the local Director of Education.

Although some of the school fees have been abolished by the national congress since 1963, students are still urged to purchase school uniforms. Students usually have to provide their own notebooks, pencils, books, and other equipment despite the fact that the Ministry of Education will provide these things if the teachers themselves take the initiative to obtain them. Relatively little was distributed through the ministerial bureaucracy.

Education: Content and Academic Performance

In view of the high enrollment and high daily attendance in Huaylas, the failure of a large percentage of the children to finish primary school deserves comment. It is not unusual to find students who have attended school for four or five years still in the first or second grade. Of all the students registered in the Iscap school in 1959, only 45 per

figures for declared literacy may be evaluated. The difference of 9.2 per cent between these percentages (68.2 per cent self-declared literates and 59 per cent literate for electoral purposes) indicates that a discrepancy exists between what people think they can do and what they can really do, that there was a failure on the part of some to register, or that there was discrimination against some of the potential electors.

cent passed. Although the percentage of passing students in the two schools of the town was somewhat higher, the pattern of failure was also pronounced. For the same year, 62 per cent of the boys and 70 per cent of the girls passed.

Language differences are important in many sections of the rural areas of the district, where it is common for children to enter school speaking, primarily, Quechua. This, of course, constitutes an obstacle to effective communication, since all classes are conducted in Spanish. Because most of the adults in the district are bilingual and because the Quechua dialect spoken in the district contains a high percentage of Spanish loan words, it is difficult to estimate the seriousness of this problem. The extensive bilingualism in Huaylas is apparently due to the fact that many children have become more or less proficient in Spanish through attending school.

Gaining some proficiency in Spanish, however, does not necessarily mean that Spanish becomes the first language of the home. The rural women constitute 66.8 per cent (761 individuals) of the people in the district who have never attended school and 40.6 per cent of those who failed to complete primary school. By the same token, rural men represent 42.0 per cent (1,184 individuals) of the total number of persons who failed to complete primary school. Thus, despite the apparently high rate of literacy in Huaylas as compared to other areas, here is a clear measure of the fact that the rural population continues to have only minimal and often unsuccessful contact with the formal educational system. Quechua continues to be the dominant language in the home for many, perhaps most, rural families. Children who come from such homes naturally show far greater fluency in Quechua than in Spanish and consequently encounter communication problems in school.

Another source of difficulty lies in the need for the children to work in the fields with their parents. Although the school records indicate that relatively few children drop out of school with this as the stated reason, it appears to be an important factor in some cases and a contributing one in others. Many children attend school every other year or every other semester, and some attend a half-day at a time because they must pasture the animals in the afternoons (or in the mornings, as the case may be). From observation and from conversations with children as well as with teachers, it seems that economic factors are often made an excuse for dropping out of school and are not always the actual cause. Nevertheless, many persons, including a number of the teachers, consider it to be one of the major factors detracting from school attendance. One teacher at the boys' school commented that "the children all like their little fields and little animals better than they do the school."

Considering the fact that many children fail in their early years of school, it is not unreasonable to suppose that they (or their parents) become discouraged and, hence, decline to attend. This reason was given by several parents to whom I spoke. A common parental complaint about the schools (also expressed by teachers) is that the children simply do not learn anything and become bored. Aside from language problems, the low level of performance seems due to the relatively low expectations manifested in the children's ability (particularly in those from the lower class) to handle classwork. The school records indicate that lower- and middle-class children tend to fail more often than do children with upper-class backgrounds.

It is common in Huaylas to feel that some children are much too young to be advancing rapidly in school, despite, in many cases, their acknowledged intelligence. The fact that the child is intellectually capable of pursuing advanced courses, is subordinate to the idea that he is too young, sufficient reason to hold him back. In many cases, the explanation of this is that upon completing primary school, the child would have to board at the secondary school in Caraz. Many parents are therefore reluctant to send their children until they are older.

Some of these attitudes emerged when I sponsored an "essay" contest between the students of the fourth and fifth grades in the two town schools. When the idea was first broached at a meeting, some teachers were reluctant to have the students participate in the contest because they felt that the children would not be capable of performing as I wished. In brief, I had proposed that the advanced students (fourth and fifth grades) of the two schools answer a series of questions about Huaylas' public works projects in simple essay form. The children were supposed to use what information they or their parents had or what information they might obtain from other adults (excluding teachers). Numerous prizes were to be offered for the best essays on the various topics suggested.

Objections were raised on four counts: that the children were too young; that they were not accustomed to essay contests of any sort;

that this would result in many arguments and conflicts;[4] and that the children were unprepared to attempt original work of this nature. There was some additional reluctance on the part of the women teachers of the girls' school because competition between boys and girls was thought to be unfair. As one of them put it, *"No es nuestra ambiente"* (It isn't our medium"). After much discussion they agreed, however, to go ahead with the contest, more or less as planned.

The objections raised by the teachers disclosed other aspects of the problem of low expectation. It was claimed, for example, that the children were not prepared to undertake an original task by virtue of their previous school experience. In day-to-day classroom work, children learn almost exclusively by rote and by copying, seldom using their own initiative or ideas without extremely close teacher supervision. Thus, the teacher puts a drawing on the blackboard, and the children copy it exactly. Arithmetic is taught in the same manner, as recounted below:

The teacher had been explaining the measurements of length. After telling the class the number of meters in a block and of blocks in a kilometer, she wrote questions on the board to be answered by the children in their copybooks. One of the questions was, "How many meters are there in a kilometer?" The teacher's pet went up to the teacher and asked for the answer saying the teacher had not included it in her previous explanation. The teacher realized that she hadn't and told the class the answer. Although the tools for answering the question had been given, she did not expect them to figure it out for themselves and considered their request justified. In giving them the answer she didn't explain the reasoning behind it even though it was simple enough for the children to grasp.[5]

It was perfectly logical, therefore, that one of the teachers should be reluctant to allow children to enter the contest. As she put it, "They will not be able to do it because they have nothing to copy." The rigid teaching methods are standard throughout most of Peru, as is, of course, the curriculum in all the schools. Since methods and subject matter are prescribed by the Ministry of Education in Lima, there is relatively little variation in schools of the same category throughout

---

[4] It most certainly did—not among the students, but between the faculties of the two schools, that is, the men versus the women.

[5] Kasakoff, 1960:10.

Peru. Most teachers simply "follow the book." [6] Reasons such as these help to account for the fact that of the two classes graduating from the schools in the town of Huaylas in 1960, only three boys and nine girls out of the total of fifty-two pupils had never repeated a year of primary school.

The inflexible curriculum is a defect recognized in Huaylas by teachers as well as by others who have expressed the wish that some schools in Huaylas become vocational schools, which would allow for the training of students in agriculture and various trades. To date, however, this has not occurred, and the only practical training offered is to be found in very elementary, recreational courses in the manual arts, such as carpentry. In two of the girls' schools some instruction was given in sewing and weaving.

The four complete primary schools in the district graduate an average of eighty students a year among them, and because the population of Huaylas has remained relatively constant, this figure has probably not altered much over the past fifteen to twenty years. Thus, over a twenty-year period, Huaylas should have produced approximately 1,600 primary school graduates. Referring to Table 36, however, we see that there are only 661 persons in the district who have completed primary school (including students who have attended secondary schools, universities, or normal schools). There appears to be a very high correlation between the level of education and the propensity to emigrate. Of the teenagers who finished primary school in 1960, the vast majority are now living in Caraz, Chimbote, or Lima. The population pyramid (Figure 2) dramatically illustrates this exodus of persons over fifteen years of age.

In addition to the typical classroom phenomenon—the teacher's pet—there is that of the class "leader." The teacher's authority for maintaining discipline in the class is delegated to student "leaders," who are often chosen by the pupils themselves. The class "leaders" keep order in the classroom and see that everyone lines up properly at assembly time in the morning and marches in an orderly fashion when the class goes from one place to another. They are permitted to administer corporal punishment to classmates and, although there may be resistance from time to time, the "leaders" are usually obeyed, since they have the backing of the teacher.

[6] Perú, Ministerio de Educación Pública, Dirección de Educación Primaria, 1955.

Table 36. Number and percentage of urban and rural population over six years of age by sex according to the level of education attained in the District of Huaylas 1961 *

	Men				Women				Total	
	Urban		Rural		Urban		Rural			
	Num-ber	Per cent	Num-ber	Per cent	Num-ber	Per cent	Num-ber	Per cent	Num-ber	Per cent
Have not attended school	27	6.2	216	12.9	89	21.8	671	34.0	1003	22.3
Primary school										
Incomplete †	251	58.0	1184	70.9	223	55.0	1134	57.4	2792	62.2
Complete	91	21.0	214	12.8	59	14.5	134	6.7	498	11.1
Secondary school										
Incomplete	38	8.7	31	1.8	25	6.5	11	.5	105	2.3
Complete	13	3.0	4	.2	2	.4	6	.3	25	.6
University or normal school	11	2.6	9	.5	6	1.4	7	.3	33	.7
Don't know	3	.5	16	.9	2	.4	16	.8	37	.8
Total	434	100.0	1674	100.0	406	100.0	1979	100.0	4493	100.0

* Excludes 24 persons incompletely censused.
† Excludes 13 pupils aged 5 who attend primary school.

In this role, which may be filled by several boys or girls for a given class during the year, both middle- and upper-class children are well represented. In some cases, a child from a lower-class background may be selected, particularly if he is older than the rest. In one grade, one of the poorest children in town acted as class leader. The boy was both bright and aggressive, factors which contributed to his selection. Through this system, authoritarian patterns of leadership are learned. At the same time, the practice provides a sanctioned channel for aggression and peer-group rivalry.

Despite the aura of authoritarianism, however, there is a considerable amount of horseplay which takes place both inside and outside of the classroom, depending on the strictness of the teacher and the respect he commands among his pupils. Misconduct, real or imagined, is usually reported to the teacher by the pupils, who seem to have little hesitancy about "tattling." Misbehavior is usually reprimanded, but if a child (particularly a boy) is especially unruly, he may be administered some form of corporal punishment by the teacher.

In the classroom, when the teacher (or a visitor) enters, the children rise and greet him with "Good morning, teacher" and remain standing until told to sit down. At the end of the day, the children are charged with cleaning the classroom and sweeping the patio, which they do under the direction of the teacher. There is no janitor in any of the schools.

Before the day's classes begin, the children line up in the patio to hear announcements, and, if scheduled, a brief assembly program is conducted. The school calendar, reproduced in Table 37, indicates the frequency with which special programs occur. After the assembly period, the pupils march to their classrooms, beginning their classwork at approximately 9:15 A.M. Classes are held from Monday through Saturday noon during the school year. In Huaylas, Saturday mornings were often devoted to manual arts, recreational activities, and, sometimes, to cleaning the school premises.

Preparation for special events, which generally last for two or three hours if they are held in the auditorium, occupy the teachers and students for many hours, arranging, practicing, and memorizing the recitations, parts for skits or plays, songs, or dances, and preparing the necessary props and costumes. Admission is usually charged for programs held in the auditorium, as a means of obtaining money for school improvements or supplies.[7] The usual attendance at such programs is 200 to 300 adults, who usually receive invitations such as the following, printed on shiny, colored paper.

A common feature of all such events is the recitation, usually touching upon themes which are patriotic, nostalgic, sentimental, or humorous. The child follows a standardized form of oratory, complete with dramatic, highly stylized gestures, and vocal intonations. Declamations are taken seriously, and the quality of the performance is judged on how well the student has reproduced the style required. Nevertheless, when younger children sometimes forget the words but remember the arm and hand movements, the humor of the situation is not lost on the audience which roars with laughter. Older students who do not perform well, however, are regarded less tolerantly, and members of the audience may comment that the teacher has not prepared the child sufficiently.

These events serve to reinforce the already entrenched pattern of ritualistic and recreational festivals which are associated principally

[7] Because there are few benches, a "general" entrance fee is charged those who wish to bring their own chairs. As would be expected, the poorer people do this. The "preferred" ticket holders are provided seats.

Literary-Musical Evening

AUDITORIUM OF PRIMARY SCHOOL NO 330

Santo Toribio, 27 of July, 1960 Hour 8:30 P.M.

TO THE PUBLIC

The Teaching Personnel of the Women's Primary School No. 330 of Santo Toribio, for the purpose of celebrating the 139th National Anniversary, has organized a Literary-Musical Evening, staging the historical drama of national acclaim entitled:

"MOTHER AND SON"

in addition, several variety acts.

On this occasion, the blessing of the new school furniture in distinct sections of the school will be carried out.

Trusting that the Santo Toribian public will know to support this performance with its presence, we genteely invite all, thanking you in **advance**.

SEATS

Preferred: $3.00   General Admittance: $2.00   Children: $1.00

GRAND SOCIAL DANCE WITH A COMPETENT ORCHESTRA

---

with the practice of religion (Chapter X). Indeed, several of the school-sponsored programs include student attendance at Mass, an activity which tends to involve the girls' schools more often than the boys' schools. Eighteen of the special events listed in Table 37 are either directly concerned with religious observance or include, as part of the activity, acts of religious significance. The attention given to religion is in accord with the stated goals and program of the national educational system.[8] Finally, the special programs, by virtue of their

[8] Perú, Ministerio de Educación Pública, Dirección de Educación Primaria, 1955:34, 47, 385-429.

Table 37. Calendar of events of boys' school No. 323 in the town of Huaylas, 1960

Date	Days of vacation	Event
Mar. 1–Apr. 30		Matriculation period (parent or guardian registers child at the school in person).
Apr. 1		Classes begin.
Apr. 12		Anniversary of the Birth of Inca Garcilaso de la Vega (short speech at assembly period).
Apr. 14		Pan American Day (program in each classroom).
Apr. 14–15	1½	Holy Thursday and Good Friday.
Apr. 23		Language Day (classroom programs in each).
May 1		Labor Day (classroom programs).
May 2		Anniversary of the Victory at Callao (1866 war with Spain; speech at assembly period).
May 3	1	The finding of the Holy Cross (local religious fiesta).
May 8		Mother's Day (program for parents).
May 11		Anniversary of the Heroic Acts of Maria Parado de Bellido (classroom programs).
May 18		Anniversary of the Execution of Tupac Amaru (assembly speech).
May 26	1	Ember Day (religious holiday).
End of May		Examinations.
June 7		Flag Day (parade by school children, Mass, program at the municipal offices).
June 16	1	Sacred Heart of Jesus (religious holiday).
June 18		School Equipment Day (meeting of parents at the school and collection of money for school equipment).
June 20		The Cry of Zela at Tacna (first cry of independence, 1811, classroom programs).
June 21		St. Louis Gonzaga, Patron of Studious Youth (Mass and procession).
June 24		St. John, Day of the Indian (programs for parents).
June 26		Anniversary of the Assassination of Francisco Pizarro, Conqueror of Peru (classroom programs).
June 29	1	St. Peter (religious holiday).
July 6	1	Teachers' Day (program in auditorium).
July 7		Anniversary of the inauguration of the Acosta Library in Huaylas (assembly program).
July 7–9	2½	Fiesta of St. Elizabeth (local fiesta).
July 10		Anniversary of Battle of Huamachuco (1883, Chilean War, classroom programs).
July 18–25		Patriotic Week (special classroom programs and activity preparing for Independence Day).
July 19		Anniversary of the Death of Gregorio M. Cano, Benefactor of the School (assembly speech and short program, Mass).

Date	Days	Event
July 27		Military Preparation Day (speech and short assembly program).
July 28	1	Independence Day (parade in Plaza, ceremony at municipal offices; Mass).
End of July		Examinations.
July 28–Aug. 11	12½	Vacation period.
Aug. 15–16		Virgin of the Assumption, Patroness of Atun Huaylas (local fiesta).
Aug. 17		Anniversary of the Death of José de San Martín (classroom celebrations).
Aug. 29		Anniversary of the Death of St. Rose of Lima, Patroness of the Americas (assembly program).
Aug. 30	1	Feast Day of St. Rose of Lima.
Aug. 31	1	Policemen's Day (assembly program).
Sept. 23		First Day of Spring, Aviation Day, Youth Day (assembly programs).
Sept. 24	1½	Feast Day of Our Lady of Mercy (Our Lady of Ransom), Patroness of the Armed Forces (assembly program).
Sept. 25		Anniversary of the Birth of Antonio Raimondi (classroom programs).
End of Sept.		Examinations.
Oct. 8		Anniversary of the Naval Battle at Angamos (1879, War of the Pacific, assembly program).
Oct. 12	1	Day of the Race (Columbus Day).
Oct. 21		Anniversary of Magellen's Discovery of the Strait bearing his name (classroom programs).
Nov. 1		All Saints' Day (religious holiday).
Nov. 2–3	2	All Souls' Day (religious holiday and local fiesta).
Nov. 4		Anniversary of the Insurrection of Tupac Amaru (classroom programs).
Nov. 27		Anniversary of the Battle of Tarapaca (1879, Chilean War); Army Day, (classroom programs).
End of Nov.		Examinations
Dec. 1		Savings Day (assembly program)
Dec. 5		Arbor Day (assembly program)
Dec. 8	1	Immaculate Conception (religious holiday)
Dec. 9		Anniversary of the Battle of Ayacucho (1824, War of Independence, assembly program).
Dec. 12–24		Final examinations and end of school year.
Total days of vacation	30	

frequency and the demands made upon both teachers and students in their preparation and performance, monopolize uncounted hours (apart from outright holidays) which might otherwise be devoted to strictly academic pursuits.

The calendar of school activities (Table 37) reflects the patriotic tenor of many school programs and the intent of the school system to indoctrinate its pupils with a nationalistic and patriotic spirit. Thus, if the children learn nothing else from their school experience, they begin to perceive that they are Peruvians and part of a larger entity, a nation declared independent by San Martin, liberated by Bolivar and Sucre, preserved by Ramón Castilla, and glorified by Admiral Grau, Colonel Bolognesi, and Jorge Chavez.

The nationalistic indoctrination places emphasis on the military aspects of patriotism, more perhaps than on citizenship itself. The tone of the school organization reflects a latent military influence, which becomes manifest in the last years of the primary school. In Huaylas the police sergeant in charge of the local *puesto* drilled the students in marching.[9] The martial influence is also seen in the boys' school uniform, which consists of khaki trousers, shirts, and ties, topped by an "overseas" cap.[10]

One of the biggest events of the school year is the celebration of Fiestas Patrias (Independence Day—July 28), which is preceded in all of the schools by a week (*Semana Patriótica*—Patriotic Week) devoted to study of the history and legends of the War for Independence and preparation for the special programs of Independence Day. The principal event is a parade of all the school children (except those from Huaromapuquiro, Tambo, and San Lorenzo) into the town and around the plaza. The children train at least a week, perfecting a vigorous stride (a "semigoosestep" being preferred) and various maneuvers. The best students are chosen to precede the others in the *escolta* (flag escort) or to march at the heads of their classes. For the sake of appearance, the few children who do not have uniforms march behind the others in their grade and, with some exceptions, are usually the poorer children. Children who do not wish to be singled out in this

[9] Those who go on to high school receive a full-fledged course in military techniques. Boys who finish secondary school leave with the rank of sergeant, second grade, of the infantry reserve. Marching is also taken seriously in the girls' schools.

[10] This is a standard uniform throughout Peru. Girls' uniforms are, of course, more feminine.

manner besiege their parents with requests for uniforms which are made by local tailors and seamstresses who normally do a lively business in July.

The impact of the national educational system on Huaylas has been great and continues to grow as the years pass. Although the apparently high rate of literacy and exposure to the formal educational system is clouded by the fact that for many persons, particularly those in rural areas, this contact is minimal at best, the influence of the system nevertheless makes its mark. The relative accessibility of primary education to all residents of the district has lead to the erasure of gross educational variation in the district and to the development of linguistic homogeneity. The traditional Quechua and regional elements of the culture are slowly but constantly eroded by the increasing use of Spanish, by the introduction of notions of patriotism and nation, and by the development of other patterns of thought and behavior sanctioned by Peruvian national culture. The schools are largely responsible for the bilingual character of Huaylas and are beginning to tip the balance in favor of Spanish. Aside from these advantages, the system serves to awaken or encourage the desire for things not readily available in the district, thus stimulating migration to the coastal cities, but schooling is not, unfortunately, aimed at imparting the skills immediately necessary for the people to develop their regional homeland. The outside contact gained through migration and strengthened ties with the coastal cities also reinforces and stimulates bilingualism.

CHAPTER X

Religion in Society

Priest and Parish

The Parish of Our Lady of the Assumption of Atun Huaylas, in the Diocese of Huaraz, has its seat in the town of Huaylas. It includes not only the district of Huaylas but also those of Huallanca and Yuramarca. Although Mass is said on Sundays in the town and often in Santo Toribio, the rest of the parish, both in and out of the district, is visited by the parish priest only on special feast days. Many parishioners, therefore, seldom attend Mass and, consequently, find themselves "on their own" in the practice of religion.

The manner in which the parish is managed depends primarily upon the energies and ambitions of the parish priest. The priest in Huaylas at the time of the study was very enterprising: he attempted to reorganize the lay brotherhoods (*hermandades*), organized catechism classes throughout the district, attempted to readjust the major religious fiestas so that they would be more in accord with modern Catholic practice, and tried to stimulate devotion to saints whom he preferred.[1] Most important, from the point of view of Huaylinos, he showed initiative in leading the people of the district in a complete reconstruction of the church.

It was during this time that the diocese took direct control of church

[1] Such as Saint Joseph, patron of married persons, and the Virgin of Fatima, patroness of Catechism. His efforts in this regard met with little success.

property in the parish whereas it had formerly been handled by the parish priest. Although I never obtained a complete record of the amount of church property in Huaylas, it was the consensus of opinion that the church was the largest landholder in the district. The tax records in the Caja de Depósitos showed the church to be the biggest taxpayer. While many church properties have been held since colonial times, other parcels have been added occasionally through gifts, known as *buenas memorias* (good memories), bequeathed by parishioners. The deeds and titles to the older properties have been lost or destroyed over the course of time, and the church today finds itself in a position identical to that of many other property owners in Huaylas, since it cannot actually prove title to some of the land. This has led to innumerable lawsuits with renters, who, as usufructuaries (in some cases, for a generation or more), consider the properties their own.

The parish priest has always exercised an important role in Huaylas. Because of his position of leadership and the expectation of Huaylinos that the parish priest will take an active part in community life, it is not surprising that seven priests, over the past seventy years, have served as district mayors or councilmen.[2] Although his status as a religious functionary is unquestioningly accepted and respected by the community, the priest's behavior and interpretation of his role are subject to careful scrutiny.

How the priest is viewed by Huaylinos involves ideas that have wide currency in Peru and Latin America as well as in Huaylas. The complicating factors center about the belief that a basic conflict of interest often exists between the church organization and its representatives and the people. In consequence an anticlerical overtone pervades the relations of many with the clergy. The antagonism toward the church organization and individual priests should not, however, be taken to mean that the people are anti-Catholic, for this is rarely the case.

For some, anticlericalism has led to a feeling of skepticism over certain religious practices and the development of a neutral or "uncommitted" philosophy with regard to the Catholic church. Such persons often referred to themselves as "free thinkers," whereas the parish priest called them "renegades." These attitudes did not, however, keep the "free thinkers" or others holding anticlerical opinions from participating in the social areas of religious practice, for such persons often served as *padrinos* or even as *mayordomos* (fiesta sponsors).

[2] Two of the priests were themselves Huaylinos.

One aspect of anticlericalism is a deeply rooted opposition to outside control over the life of the community. In order to obtain the affection and good will of the people, the parish priest must overcome a latent reservoir of doubt in the public mind by demonstrating his sincerity and his interest in the people.

In the light of what has been said in the preceding chapters, we might suspect that in Huaylas the parish priest who wins the greatest support is the one who lends his prestige and enthusiasm to community activities and projects. The priest who opposed the keeping of an official register of vital statistics at the turn of the century is not remembered with much fondness, but his successor is remembered as a great man because he actively supported projects in the public interest. The priest in Huaylas at the time of this research was also judged on this basis. When he first arrived, he began the reconstruction of the church which is, like the library, the pride of Huaylas. He drew much support for his activities and enjoyed considerable prestige as a result of his work. But few persons mention the fact that he instituted catechism classes. His attempted reforms in the lay organizations accentuated existing factionalism and eventually led to a growing mistrust of his motives. Huaylinos interpreted these attempts at reform as mere capriciousness, if not as an overt attempt to seize power in the district. In the end, the people accused him of stealing their church bell, which disappeared, they say, at the time of the reconstruction, and of misappropriating church goods.[3] So Huaylinos say, "He was a good man; he rebuilt the church making it one of the most beautiful in the entire Callejón; but he was a very ambitious man and not the kind of person who should be the priest."

The upper-class men tend to be the most vocal exponents of anticlericalism, often basing their objections on their feeling that the women of the community and the people of lower-class status are "dominated" by the priest and follow him unquestioningly. "They think that the priest is a kind of God," said one man. The participation of women in church life is viewed in similar fashion, because women are thought to be

[3] Mentioned particularly were gifts of food from "the people of the United States" distributed by Catholic Relief Agencies. These charges were never substantiated but remained as rumors with some persons denying them and others giving them credence. At the time that these rumors were circulating widely, the priest was transferred to another parish and was not immediately replaced. When this occurred, the supporters of the priest sent a petition to the Bishop requesting his return.

"naturally prone to such activity," thus facilitating the priests' efforts to influence the women's religious organizations and participation in church life. Hence, many upper-class men consider it impolitic to participate very fully in church affairs. Those who do are regarded as being "too attached to the church," that is, somewhat deviant.

Many suspect that the priest uses his power to gain political, social, and economic advantages. Upper-class Huaylinos often remark that the priests are *muy metálicos* ("very metallic," implying that they are always thirsting for money). "These priests die wealthy men," said one prominent Huaylino, "and what do they need wealth for anyway? They have no families to support as we do. They just exploit the people."

The anticlerical attitude of many has also a strong sexual content, which is not without some basis in fact. Over the years, several parish priests in Huaylas not only have produced a number of offspring but have, at times, lived openly with women in the town. Jokes and stories about the sexual exploits of priests in Huaylas and other highland areas are common, and, no matter what their foundation happens to be in fact, they are accepted as reflections of actual situations. While not necessarily approving of this, many persons do not view the situation with alarm, for they incline to the opinion that a priest is subject to the same needs and desires as other men—and, like other men, some are able to check their impulses and others are not. Some persons, in fact, expressed the opinion that it was "abnormal" for priests to be required to live in celibacy. While these attitudes are by no means held by everyone, there can be little doubt that deviant behavior by members of the clergy is understood or excused on this basis.

The anticlerical attitudes and the bases for them help to explain some of the patterns of attendance and participation in church activities in Huaylas. Women, for example, usually outnumber men by at least five to one at any given church service. Although male attendance is limited, feminine participation begins at an early age and is actively encouraged by the schools. Schoolgirls, accompanied by their teachers, frequently march to church to hear Mass and walk in the procession. The boys, on the other hand, attend less often as a group. The greater emphasis given religious instruction in the girls' schools is seen in the fact that the priest made a special effort to teach the courses in religion there, but not at the boys' school. Further, the girls' schools had a small religious shrine, whereas the boys' schools did not.

This is not to say, however, that the males of the community do not have important, traditional roles in religious activities, for they do: as acolytes, as members of the *hermandad*,[4] Los Santos Varones (The Holy Men),[5] and as caretakers of particular saints or of the chapels that dot the rural countryside. With the exception of the acolytes, however, these are active roles only on appropriate feast days.

Middle- and upper-class women, on the contrary, are active in a number of religious societies: The Daughters of Mary, Our Lord of Miracles, The Sacred Heart of Jesus, The Virgin of Copacabana, Our Lord of Perpetual Help, Our Lady of Mount Carmel, The Virgin of the Rosary, and The Third Order of Saint Francis.[6] Another *hermandad*, that of Saint Elizabeth, with both male and female members, was organized within the past four years, but it does not have official status. Not all of the religious societies function with the same degree of cohesiveness, however, and some have almost ceased to exist because of lack of interest in the particular saint or because its members are busy with other activities. The priest said that one of the greatest problems of the *hermandades* was that their members were always quarreling among themselves. He described the situation as a *leonera* (a lion's den).

The *hermandades* are supposed to have monthly meetings with the parish priest to conduct their business. Each has a president, a secretary, and a treasurer, and each collects dues amounting to twenty centavos ($.005) a month from each member. The *hermandades* actually have little to do outside of planning the celebration of the Feast Days of the Saints to which they are devoted. As may be seen in the calendar of events (Table 38), the various *hermandades* pay some of the expenses connected with different fiestas, sharing the costs with the *devotos* (individual devotees of a saint).

The *hermandades* are quite impecunious. According to the parish priest, the only *hermandad* that owns any property is that of the Santos Varones, which owns two white burros used during the Palm Sunday processions. Branded with a cross, the burros are allowed to roam at will throughout the district during the year, eating where they please,

[4] This term refers to the lay societies or brotherhoods of both men and women in Huaylas. *Cofradía*, a term often used with this meaning elsewhere, designated land belonging to the church in Huaylas.

[5] A *hermandad* consisting of twelve men who take care of arrangements during Holy Week (Easter). The *hermandad* also goes under other names associated with Christ's Passion and the Stations of the Cross.

[6] Only the women's branch is active.

like sacred cows. Farmers generally allow the animals to graze for a short time in their fields before chasing them out. They are not supposed to be used for work, although it was noticed that the older burro bore the marks of having carried packs. In addition to this, the Virgin of the Assumption was given a "cantankerous" calf by a *devoto*, according to the priest.

Membership in lay organizations follows sex and class divisions. Except for the twelve members of the brotherhood of the Santos Varones, who are men of middle-class status, the majority of participants are upper- and middle-class urban women. Apart from the members of the *hermandades*, there are lay officials called *depositarios* (caretakers) and *procuradores* (procurators), who take care of specific saints, their wardrobes, litters, and donations. Most of the statues of the saints in the church are primarily in the care of upper-class women, although there are some middle-class men and women who also hold these positions. In all, there are twenty-two saints represented in the church. At least eight of them have no specific caretakers, and their feast days are not celebrated.

In the rural areas, there are twelve chapels devoted to various saints and thirteen to the Holy Cross. Each of these is in the charge of a *depositario*, who opens the chapel when there is to be a celebration there. For the most part, the *depositarios*, many of whom are men, are persons of middle- or lower-class status in the district. The presence of so many chapels in the rural areas bespeaks an active religious life outside of the urban area of Huaylas, apart from upper-class influence and often outside the control of the parish priest, although this independence appears to be diminishing.[7] Middle-class participation in the formal life of the church is not limited, however, to the role of caretaker or of organizer of minor fiestas. The majority of acolytes come from middle-class families, as do the catechism teachers in both urban and rural areas. Thus, the boys from Huaylas who attend seminary (usually four or five a year) come principally from this social class.

The Practice of Religion

The fiestas celebrated in the district of Huaylas are summarized in Table 38. There are also minor, private religious celebrations held from time to time at the request of a particular *devoto*. Only three of the

[7] In 1963 a loud-speaker system was purchased from donations, thus enabling Huaylinos "as far away as Iscap" to hear Mass on Sundays.

Table 38. Calendar of major religious events, 1960 to 1961, in the District of Huaylas

Time	Event
January 6	Epiphany. The adoration of the Magi. The story of the Three Wise Men enacted by costumed children's groups in the plaza in town and in Santo Toribio, followed by Mass; children accompanied by harp, violin, and mandolin music; primary orientation is religious. Sponsored by *devotos.* Participants number around 100 of rural, middle-class background, equal number of men and women. Expenses are probably under S/500.00, but may vary with devotee enthusiasm.
Pre-Lent	*Carnival.* Three days. Several *mayordomos* sponsor small fiestas at their homes, honoring the household shrine or saint. Special events sponsored include the *tumbamonte* * *tabladas,* * *condor racchi,** *carreras de cinta.** Social dancing, water, flour, and talcum powder "fights" occur everywhere in the streets. Primary orientation is secular and recreational. Participation widespread but primarily rural, middle-class groups, both sexes active. Expenses varied, minimum around S/1,200.00 per *mayordomo.* Dances in town attended by upper class, often for raising funds for some project.
Ash Wednesday	Mass is celebrated in the church, paid for by the church. Attendance small and of mixed social class, mostly women.
Passion Week	Feast of the Seven Sorrows of the Blessed Virgin Mary. The image of the Virgin is placed on the litter after being lowered from the altar (*bajada de la Virgin*) for the *alumbrado;* * Mass and *alumbrado* sponsored by *devotos.* Costs minimal and orientation is strictly religious. Participation mainly feminine, middle and upper class, 50–100 persons nightly. Arrival of Franciscan friar to assist parish priest during the week.
Palm Sunday	*Domingo de Ramos.* Mass held in the morning at which palm branches are given to the *notables* and others. Procession through streets in afternoon, with the image of Christ mounted on a white burro, lasting about 2 hours. Most of the costs and arrangements are undertaken by the Hermandad de los Santos Varones for the week. Music provided by a band. Participation general, all social classes and areas. Attendance at Mass over 400 and around 600 in procession. District authorities attend. Activities strictly religious.
Holy Wednesday	*Miercoles Santo.* Essentially same as above. Solemn High Mass attended by all *notables* and authorities who are given special seats in entry of the nave. Special service and procession in evening, ending at midnight. Approximately 600 persons at Mass and procession.
Maundy Thursday	*Jueves Santo.* Same as Wednesday.
Good Friday	*Viernes Santo.* Essentially same as previous days. Collection is taken from all present. Attendance largest of the entire year, over 1,000 at Mass. Special sermon in afternoon lasting 3 hours, attendance about 500. Evening vespers and procession attended by about 1,500, lasting to midnight.

* See Glossary.

Table 38 (cont.)

Time	Event
Holy Saturday	*Sábado de Gloria.* High Mass offered by parish priest. Attendance around 400 in church. No procession.
Easter Sunday	*Pascuas de Resurreción.* Mass and procession beginning at 4 A.M. About 300 present, mostly women of middle- and upper-class background from town. Mass said at 10 A.M. in Santo Toribio.
April 17	Virgin de Checta Cruz (Virgin of the Assumption, Shuyo). Mass, procession, fireworks, and dancing sponsored by a *mayordomo* and *barrio* of Shuyo officers; in some years, a band is hired. Fiesta is principally recreational. Participation limited largely to middle-class residents of Shuyo. Costs variable, between S/800.00–1,500.00.
April 26–28	*Fiesta de Santo Toribio* in Santo Toribio. Mass, procession on the 27th. Fireworks and music, some commercial activity. Orientation both religious and secular. Participation general in Santo Toribio, but some townspeople attend. Mostly middle and lower class. Expenses variable and spread among the *devotos* and *barrio* organizations.
May	The month of the Blessed Virgin Mary. Evening prayers and candles given by *devotos* throughout the month. Participation limited mainly to about 20 middle- and upper-class women from the town.
May 3–5	*Fiesta de Amankaes* (The Finding of the Holy Cross). Formerly celebrated only in Santo Toribio, it is now also observed in town, due to factionalism between these areas. The large crosses on the hills of Chupacoto and Amankaes (Huantar) are lowered and taken to the church and chapel of Pallpo respectively. Mass and processions at each on the 4th and 5th. Crosses returned to the sites on the 5th in the afternoon. There are *mayordomos* for the raising and lowering of each cross, whose expenses are about S/1,200.00 each (minimum). In town, participation limited to middle- and lower-class relatives, *compadres*, and friends of *mayordomos* except at Mass when some upper-class women are present. In Santo Toribio, pattern is similar. Music, dancing, rockets, and eating highlight activities; strong religious orientation but more time spent on recreational activities.
June	Month of the Sacred Heart of Jesus. The Hermandad of the Sacred Heart sponsors the *alumbrado* and prayers each evening.
June	Corpus Christi. Mass and procession given by the parish priest or a *devoto*, with girls' and boys' schools attending. A "queen" is chosen for the occasion. Principally upper-class participation. Orientation religious.
June	Feast Day of Sacred Heart of Jesus. Mass sponsored by the parish priest and Hermandad of the Sacred Heart. No *mayordomos*. Procession held. School children attend, coming from town and nearby *barrios*.
June 24	Feast Day of Saint John. Candles burned at household shrines. A special event is the *quemazón* or burning of a special cactus on the hillsides in the evening by young people and shepherds, since

Table 38 (cont.)

Time	Event
	St. John is patron of shepherds and cattle breeders. No *mayordomos*. No fiestas.
July 1–10	*Fiesta de Santa Isabel* (Visitation of Our Blessed Lady to her cousin Elizabeth and the Feast Day of Saint Elizabeth, July 2). This is the biggest fiesta of the year. Daily Mass and processions are sponsored in turn by the different *barrios* which raise money through public collections. Activities are organized by the Concejo and *barrio inspector*. Each *barrio* hires a band which arrives on the afternoon of the 6th for the "rompe" or start that evening. Each *barrio* also organizes its clowns (*pashas*), floats (*buques*), children's dance groups, and other special dance groups. From the 6th through the 9th, each night there is general dancing in the plaza till midnight. On the 7th, the children's dance group contest is sponsored by the Concejo. On the 8th, the Feast Day of Santa Isabel, the Mass is sponsored by the *barrio* of Delicados and all the district authorities attend. All the *barrios* accompany the procession. Hundreds of rockets and sometimes other fireworks set off daily. Contest winners are announced on the 9th and the bands leave on the 10th. Participation by sex and social class is general throughout the district. Many persons return from Lima for the occasion. Expenses are shared by the *barrio* residents, about S/15,000.00 per *barrio*. Primary orientation is recreational and commercial, since over 100 merchants come from outside Huaylas and set up stands in the streets. The separatist factions in Quecuas and Huayrán have a similar fiesta in Santo Toribio. Separate celebrations occur in Tambo and San Lorenzo. Almost the entire population participates at one time or another.
July 16	Our Lady of Mount Carmel. Mass and procession sponsored by the Hermandad de Nuestra Señora de Monte Carmelo. Participation limited to middle- and upper-class women. Strictly religious in orientation.
July 31–August 1	*Mamanchic Taripé* (commemorating the Finding of the Virgin of the Assumption, the Patroness of Huaylas, in 1789).* On the evening of the 31st, vespers are held followed by fireworks and dancing with the band to a place on the road called Misa Rurana ("place where Mass is said"). Lasts to midnight and after. Participation of people from Yacup, Delicados and Shuyo, and Santo Toribio. All social classes and sexes. *Mayordomos* and *devotos* are usually of upper-class standing. On the 1st, Mass and procession held in the morning. Dancing and banquets held at houses of *devotos*. Principally upper-class participation from town. Orientation religious, but most time is devoted to recreational aspects. Total expenses around S/3,000.00, but variable from year to year.

* An account of this event is recounted by Rodriquez (1958) and also by Veliz Alba, 1947:124–125.

Table 38 (cont.)

Time	Event
August 12–14	The Vigil of the Assumption of the Blessed Virgin Mary. The Host is exhibited for adoration. Daily Mass, vespers, communion and confession held. Sponsored by *Devotos* and parish priest. Strictly religious orientation.
August 15–16	Assumption of the Blessed Virgin Mary, Patroness of Atun Huaylas. High Mass and procession held on the 15th with the attendance of the district authorities. About 300 participants, all social classes, principally from town, Yacup, and Shuyo. In the afternoon, the Concejo and *barrios* sponsor a "sierra"-style bull-fight.* About 2,000 persons watch and participate. Some dancing, much drinking. On the 16th, the events are the same, but Mass is attended by fewer persons. Bullfights in afternoon have same participation. All social classes, districtwide. No *mayordomos*. Expenses met by *barrios* and by persons to whom the bulls are dedicated, each spending from S/200.00 to S/400.00 each. There are usually 18 such sponsors. Orientation is primarily recreational.
September 14	Exaltation of the Holy Cross. Fiestas are sponsored by *mayordomos* at the rural chapels dedicated to the Holy Cross. Some have no fiesta however. Participation is in rural areas, almost exclusively among lower- and middle-class relatives and friends of the *mayordomos*. Expenses variable, around S/1,000.00 for each *mayordomo*. Mass may be sponsored by a *devoto*. Orientation is, however, principally recreational. Dancing and eating.
September 24	Our Lady of Mercy (Our Lady of Ransom). Mass sponsored by a *devoto* in town, or by the veterans' organization which sometimes also sponsors a bullfight as on August 15th and 16th. Participation very limited and expenses nil (if no bullfight). In the sector of Quenti in Quecuas, there is a larger fiesta, with a Mass and procession sponsored by a *devoto* or *mayordomo*. No estimate of expenses. With no bullfights, orientation is religious, but strong recreational aspect as well.
October	The Month of the Holy Rosary. The Hermandad del Santo Rosario sponsors daily prayers. *Alumbrado* in the church. Mass and procession on the final Sunday of the month. Participation limited to upper-class women principally.
October 22	Virgin of Perpetual Help. Mass and procession sponsored by *devoto*.

* For this, the bulls (and cows) are brought down from the *puna* regions. Only the most *bravos* (fierce) ones are selected. The animals are sent into the ring decorated with cloth trappings which the men try to take off as they play at bullfighting. The animals always "win" what is expected to be a humorous contest in which the bulls leave the field without a scratch. This contrasts greatly with the dangerous bullbaiting practiced elsewhere in the sierra. For a dramatic fictionalized account of the latter, see José María Arguedas' classic, *Yawar Fiesta*, n.d.

Table 38 (cont.)

Time	Event
October 28	Our Lord of Miracles. A Mass and procession are sponsored by the Hermandad del Señor de los Milagros, with very limited participation, almost exclusively upper-class women, about 50. Strictly religious orientation. Some women wear the purple habit of the cult for the month.
November 1	All Saints' Day. Mass said in church by parish priest. Participation light.
November 2	All Souls' Day. Mass celebrated in church and special ceremonies held in cemetery for individual families. Families decorate graves with flowers and prayers are said. Primarily religious orientation in the activities of the two days.
December 24–25	Christmas Eve. High Mass celebrated at midnight (Misa de Gallo). As many as 500 persons attend, all social classes and many children, as members of the catechism classes come dressed as "shepherds" and have a special ceremony at the image of the Virgin Mary which rests on a litter. Afterwards, upper-class families often entertain their friends at home with hot chocolate. Principally a religious tone to the events of the day. Most families prepare "nacimientos" or manger scenes, which they display in their homes. Some Christmas cards are exchanged. On Christmas Day, upper-class families have family dinners.

fiestas simultaneously incorporate a broad cross section of the public as participants: the strictly religious celebrations during Holy Week (Semana Santa), the Fiesta of Saint Elizabeth in early July, and the celebration of the Patroness of Huaylas, the Virgin of the Assumption, in the middle of August. All of the other fiestas are smaller and are celebrated by particular sectors of the population.

The various minor fiestas wax and wane so far as the interest they engender over the years is concerned. For example, according to informants, the celebration of the Exaltation of the Holy Cross in September has declined drastically from the time, two or three decades ago, when it was a major event throughout the district. Other fiestas reported to be declining included those of Our Lady of Mount Carmel, Epiphany, and Carnival. But, while these have lost in importance over the last several decades, others have gained in popularity: the fiestas of the Virgin of the Assumption of Shuyo (celebrated in the *barrio* only), the Finding of the Holy Cross (called the fiesta of Our Lord of Amankaes), Mamanchic Taripé, and Our Lord of Miracles. The Fiesta of the Finding of the Holy Cross in May is celebrated mainly by persons of the middle and lower classes, the upper-class townspeople defining it as pertaining to them. The growth of this fiesta in the town was stimulated primarily by the schism between the town and Santo Toribio, which, prior to 1950, was the only place to celebrate it. The Fiesta of the Mamanchic Taripé (the Finding of the Virgin of the Assumption), however, as well as that of August 15 (the Fiesta of the Virgin of the Assumption), are celebrated by a broad cross section of the populace, even though they are sponsored by members of the upper class.

The fiestas recorded in the calendar are classified as either primarily religious in orientation or primarily recreational (secular), despite their religious origins. Those feast days in which the primary activity takes place at the church with the participation of the parish priest and with little or no feasting, drinking, dancing, or commercial activity are classified as religious in orientation. In these, the Mass, procession, vespers, or prayer services are the principal, if not the only, events. Eight of the fiestas are classified as primarily recreational and secular in orientation. By this it is understood that, while these events do have a religious aspect, and sometimes a very important one (as in the celebration of the Feast of Saint Elizabeth or the Feast of the Patroness of Huaylas), the celebration is primarily associated with other special events and activities, and these events attract many more participants than the religious ceremonies.

The two types of fiesta may be further differentiated with respect to costs and participants. Secular and recreational fiestas involve relatively high expenses, a large number of participants, a broad cross section of the population, and equal numbers of men and women as participants. The strictly religious fiesta, on the other hand, is generally characterized by a relatively low cost per participant, a small number of participants, a closer identification with social class or clique, and a greater number of women than men as participants.[8]

The expenses of the *devotos* or *mayordomos* of strictly religious fiestas include payment of the priest, payment of the cantor (if there is one), and the purchase of flowers, candles, and rockets, which are considered necessary for the celebration. Fiestas with strong secular and recreational elements involve much higher expenditures because of

---

[8] The Holy Week celebration is an exception with regard to the last three characteristics.

the sponsor's obligations outside of the church. These may include several meals for his guests, music, great quantities of alcoholic beverages, fireworks of various types, and sundry other things.

There are five recreational fiestas during the course of the year for which these expenses are underwritten primarily by *mayordomos*. While exact data were not obtained for all of these fiestas, the maximum expense a *mayordomo* has to meet does not normally exceed S/2,000 ($74.00), and in meeting it he is usually aided by his relatives and *compadres*. Although this is a considerable sum in view of the fact that most residents of the district do not have very high monetary incomes, it can by no means be regarded as extravagant, for elsewhere fiesta costs for a *mayordomo* may be many times higher.[9]

There are two principal reasons for serving as a *mayordomo*. The first is to increase one's prestige in the community, and the second is to solicit or give thanks for some spiritual help, particularly in a case of illness. Most *mayordomos* volunteer for the position a year in advance, often during the time of the celebration, thus allowing time for adequate preparation. One of the duties of the *depositarios* and *hermandades* is the recruiting of *mayordomos*, for unless suitable ones are chosen the fiesta will not be celebrated properly, or else they themselves will have to underwrite the expenses.

Despite the fact that the position of *mayordomo* is assumed voluntarily, some have regretted their decisions and have been reluctant to meet the costs involved, as occurred in one instance during Carnival in 1961. The *mayordomo* sponsoring a neighborhood fiesta (*cortamonte*) was reported to have cut down the *monte* (tree), which had been planted in the street outside of his house, and to have cursed himself for having been so foolish as to have accepted the obligation.

The two fiestas that involve the greatest expenses, those of Saint Elizabeth (in July) and the Virgin of the Assumption (in August) are organized in such a way that financial responsibility is widely shared. The fact that only two fiestas (that of Saint Elizabeth and that of the Epiphany) involve the participation of costumed dance groups helps to reduce the total cost of the fiestas in Huaylas. In contrast to many areas in Peru, where the special costumes used must often be rented or the

---

[9] Castillo, Castillo, and Revilla (1963:91–94) report that a *mayordomo's* expenses in Carcas, Ancash, may amount to S/160,000.00 ($600.00) requiring the *mayordomo* to mortgage his land to meet the costs. This does not occur in Huaylas.

dancers themselves hired, the special garments for the Huaylas fiestas are usually homemade and owned by the celebrants.

As was noted, special emphasis is placed on the role of upper-class men in the Holy Week celebrations. During the Fiesta of the Assumption, it is also the custom for *notables* to attend church and afterwards to lead the parade of the *barrios* to the *plaza de toros* (bull ring), as the soccer field is called for the occasion. *Notables* and authorities who wish to do so, on the second day of the Fiesta of the Assumption, ride to the *"plaza de toros"* on their best horses, or on borrowed horses, waving to the crowd and accepting bouquets of flowers and small gifts. Not all of the *notables*, however, engage in this, and, on the occasion observed, several persons of middle-class status took part.

It is said of Huaylinos that they are *muy católico* (very Catholic). Indeed, one of the few Protestants in Huaylas once told me that it was almost impossible to make conversions there because the people were very fanatical in their religious faith.[10] Roman Catholicism is the official religion of the country and is "protected" by the government, its *doctrina* being taught in the public schools.

Of the seven sacraments of the Catholic church, baptism is, without a doubt, the most important to the average Huaylino. It is considered an absolute necessity for everyone. The age of baptism, however, is extremely variable, some being baptized in their first year and others as late as their tenth year. If the child is healthy, most parents defer the ceremony until such time as convenient for relatives and godparents to be present for the ceremony and a family fiesta. Since the godparents of baptism are considered by Huaylinos to be the most important ones acquired during a lifetime, the responsibility is taken quite seriously by all parties.

In contrast to baptism, the sacrament of the Eucharist, or Holy Communion, is taken by relatively few in Huaylas and then usually on the feast day of a saint to whom one is particularly devoted. The sacrament of confirmation is taken during adolescence after special instruction in catechism classes. The schools and the parish priest were responsible for organizing the observance of this sacrament during the time of study. Many of the teachers served as godparents for the occasion. Most married persons are married in both civil and religious

[10] Adams (1959:79–80) states that in Muquiyauyo no mestizo had been converted to Protestantism.

ceremonies, these being followed by a fiesta at the home of the bride and groom. As with communion, relatively few Huaylinos concern themselves with the sacrament of confession [11] and penance, and, finally, many Huaylinos are buried without benefit of clergy, particularly in the outlying rural areas.

During the course of the year, aside from the special occasions, Mass is said once a week on Sundays in town and, if the priest is so inclined, also in Santo Toribio and in Iscap. The Sunday attendance at any one of these places does not usually exceed 100 persons, the vast majority of them women. The benches in the Huaylas church could seat only 200 comfortably, and there were but two small benches, located behind the rest and at right angles to the altar, reserved especially for men. With the exception of perhaps forty or fifty who are directly involved in church affairs, most women do not attend Mass more than once a month. Yet when the parish was left without a priest for several months Huaylinos bemoaned the fact that they couldn't "hear Mass" or receive the other sacraments.

It is also the women who make the greatest effort to adhere to such things as dietary restrictions. They strongly identify themselves with the Virgin Mary. They were frequently reminded in sermons (particularly at Easter) that a woman's life is full of pain, and in a spirit of penitence or thanksgiving many women wear the purple habit of Our Lord of Miracles or the *escapulario* of the Sacred Heart of Jesus or of Our Lady of Mount Carmel for certain periods during the year. Despite intense devotion on the part of a few, the majority of Huaylinos, irrespective of social class or other distinctions, consider the formal practice of religion a duty or even something owed in fulfillment of a vow or to guarantee the attainment of an aspiration.

Thus, except for the most devout, an attitude of calm aloofness often prevails among the congregation. While many genuflect and cross themselves at the proper times during the Mass, others merely pattern their behavior after that of those who seem to know what they are about. Many do nothing. Indeed, there were times when it appeared that those who gave the proper responses were in error. Consequently, it was not surprising to find that the conduct displayed in church is

[11] Many persons take the opportunity to confess at Easter time, when the priest and the visiting Franciscan friar urge the people to do so. Many wait to make their confessions to the Franciscan because he is considered to be "more religious" and because there is greater anonymity.

quite varied. The following excerpts from my field notes illustrate some of the differing patterns of behavior by social class, age, and sex, which were observed during Holy Week and on Good Friday when church attendance was by far the greatest of the entire year.

The Mass continued and the men stood and sat down at different intervals. While sitting, I saw at least three persons with their eyes closed and heads drooping, sleeping lightly. The "notable persons" for the most part maintained very noncommittal expressions. . . . A good deal of the time, many were gazing at the floor or merely straight ahead. . . . Some looked toward the altar with occasional flashes of interest, but rarely. In contrast, the women and other men about us gazed fixedly at the priest although most wore the similar (apparently) emotionless expression. Some stretched to see better. The poorer women sat on the floor, behind or alongside the pews. These persons usually remained in their sitting position throughout the ceremony unless necessary to kneel. Many of the poorer women wore no head covering although the majority seemed to wear woolen shawls. . . . Some of the women had their faces almost completely hidden by their shawls. One woman on the floor behind the notable persons was crying throughout the Mass. . . .

The children, boys in particular, (were) at times playing with the candles, throwing wax balls and pinching each other. They were reprimanded only when they got in the way of things. Faces of the adults were solemn, seldom smiling.[12]

Because of the small number of benches, more than half of the members of the congregation must accommodate themselves as best they can. Lower-class members of the congregation generally sit on the floor or at the base of the side altars, while the rest who have no seats prefer to stand. At Mass, on Good Friday:

I noticed . . . for the first time, that many men were seated in the front pews with their families. Many of the men were holding infant children. There were a number of *campesinos* [13] also seated in the front pews. . . . There were a number of well-dressed women present.[14] Generally they had brought their own prayer stools.[15] The wealthier women wear black lace

[12] Doughty, Field Notes, April 14, 1960: 1–4.
[13] Middle- and lower-class farmers.
[14] Upper and middle class.
[15] The prayer stools are specially constructed with high backs and low seats so that one can kneel comfortably on them, resting the elbows on the flat top surface of the back. They are used only by middle- and upper-class women, particularly the latter. Social status is often reflected by the elegance of the prayer stool, some

scarfs, black dresses and shoes with black stockings. They also carry . . .
missals . . . and a rosary. The poorer women do not often have these things
and generally wear long black shawls which they wrap about the lower
half of their heads, covering their mouths, ears, and shoulders completely.
Old women come . . . (in) dresses, generally ankle-length, and long shawls
which cover their heads like a hood with one end being thrown across the
front of the chest from right to left shoulder. . . . They are treated with
respect and . . . seem to participate in all the singing (and responses),
knowing the verses from memory. The older women usually find seats.
(Most of the lower-class people) . . . sat at the base of the side altars
around the walls or else sat on the floor in the aisle next to the pews and
behind them, even though their view of the ceremony was completely
blocked by someone standing in front of them. Some of these women sit
sideways at the altar, rarely looking toward the proceedings. A large
number of these persons do not participate in the singing. They are
frequently holding small children next to them. . . . (One woman) held a
small child in her lap and rocked it gently to and fro. She and the child
were wrapped in her dark blue shawl. The child was also swathed in a red
homespun blanket. She nursed it when it awoke, covering her breast and
the child partially with the shawl. She was seated behind the rear pew and
never once looked at the ceremony for over an hour, neither did she sing
or pray aloud. . . .[16]

At night the procession moved through the cobbled streets. It was a
solemn experience for most—heightened by the atmosphere created by
the flickering candles which everyone carried, and by the repetitive,
sorrowful singing: ". . . Mercy Lord, mercy Lord, if my sins are
many, your bounty is greater."

There were many children in the procession and the (little boys) were
constantly underfoot—nudging their way in and out, between the adults.
They moved about in groups of three and four, wearing their little brown
ponchos and carrying stubby candles which were not always lit. One time,
two or three small boys found their way to the litter and walked along
underneath it, smiling mischievously that no one was taking notice. . . .
(Accompanying the litter of the Virgin Mary) there were about one
hundred persons being led in a prolonged series of verses about . . . the

---

of which have upholstered seats and are made of nicely stained and finished wood.
Most, however, have simple wicker bottoms and are made of unfinished wood
with the owner's initials carved on them, since they are often left at the church.
Some families also have their own marked benches in the church.

[16] Doughty, Field Notes, April 15, 1960:3.

Virgin Mary . . . during the Passion of Christ. After the leaders sang a verse, the women and some men joined in the chorus. The man leading the song was a member of the *hermandad*. He wore sandals and a green shirt with dark blue pants; his hair was uncombed.[17] He sang in a loud voice which at times bordered on a shout as he had difficulty in reaching many high notes and the veins in his neck stood out sharply as he sang. He read the verses from a weathered notebook in which they were handwritten; the pages were turning brown with age. Another man looked over his shoulder as they stumbled along singing. The second man held a candle for the first to read by although he sang too (at times). Another, much older man with a handle-bar mustache flecked with grey, and wearing a brown poncho sang along although he did not read from the book. He apparently knew most of the verses by heart for he sang in a loud, wavering voice, faltering occasionally to recall the words as he heard the others sing them. . . .[18]

Thus, a wide spectrum of moods is reflected by the people. There are those who demonstrate an intense and constant interest in religious events, but the majority of Huaylinos in all social classes do not.

The social prestige to be gained from selective participation in religious affairs is considerable, irrespective of one's social class. Gifts to the church of any size seldom go unnoticed and are usually brought to the attention of the public by the parish priest. On one occasion the priest read to the congregation the names of contributors and the amount of their individual contributions. Those who donate such things as an altar or other large material object to the church invariably have their names inscribed on them.

Many persons, nevertheless, depend upon the saints for the blessings of health, prosperity, and success in one field or another. Such assistance is sought through prayer and devotion or through invoking divine intervention in other ways. During the fiesta of the Finding of the Holy Cross in May, a number of persons avail themselves of the opportunity to have the small glass case containing a bust of Christ (Our Lord of Amankaes) held over their heads so that they may ask for some special favor, the petitioner later depositing a few centavos in the alms box as an offering. Again, at the time of the Fiesta of the

[17] In all processions, as in church, both men and women take off their hats. Thus, middle- and lower-class women, upon entering a church, leave their heads uncovered, just as the men do. Upper-class women usually cover their heads with a scarf or shawl, as noted. No one wears a hat in church.

[18] Doughty, Field Notes, April 15, 1960:4–5.

Virgin of the Assumption, others go through the ceremony known as the Manto de la Virgen (the Virgin's mantle) in which persons desiring assistance cover their heads with the robes of the Virgin. A godparent, specially chosen for the occasion, holds a lighted candle in one hand and rests his other hand on the petitioner, while a third person (or the priest) recites a short prayer. On feast days, some persons in moments of great fervor caress the feet or robes of the statues or carry their litters during processions. Devotees and those who feel that they have received some divine blessing often pin money (in bills) to the robes of the saint's statue, sometimes during the course of a procession.

Unusual occurrences are often attributed to miraculous or divine intervention. At Christmas time, for example, the small images of the Niño Jesus (the Child Jesus), which are placed in the *nacimientos* or manger scenes set up by many families in their homes, are often considered to be "miraculous." A story is told of the Child Jesus and a parish priest of many years ago. The priest was ill-mannered, drunken, and not well liked in Huaylas. After the Misa de Gallo (midnight Mass on Christmas Eve), when this particular priest went to pick up the statue of the Christ Child so that the people could kiss it, the Holy Child reportedly turned away from the corrupt priest, thus indicating his disgust. It is said that the priest died shortly afterward.

At the Christmas Eve Misa de Gallo in 1961, which I attended, the parish priest who had been having personal difficulties with various townspeople asked me to photograph the distribution of powdered milk and flour [19] to the children of the catechism class. However, the flash synchronization of my camera, which had not been working properly, failed to function and the pictures were lost. When I recounted this to one of the prominent lay religious leaders in town, she said that it was because the Christ Child did not want me to take photographs for "that evil priest." Thus, the hand of God is felt by many to enter directly into the day-to-day life of the community.

There are few Huaylinos who do not think of themselves as reasonably good Catholics. Few, in fact, could envision themselves or their neighbors professing any other religion. Protestants are generally considered "odd," although it is often conceded that the *evangelistas* (as they are called) are honest and abstain from smoking and drinking. This abstention is considered vaguely good, but unnatural. There are,

[19] A gift of Caritas, the Catholic Charity. The food is obtained from U.S. Government surpluses.

consequently, very few Protestants in Huaylas (perhaps fifty members of the Assemblies of God and Jehovah's Witnesses) and only one is of upper-class status. One Protestant said that it was very difficult for him to practice his faith because of the tremendous social pressure to which he was subjected. Some Protestants have constructed a small chapel in Santo Toribio.

The implications of renouncing the Roman Catholic faith in a high-land community such as Huaylas are serious. It means giving up *compadres* and responsibilities to *ahijados* and also foregoing the many private and public fiestas of the Catholic religion with all their recreational and social aspects, thus cutting oneself off from a large number of the basic social relationships of the society.

It has already been noted that, because it is the official religion of Peru, Catholicism is taught in the public schools, and attendance at church is expected of school children at special times during the year. In addition, overtly anti-Protestant attitudes have been fostered. Members of the catechism classes, carrying *faroles* (fancy tissue-paper lanterns) through the streets of the town on the night of the Mamanchic Taripé in 1960, shouted such things as "Death to Protestantism." In fact, perhaps because both are roundly attacked from the pulpit, some persons even regarded Protestantism as an aspect of Communism.[20]

A funeral in Huaylas is a solemn occasion, whether it is a first-class or a second-class burial or one without a priest. A wake is usually held before the interment, and friends, relatives, and neighbors of the deceased assemble and pass the night talking quietly and sipping an occasional glass of vermouth or pisco[21] to keep away the cold. Often on the death of a very small child, a group of the older children will carry the coffin from the home to the cemetery. The priest accompanies the mourners to the cemetery only in a "first-class" funeral—which costs twice as much as a "second-class" burial. Although the wealthy generally bury their dead in special niches and mausoleums made of brick, a new style in Huaylas, the coffins of the poor are simply buried in the ground with the graves marked by a small wooden

---

[20] This has some interesting consequences for the United States and its citizens, since most rural Peruvians, Huaylinos included, think that almost everyone in the United States is an *evangelista* or *adventista* (Seventh Day Adventist). Thus, North Americans are suspect on these grounds, as being missionaries and attempting to undermine the foundations of the society—just like the Communists. See Doughty, 1961.

[21] Often donated by the mourners to the family.

cross. Two persons in Huaylas offer undertaking services, renting funeral paraphernalia and sometimes assisting with arrangements.

As a sign of mourning (*estar de luto*), those particularly close to the deceased wear black suits or dresses, shoes, stockings, shawls, ties, and sometimes hats. Mourning is usually worn for a year, although there are a number of persons who have continued to wear it for as many as four years. After the period of deep mourning, many men simply wear a black tie, arm band, or patch on their shirt pockets to indicate that they are in *medio luto* (partial mourning or second mourning). Relatives not of the immediate family of the deceased also express their sorrow in this way.

For the lower class, a complete change in wardrobe for mourning is expensive, and many cannot afford it. Thus, only the more well-to-do wear complete mourning. It is said that ponchos used to be dyed black for this purpose, but now they are not. It is common to see people dressed in mourning in Huaylas, the women being most noticeable, for they wear full mourning more often and for longer periods than do the men as a general rule.

The Fiesta of Saint Elizabeth

The fiesta of Saint Elizabeth is one of the best-organized events of the calendar year in Huaylas.[22] About a month in advance of the fiesta, the *barrio inspector, brazos,* and *repartidores de aguas,* together with the family heads in each *barrio,* meet to plan their participation in the fiesta. The skit to be performed by the dance group (called *conjunto Incaico*) is planned and the children selected to play the roles. Each *barrio* selects a committee to hire a brass band and to handle the arrangements for feeding and housing the band members for the four days that they are in Huaylas.

To cover the *barrio* expenses during the fiesta, the *inspector* and the *repartidores de aguas* solicit money or promises to supply food or drink from all the families residing in their *barrios.* In addition, everyone who owns and cultivates land in each *barrio* is contacted and asked for a contribution. Accompanying the solicitations is a veiled threat that if the owner or renter of the land does not make a contribution in proportion to his landholdings and the extent to which he makes use of the irrigation system, he will be denied the use of irrigation water. In

---

[22] A brief description of the fiesta is to be found in Toor, 1949:164.

essence, then, the collection of money is a graduated tax. Those persons (particularly of the upper class) who own more land are obliged to make contributions to several *barrios* if they have land in them.

As plans are laid for the formal aspects of the fiesta celebration, the young men of the *barrios* begin to practice with their bullwhips,[23] which they carry when they disguise themselves as *pashas* (masked clowns) in multicolored robes. Each man who intends to be a *pasha* must register with the *barrio inspector* or the person who has been given the responsibility for them. The number of *pashas* representing each *barrio* may vary from twenty to as many as sixty.

Two weeks before the fiesta, a meeting is called at the office of the *Concejo*, of all the *barrio inspectores* and their *brazos* with the mayor and the councilman in charge of "spectacles." Here, many decisions are made: the days on which each *barrio* will sponsor the Mass and procession (with the exception of July 8, which is the day traditionally reserved for the *barrio* of Delicados); the time to be allotted for each band and dance group during the contest held between *barrios* on July 7; the kinds of prizes or diplomas to be awarded on July 9 to the winners of the contest; and the order in which the members of the different *barrios* will accompany the procession of Saint Elizabeth and the Virgin Mary on July 8 (on that day, each *barrio* and its band accompanies the procession part of the way around the plaza). Lots are drawn to decide the order of appearance of the *barrios*. The *inspectores* also agree to try to control disorderly conduct and report any persons who violate municipal ordinances. The program of the fiesta, then, is drawn up by the *barrio* and district officials. The *Concejo* contracts a printer in Caraz to make several hundred copies of it for distribution at the time of the fiesta.[24]

All *pashas* are registered, and it is usually agreed that if any are caught stealing or fighting, the *barrio* officials will assist in the capture of the offenders.[25] The intense inter-*barrio* rivalry was, at one time, the major cause of fighting and disorders during the fiesta. While large-scale violence has stopped, the rivalry remains, becoming manifest in

[23] These have several names such as *chicote*, thunderer, and *látigo*.

[24] For the fiesta, the *barrios* sometimes publish their own programs, emphasizing their own activities and mentioning the names of the *barrio* officials and of all those involved in their skits.

[25] Because the *pashas* wear disguises, it is feared that they could perpetrate disorders or steal things from the street vendors without being identified. This, apparently, was a serious problem at one time.

the interchanges at the meeting to plan the fiesta and, later, during the contests.[26]

The problem of selecting contest winners for the best band and best children's dance group has never been satisfactorily resolved and each year new solutions are sought. One year all the participating *barrios* received "diplomas de honor"; another year I was asked to head a board made up of visitors to Huaylas, to select the winner; and a third year three leading district officials (thought to be above reproach) were asked to serve in the same capacity. Each time fault was found with the result. In the last instance mentioned, in 1964, the board decided that there was a tie for first place in the dance contest. One of the co-winners, defiantly, with band playing and with loud *guajes* from the *pashas,* marched past the reviewing stand, snubbing the district officials and rejecting all of the rewards the group was to receive in a grand gesture of contempt for the decision. This caused a great turmoil. Tempers flared and considerable animosity was expressed toward the offending *barrio* whose leaders were accused of being *envidiosos* and *egoistas.*

The contest organization, however, is of relatively recent origin, having emerged in response to the problems posed annually by the fiesta. The following article recounts this development:

Within a few days the celebration of the fiesta of the Patroness of the Harvests, Saint Elizabeth, will have its start: the vernacular fiesta in which all the district, regardless of locality or person, participates.

In the olden days, the fiesta was held on the second of July, the day of the Catholic calendar commemorating the Visitation of the Virgin Mary to her cousin, Saint Elizabeth. In those days, the whole district divided into two groups, the "mistis" and the "indios"; they filled the plaza and streets of the town where in their overwhelming enthusiasm a fierce battle between the two sides broke out, resulting in wounds and even deaths. The authorities who felt themselves incapable of stopping these fights chose to decree that the "indios" celebrate independently from the "whites"[27] on the eighth, hoping in this manner to avert the brawls. But with the passage of time the festivity of the "indios" reached the greatest heights, the fiesta of the "whites" diminishing to the point of extinction.

[26] The intense, often bitter, feuding in Santo Toribio continues, however, between the faction which wishes to celebrate the fiesta apart from the town and the group which does not. In 1961 a serious fight took place and several men were sent to jail for a few days in Caraz.

[27] Also called *"mistis."*

Alone, the "indios," being accustomed to the fights, divided themselves into two sides, "itzoc" and "allanca" (the upper ones and the lower ones), who for some insignificant thing would give each other a good thrashing. This form of celebration persisted up until a short time ago because there was no authority that could suppress or vary it. It is remembered that a certain *gobernador* attempted to eliminate the bullwhips. Thus it was that on the first day (of the fiesta) all of the disguised ones (*pashas*) came with little handkerchiefs in hand, dancing in front of the band, and the *gobernador* raced about the plaza flushed with his triumph. The *pashas*, however, felt their manhood deflated and said that they had been like "jerks" with their little handkerchiefs. On the next day hundreds of *pashas* invaded the town, each one carrying his best thunderer, so that the fiesta was celebrated as it should be. They gave each other the infamous thrashing. They looked for the cause of the ridiculous affair but did not find him. Mr. *Gobernador* and his lieutenant greeted the dawn in Socoyaco,[28] where they remained until the fiesta was over.

On many occasions incidents have been aired before the judicial authority (courts); and how many brave men have passed a little time in the jails of Caraz and Huaraz! Nevertheless, the fights did not diminish.

Then in the year 1934, the *alcalde*, Don Demetrio Sarmiento, and his secretary, Don Aurelio Ardiles, conceived the idea of changing it by suggesting the organization of contests between the six *barrios* in music and dancing, with prizes to be offered by the municipality. The idea [was agreed upon] and the affair was a success. Since that year and through the following ones we see the interest of each *barrio* in preparing its dance groups to celebrate the Fiesta of Saint Elizabeth.

The *barrios* of Huayrán and Quecuas celebrate in the Campiña and, on the other hand, the *barrio* of Iscap comes down to the capital of the district with all its celebrants to precede the others, celebrating on July 2, the true day.

The fiesta is the best that is celebrated in the district since it attracts a large number of visitors. Many days before, the principal plaza becomes an immense field of commercial activity with the coming of ambulatory merchants, sutlers, photographers, etc. So the town is packed with people eager to watch the parade of the *Incaicos, pashas, caballitos, danzantes, chapetones, pallas,*[29] etc., who with their orchestras, bands, bullwhips, and shouts at one time offer an extraordinary spectacle.

This year the authorities in charge of the organization have neglected to

---

[28] A place in the *barrio* of Tambo, farthest from town.
[29] Names of the various costumed groups, representing in order the Incas, clowns, Spanish conquerors on horseback, dancers, the haughty Spaniards, and Indian maidens.

take care of it in time. The *barrios* alone, headed by their respective *inspectores* and water distributors have had to react a little late in order to honor the Patroness of their crops and not forget the custom so deeply rooted in the people. So we hope that the fiesta be good and that our visitors enjoy themselves very much.[30]

Preparations are also made by the public in general. During the weeks prior to the fiesta, truckloads of supplies are brought to the stores to be sold during the fiesta. These include hundreds of cases of beer and other beverages and manufactured articles of all kinds. Many families receive packages from their relatives in Lima. In late June, Huaylinos who live outside the district begin returning for the fiesta —it becomes a kind of "homecoming" day. The traffic record kept by the police in Huaylas in 1960 indicated that between June 21 and July 8 of that year, some 657 persons came into the district for the fiesta.[31] The fiesta is a time for reunions with family and friends.

The first days of the fiesta are relatively calm, with the *barrios* designated to sponsor events on those days attending Mass and accompanying the procession. The evening of July 6, called the *rompe* (the real start of the fiesta), marks the first widespread public participation and is purely social in nature. On this night, three *barrios*— Delicados, Yacup, and Shuyo—prepare floats (*buques*) in the shape of boats (said to represent the naval vessels of the war with Chile in 1879), which are carried to the plaza on the shoulders of many men. The people of the *barrios* follow, dancing with their band. The dancing and merriment reach great heights as the floats are carried through the streets and, eventually, to the plaza which is crowded with 2,000 or more persons, many of whom sit along the sidewalks to watch or rest. Young men arrange to meet their "dates" (*parejas*) to dance during the evening. Huaylinos who have returned from Lima and members of the upper class "disguise themselves" (*disfrazarse*) by dressing like everyone else: the men wear ponchos, high-crowned hats made of *jipe*, and white woolen scarves covering the lower halves of their faces; the women wear long skirts and often *polleras*, shawls, and hats. The men

---

[30] *Atun Huaylas*, June 30, 1952:1–2 (my translation).

[31] This figure is minimal, since the police neglected to record all of the arrivals at this time. The list included those who arrived in commercial vehicles and not those who came by private means of transportation or who may have walked or ridden horseback up the hill from the Huallanca railroad station. I estimated that about 1,000 persons returned for the fiesta.

usually carry bottles of *pisco,* vermouth, or *washco* in their back pockets.[32]

Couples lock arms and, raising handkerchiefs (or bottles) high in the air, dance around the plaza amid the great noise of the fiesta—three or four bands playing simultaneously and frequent *guajes.* Drinks are shared with everyone, often for the purpose of making the dancers reveal their identities when they lower their scarves to drink. The spirit of the fiesta that prevails on July 6, 7, 8, and 9 is conveyed in these words, written in an impressionistic, staccato style by a Huaylino for the local newspaper.

This night I am disguising myself. . . . Thou wilt wear a pollera down to thy ankles and a mantle that will cover thy face and a hat of *jipe* or however thou may wish . . . let's go with the band from Yacup, it's better . . . but hurry-up, a drink, thou must be thirsty. . . There's the "boat" from Shuyo, let's go. . . . How sweet it is to live, knowing how to enjoy . . . thy health! . . .

I danced so much at the *alba gané* [33] that my feet can't continue . . . Saint Elizabeth will make them better. . . . Those from Delicados thought they would beat us to the plaza by going quietly . . . but we were at the atrium, already dancing. . . . Commerce Street is like a blanket of products for sale. . . . So many people have come this year. . . . What beautiful girls from Lima showing off their figures and dresses and good humor. . . . Won't many return saying that "Our Patroness Saint Elizabeth was at fault. . . ." [34]

It is now time for the procession . . . the contrite *pashas* whispering their prayers, cease to snap their "thunderers," the *toros,* with deep genuflections seem as souls in pain, purging themselves of their errors . . . the smiling *pallas* dressed like flowers and singing their songs finishing with the classic chorus, "qu-yaya," waving their kerchiefs in the air . . . the *chapetones,* white and elegant, dance together, swelling with pride, remembering the arrogance and nobility—mark of the intrepid Spaniard. . . . One after another *caballudanza* goes meandering about. . . .

---

[32] *Washco* is cane alcohol mixed with water or soda. Other popular drinks are a mixture of *pisco* and vermouth, called *capitán,* and anisette.

[33] To "beat the dawn." The most hardy celebrants go to the plaza at 5 A.M., on the morning of July 8, with the bands to dance for an hour or more. Many persons dance all night for two or three days.

[34] A certain amount of sexual license is common during the fiesta. Those who indulge themselves, particularly the middle- and lower-class women, excuse their behavior by saying that it was the "fault" of Saint Elizabeth for allowing them to abandon their restraint in the gaiety of the fiesta.

Today is the last day. . . . Let's go dance. . . . It is the *shillca*.[35] Perhaps we won't be here next year . . . perhaps our bones will rest in a coffin. . . .

Long live the Fiesta of Saint Elizabeth! . . . Long live my *barrio!* . . . Long live Huaylas! [36]

The nature of the social structure is clearly reflected by such things as the differential participation of men and women in the practice of religion, differences in behavior and dress, and the tendency of the important fiestas to generate almost equal interest in all classes. The attitudes of Huaylinos toward the clergy, in a sense their rejection of external controls and the assertion of their independence, parallels, to some extent, their attitudes toward the national government. The Catholicism practiced carries the flavor and stamp of the region—it belongs to and is part of the Huaylas homeland.

The religious fiestas can be differentiated in terms of their primary functions in the collective life: those that fulfill an essentially spiritual need, and those that, while prompted by the feast day of a particular saint or by some other religious occasion, satisfy recreational and secular needs more than spiritual ones. The biggest and most important religious events—Holy Week, the Fiesta of Saint Elizabeth, and the Fiesta of the Virgin of the Assumption—are all identified as public events and are not exclusively associated with a particular class or a particular sector of the population, despite the fact that two of them place special emphasis upon upper-class participation.

None of these major fiestas seems to be diminishing either in strength or appeal, as might be anticipated because of the great outmigration and the close ties maintained with the large urban centers of the coast. In fact, as in other areas of life the emigrants lend their wholehearted support to the aggrandizement of fiesta activities.[37] From time to time, there is some inclination on the part of urban upper- and middle-class persons (usually women) to create special activities or associations among their own subgroups or cliques.[38] Although this has been the case for many years, apparently few of the resulting organizations

[35] Last night of the fiesta.

[36] Rodomiro Flores V., 1948:29–30 (my translation).

[37] Huaylinos in Lima celebrate the fiestas of Saint Elizabeth and the Virgin of the Assumption there, too, often reporting it in the Lima papers (*La Prensa*, August 14, 1960:4).

[38] Adams (1959:80) also reports this in Muquiyauyo and feels that such organizations were taking over the *barrio* functions and structuring fiesta events more along class lines.

endure. Because of their transitional nature and because they include individuals of both middle- and upper-class status, the lay organizations facilitate rather than obstruct social mobility, a fact lamented by a few of the upper-class women.

In the context of Spitzer's useful classification of Roman Catholics in the Latin American setting, there are several points of similarity with his system as well as some exceptions to it.[39] Most Huaylinos would be classified as what Spitzer calls "nominal" and "cultural" Catholics at all levels of society, with a nucleus of persons, principally of upper-class standing, being considered as "formal," or thoroughly knowledgeable Catholics. In Spitzer's Yucatan study, the "formal" Catholics were of lower social status. His remarks, however, to the effect that, at the lowest level of participation in the Catholic church (referred to as "folk" Catholicism), there is but a vague comprehension of the meaning of the sacraments and saints, that the cross is often treated as an idol, that failure to observe devotion to a particular cross or saint is believed to result in punishment, and that the largest church attendance is on Good Friday (when "Christ is dead from a liturgical standpoint") would seem to have a much wider application in the Huaylas setting than in the one he describes.[40]

[39] Spitzer, 1958:1–20.
[40] Spitzer, 1958:15–16.

CHAPTER XI

A Different View
of Peasant Society

After a year's absence I had occasion to return to Huaylas in 1963 and in 1964 for short visits, and then again in 1966. Some of the people I had known had left for the coast or had died. The electrification program continued and, of an evening, lights could be seen in the far corners of Huayrán and even over the hill of Amankaes in Iscap. Indeed, the Concejo had created a special office to handle electrical installations, read meters, and collect what was owed. Four persons had been added to the municipal payroll as a result.

There was a variety of new things in the community as the result of having the "good" electricity. An ever-increasing variety of appliances was being purchased, a shoemaker from Santo Toribio had opened a shop equipped with an electric stitching machine on Commerce Street in the center of town, and a roaring juke box (called a "Wurlitzer" although not of that make) in the bar on the corner of the plaza played *huaynos* that could be heard for blocks. A new truck owned by a man in Santo Toribio made scheduled runs to Caraz and on July 8, 1963, mercury vapor lights were installed around Raimondi Park in the plaza. These were a gift of the Huaylas District Association in Lima.

The new parish priest wearing a beret and driving a Volkswagon had come and, through public contributions, had purchased an elaborate loudspeaker system for the church. Construction had begun on a new school in the *barrio* of Shuyo after the migrants from that *barrio* in Lima and Callao had purchased and donated the land for it. A massive concrete bridge had been built to replace the one over the Huaylas "river" gorge in town. The Parents' Association of the boys' school in town was sporadically at work, reconstructing a portion of the school that had fallen down. Our house was now a restaurant, and the billiard parlor had moved to a new location. In 1966, a high school was functioning, the road to Huallanca was almost finished, and a potable water system was being installed, among other things.

In the fall of 1963, a Peace Corps couple, Bill and Jackie Daley, had established themselves in town, sponsored by the Concejo. They were soon busy at a variety of tasks, consulting with farmers, surveying the town for the installation of a water and sewerage system, conducting English and home-economics classes, and studying the irrigation system for possible canal improvements and the lakes on the *puna* for the dams, so desired by the farmers. With a Peruvian government grant, work had begun on the dams in 1965. With the help of Bill Daley and the provincial extension agent a group of six middle- and upper-class farmers, called the Committee for Agriculture, had begun using new agricultural techniques, with the hope of starting a producers' cooperative. In early 1965 they purchased a small tractor for common use and seemed to be enjoying some success in their pioneering efforts. A large group of farmers in Iscap also pooled their capital and rented the hacienda in the neighboring district of Huallanca in 1963. How they were faring in this innovative venture, however, I cannot say.

The many small changes that had been taking place in Huaylas over this period of six years had, of course, some relationship to what was taking place elsewhere in the world, however indirect. On revisiting Huaylas I became acutely aware of just how closely, indeed how quickly, this small district in the Peruvian Andes was becoming integrated not only into the national society, but also into international life. In 1963 a travel-leadership grant for farm leaders was made available to a Huaylino through USAID and the National Farmers' Union of the United States. The young man spent six months in the United States on a farm in South Dakota, returning full of ideas and ambitions.

In May 1964 while returning to the town from Santo Toribio, I stopped to listen to the music of a *caja* and *roncadora* emanating from a new and rather elegant house. To my astonishment a man approached me and in impeccable English invited me inside. Where was he from?

La Campiña, Huaylas. Where did he learn his English? Miami, Florida.
It seems that he was home from the United States on vacation, and was
building himself a "little chalet." The following week he planned to
return to Miami, with his new bride and mother, to join his two
brothers who also worked there.

I had known of other Huaylinos living in the United States including
the donor of the Huaylas library, Mr. Eusebio Acosta, who has resided
in New York City for almost forty years. Other Huaylinos have served
in the United States Marines and worked as servants in the United
States. Nevertheless, these two contacts underscored the importance of
the international influences in Huaylas. The relationships were no
longer one-way affairs with North Americans visiting such places as
Huaylas by chance. Now, the process was reciprocal. A kind of egalita-
rian atmosphere now enveloped our conversations with the unstated
premise being, now we know about you, just as you know about us.
Thus, the social, economic, and cultural horizons of many Huaylinos
are directly broadened by international influences.

Huaylinos continue to transform their highland environment at a
piecemeal, plodding, but nevertheless steady pace. As in the past, they
continue to utilize their own and whatever other resources they can
obtain. Despite internal factions, *envidia*, and migration, cooperation is
achieved in one way or another.

Huaylas cannot be routinely classified as a "typical" district if indeed
there is such a thing, as Tschopik pointed out long ago. He remarked
that his study of central highland communities

. . . will serve in some measure to correct the widespread misconception
that the entire sierra of Peru is "Indian" and that its peoples are uniformly
primitive, backward, and nonprogressive. Indeed, our survey can claim to
have revealed a diversity of patterns and an essential lack of cultural unity
in the Central Peruvian Highlands. Marked differences from one community to the next have been described.[1]

Today the Indians are largely "gone" from Huaylas. Huaylinos are
measurably distinct from neighboring areas not only in cultural terms,
but in social and economic terms as well. The Huaylas standard (and
levels) of living are noticeably higher, particularly in rural areas, than
for comparable populations in the region. Moreover, the elements of

[1] Tschopik, 1947:55.

deprivation, common in Vicos [2] and Hualcán [3] are absent. Why should this be so? The hypothesis has been advanced that where the traditional manorial system is dominant, a rigid social structure prevails, permitting the lowest class—the Indians—only the barest minimum level of existence and blocking any changes that might occur.[4]

There can be no doubt that the traditional highland manor with its resident population of ragged and unenlightened serfs is a barrier to change as has been thoroughly demonstrated in Vicos.[5] But the absence of the manor from the scene is not a guarantee that "progress" must necessarily occur or that the people will take it upon themselves to initiate a process of change, with or without outside assistance.[6] There may exist, in fact, other kinds of barriers which shut out alternatives and stifle opportunities which may beckon. In the Andes, such barriers as isolation, either physical or social, a lack of education or resources, limited freedom of movement, and attitudes which militate against change in the status quo, of course play a vital role in community histories. Of particular importance to cultural and social change, as Adams pointed out in the case of Muquiyauyo (Department of Junín), has been the continued ability of the community to resolve its problems to the general satisfaction.[7]

In reviewing the present situation in Huaylas we can see that many of the physical and structural barriers have been set aside. Huaylinos are not caught in a situation that precludes their freedom to participate in the national society, nor are they burdened with an oppressive poverty. Although Huaylas has never been truly isolated in a social sense from the rest of the country, geographic mobility and outside contact were greatly increased when the railroad reached Huallanca in 1927. This mobility was further increased upon completion of the vehicular road in 1942.

The role of emigration in the social history of Huaylas is exceedingly important. Many of the families which constituted the upper class at

[2] Holmberg *et al.,* 1965.

[3] Stein, 1961.

[4] Vázquez, 1961a:50.

[5] Holmberg, *et al.,* 1965.

[6] Dobyns (1964:44) surveyed 640 Comunidades Indígenas in Peru finding that 71.6 per cent felt that some governmental agency should be responsible for initiating or backing changes and community reforms.

[7] Adams, 1959:201–211.

the turn of the century and into the second decade of it, migrated to Lima, following a pattern which was noted throughout the region. There can be no question that this was one of the basic factors underlying the evolution of the relatively open society that exists in Huaylas today. But this alone does not account for the present pattern of social mobility in Huaylas. The common economic base, the absence of those contrasts that are always referred to in the literature, of extreme wealth in intimate juxtaposition with desperate poverty, and equal access to the primary schools are at least of equal significance. The combined impact of these factors has diminished the outstanding, visible cultural differences between the different sectors of the population.

I have placed special emphasis on the attachment that Huaylinos have for their homeland, for it seems to me that this is the warp which holds the social fabric together. Without some unifying force at work, the independence which characterizes these people could well have a centrifugal effect tearing the society apart. There have been these tendencies in Huaylas, particularly in the case of the feud between the town and Santo Toribio.

Despite this, the people identify with the homeland. The migrants maintain this kinship even after many years of absence from the district and actively support its development. The firm and positive sense of belonging to the community is a powerful sustaining element in Huaylas and perhaps vital in controlling, to some extent, the vastly disruptive consequences of emigration. Thus, rather than contributing to a breakdown of local institutions (although some have suffered for this reason, particularly social clubs), the migrants have played effective community roles in absentia.

The sense of community is widespread. Huaylas organizations are characterized by a broad sharing of power and responsibility. The political system not only makes possible the participation of persons of all social classes but encourages it. Creditable performances in support or leadership roles gain prestige for the individual, thus providing a reward for public service as well as an inducement. The concept of leadership is linked with that of civic responsibility, and persons who fail to demonstrate the degree of dedication to civic affairs that is expected of them are strongly criticized.

Against a background of diminishing social and cultural differences, the concept of district unity and individual identification with the homeland (*tierra*) provide the basis for translating group needs and desires into concrete projects for their attainment. The needs of the community can be agreed upon. Most Huaylinos can and do feel that the benefits from work on *repúblicas* and committees accrue to the community at large and not merely to a small group or clique. The fact that Huaylas is able to utilize almost all of its human resources for community enterprises is of major significance, considering the limited monetary, technological, and other resources at its disposal.

While the common cultural background and diminished social distinctions have created the basis for integrated action and decision, the common economic base has provided the necessary time. Because the rhythm of economic activity is derived from the agricultural cycle, periods of relative inactivity occur, which allow time for voluntary, large-scale undertakings of an individual or collective nature. The fact that most Huaylinos are farmers, enables the majority to engage simultaneously in public works projects.

Success in their undertakings has created a notable degree of pride and self-reliance among Huaylinos at the community level. This is particularly true of the confidence expressed in the ability of the district to surmount problems that do not call for special skills or unobtainable materials in order to resolve them. Huaylinos have not developed an excessive dependency upon outside intervention, as is the case in many other highland communities, and, although they do make frequent appeals to the government for aid, it is usually on the basis of sharing the responsibility for the execution and cost of the project. Continued success in public projects has reinforced the community institutions and attitudes, thus stimulating further undertakings. A positive, rather than negative, cycle of events is, therefore, fostered.

An outgrowth of this situation has been the continued positive emphasis on work and public service, two features of their society which Huaylinos feel are lacking in neighboring communities. The continuance of this emphasis has underwritten the survival of the institution of the *república* in the changing cultural milieu. Such personal involvement in public affairs is functional in terms of the collective and individual wants inspired by modern Western society. The *barrios*, regional associations, clubs, and individuals can be asked for their contributions and work, often at a considerable sacrifice. Thus, it was possible for the District Council to place signs along the high-tension line and at the transformer station of the new electrical system, reading: "This is yours, Huaylino—take care of it!"

The situation in Huaylas, when considered against a background of studies of peasant societies, particularly those of Hispanic or Mediterranean cultural tradition, exhibits a striking contrast. In a useful review article concerning interpersonal relationships in peasant societies throughout the world, Foster (dismissing Redfield's study of Tepotzlan as one-sided) demonstrates with great clarity that the romantic idea of the friendly, cooperative, sturdy peasant—the "noble peasant" if you will—is rarely to be found in fiction and certainly not in ethnographic reporting.[8] There, peasant life is viewed as rent by mistrust, latent and overt hostility, and extreme factionalism, which inhibit collective activity and obviate the possibility of work for the common good.[9] Foster attributes much of this, particularly as it relates to rural development programs, to the peasant's view of his resources. He sees land and technology as essentially static in dimension and believes that "there is no way to increase it however hard the individual works unless new land and improved techniques become available." Thus individual progress and betterment is possible only at the expense of one's neighbors because "the pie is constant in size." [10] Since the economy is viewed as static, rather than expanding, in nature, Foster concludes:

(a) A village must be approached with the assumption that most of its people are naturally uncooperative, not that they are cooperative.

(b) A major educational effort must be made to break the traditional image of a static economy in the minds of villagers. More effort must be devoted to help them see, through demonstration and continual explanation, how it is possible for some to have more without others having less. I suspect that, to the degree that people can come to appreciate this fact, it will be easier and easier to obtain real cooperation.[11]

How then is the situation in Huaylas to be explained? In the preceding chapters, I have attempted to present a well-rounded view of Huaylas culture, to discuss the harmonious and cooperative aspects of district life along with the conflicts and hostilities that also characterize

---

[8] Foster, 1960–61:174–178. See in the same volume "Comments" on Foster's article by Lewis and Pitt-Rivers and "Rejoinder" by Foster, 179–184. Also commenting on Foster's article and extending it somewhat is Lopreato, 1962:21–24.

[9] This is a condition of peasant life which the Banfields (1958) have described as "amoral familism."

[10] Foster, 1960–61:177.

[11] Foster, 1960–61:178.

it. The indices of disorganization and conflict, such as the constant entanglements over landownership, marital instability, gossip, enmities, the types of crime, and factionalism are reminiscent of, if not identical with, those discussed by Foster and others. The picture one draws from the literature about these societies is bleak indeed; integrating and cohesive forces within them appear to be almost nil.

In Huaylas, hostility is vented through traditional channels such as *barrio* rivalry in the fiesta of Saint Elizabeth and also in the *repúblicas* themselves. As one *barrio inspector* put it: "There is always a little counterpoint." Thus, much of the aggression and hostility emerges under "controlled" conditions, which often render them harmless or even turn them to constructive purposes. Although many Huaylinos note that the fights which occur during the fiesta are "forgotten" as soon as the fiesta is over, the schism between the town and Santo Toribio remains a serious one and awaits resolution.

The key to cooperation is linked by Foster to the emergence of an image of a dynamic economy. On this point we note that it is characteristic of Huaylinos to view their resource base and potential optimistically. Both individually and collectively, Huaylinos feel that there is much that could be done. They are always talking of *superandose* (improving oneself) or *perfeccionandose* (perfecting oneself, referring to a skill) and, by these means, hoping to alter their condition.

Although the land base in Huaylas is not expanding at the present time (and has probably declined since the time of the Conquest), Huaylinos nurture the hope that the amount of land now cultivated can be expanded and existing fields greatly improved through amplification of the irrigation system by increasing the water-storage capacity of the small lakes in the *puna* region. If there is one thing upon which all Huaylinos can agree, it is this.

But an optimistic view of the economy is not the only factor involved. Huaylinos have always had to cooperate with one another to a certain extent in order to assure reasonable success in their individual farming ventures. The scarcity of water is a great preoccupation among Huaylinos, and it is not surprising that there are almost constant conflicts over the use of water. Practical necessity, however, appears to override most of the grosser effects of such disagreements, and there is considerable collaboration in keeping the irrigation system operative. Moreover, the persistence of the desire to improve and expand the irrigation system after years of frustration and lack of government interest is strong testimony to the fact that Huaylinos have accepted the idea of the expanding economy.

The concept of an expanding society and economy has been manifested in Huaylas in other ways too. Huaylinos, for example, have long been aware of the relationship between the district's emigration rate and the static nature of the agricultural economy. They assert that, in order to maintain their population, industry is needed in lieu of improvements in the agricultural system. In apparent preparation for the role of participants in an industrial society, Huaylinos of middle-class status particularly often refer to themselves as the "working class" (*clase obrera*—industrial workers), and those persons who own machinery of one sort or another are considered "industrialists" (*industriales*). Individual entrepreneurship is looked upon as "progressive" and, although limited by the insufficiency of capital, is nonetheless nourished in an atmosphere of favorable attitudes. Further, Huaylinos are most insistent on the need to expand and modify the educational system. Many express a desire for a vocational school that would provide training in agricultural or industrial technology.

The preconditioning in terms of attitudes toward industrial society undoubtedly serves a positive function in facilitating individual adjustments to the coastal cities, where many seek work in factories. Be that as it may, the migration rate has clearly relieved the population pressure on the stable land base. As a consequence, the almost even level of the population from 1876 to the present has permitted a greater degree of economic stability and security than might otherwise have been the case among those who remained in the district.

The role of outside agencies in the development of these attitudes should not be overlooked. Huaylinos have been engaged in major construction projects since the start of the construction of the Chimbote-Huallanca railway in 1872 and, as this project reached further into the mountains, Huaylino involvement increased proportionately. The road law of President Leguia also contributed to this. Huaylinos formed an important element in the labor force that blasted out the tunnels of the Cañon del Pato and were solely responsible for the construction of a difficult seventeen-kilometer road. The building of the hydroelectric plant used and developed Huaylas manpower. Huaylinos learned through their participation in these projects that it was indeed possible to move mountains and that they could do it.

The emergence of capable leaders in Huaylas has provided a continuing, if sporadic, stimulus for the changes that have occurred. The administrative and political organization of the district has developed leaders at all levels of the society who have been able to galvanize community interests, manpower, and organizations to achieve common goals. With such leadership, Huaylinos have been able to take advantage of outside agencies and obtain assistance from them, while at the same time they have avoided excessive dependence upon them for direction or resources. Local pride and self-respect have therefore been maintained, if not bolstered.

In the final analysis, then, Huaylas' progressiveness is accounted for by a special constellation of interrelated factors, no one of which, if taken alone, would account for the level of community initiative and enterprise that has been and continues to be manifested. Given the success they have achieved, it is reasonable to predict that Huaylinos will continue their own natural experiment in community development, as they assume an even more active role in the modern world.

POSTSCRIPT

While this book was in press, the District of Huaylas was named winner of the "Lampa de Plata" (Silver Shovel) award given each year by the President of the Republic of Peru to a community, district, or province in national recognition for what it has accomplished in its own behalf.

Glossary

abrazo, embrace.

abrigo de cuatro puntas, poncho (literally, "four-cornered overcoat").

acción cívica, civic action, collective work (see *república*).

acción popular, popular action, collective work (see *república*), name of a national political party.

acéquia, irrigation canal.

adventista, Seventh Day Adventist, Protestant.

agente municipal, municipal agent or representative (see *inspector*).

agricultor, agriculturist, farmer, owner and operator of a small farm.

ahijado, ahijada, godchild, godson, goddaughter (term of address or reference used by godparents to the godchild).

alba gané, dancing at sunrise during a fiesta, particularly during the Fiesta of St. Elizabeth on the morning of the eighth of July (literally, "beat the dawn").

alcalde, mayor (of the district).

alumbrado, lighting of candles in honor of a saint.

anda, litter on which a saint is carried in procession.

apodo, a derogatory nickname, not used to a person's face.

asiático, an Asian, a person with Mongolioid racial characteristics, or a person of Chinese or Japanese ancestry (see *injerto*).

atrasado, backward, underdeveloped.

bajada de la Virgen, lowering of the statue of the Virgin Mary from the altar niche to the litter.

barreta, crowbar used in general farm work.

barrio, ward, a subdivision of the district.

barro, clay or mud used in making adobe brick or tile.

bayeta, baize, woolen cloth of simple weave, which is made in the district for clothing.

Botiquín Popular, government drugstore.

bracero, worker.

buenas memorias, land bequeathed to the church.

bravo, brave, fierce, valiant.

brazo, assistant to the *barrio inspector.*

buque, a "boat" or float carried by the men of the barrios to start the celebration of the Fiesta of St. Elizabeth on the evening of the sixth of July (see *rompe*).

caballudanza, horse dance, a costumed dancer imitating the Spanish *conquistadores* on horseback during the Fiesta of St. Elizabeth.

cabildo abierto, open meeting of the municipal council (*Concejo Distrital*).

cacique, political boss.

caijua, momordica pedata, an edible Andean plant.

Caja de Depósitos, Government Tax Office. Now called, *Banco de la Nación.*

caja y roncadora, drum and flute, played simultaneously by one person. Two men often play together.

calamina, corrugated, galvanized-metal roofing material.

camino de herradura, trail not traversable by motor vehicle.

campesino, farmer, peasant, a person who lives in the rural area.

campiña, countryside

cancha, toasted or parched corn.

capitán, captain, a mixed drink of half vermouth and half *pisco.*

Carnavales, days of carnival preceding Lent.

carrera de cinta, contest during *Carnavales* in which horsemen attempt to grasp ribbons suspended from an archway.

carrizo, arundo dona, a kind of bamboo that grows in wet ground, usually in gullies or swampy areas; used for various construction needs and for many other miscellaneous purposes.

caserio, hamlet or group of houses in a rural area; a rural area.

caudillo, political boss or strongman.

cebón, hog fattened on barley.

cívico, assistant to the lieutenant governor.

coca, erythrozylon coca, the dried leaves of the plant, which are chewed by lower-class men particularly. The plant itself is grown elsewhere.

co-distritano, fellow resident of a district.

cofradía, lands owned by the church or a *hermandad.*

colca, grain storage bin, often in the second floor of a house.

colecta, collection of money for some public enterprise.

colectivo, taxi operating on a fixed route like a bus.

comadre, godsib or gossip, the title and term of address used by the godparent or ceremonial sponsor of a child or object in speaking with or about the mother of the child or female owner of the object sponsored, and vice versa, if the godparent is a woman.

comadrona, midwife (literally, a woman with many *comadres*).

comité, committee.

compadrazgo, gossipred, copaternity, the ceremonial relationship established between godparents or sponsors and the parents of a child or owners of an object.

compadre, godsib or gossip, the title and term of address used by the godparent or ceremonial sponsor of a child or object in speaking with or about the father of the child or male owner of the object, and vice versa, if the godparent is a man.

compromiso, compromising situation, a situation with too much or unwanted responsibility; an appointment.

comunero, member of the *Comunidad Indígena*.

comunidad, see *Comunidad Indígena*.

Comunidad Indígena, an officially recognized, landholding "community" of "Indians" who have held collective title to their land since colonial times (also, *Comunidad de Indígenas*).

concejal, member of the *Concejo Distrital*, a councilman.

Concejo Distrital, the District Council headed by the *alcalde*, in charge of public administration in the district, particularly in the urban areas (also, *Concejo*).

condor racchi, a contest staged during *Carnavales* in which horsemen using their hands attempt to kill a condor which is suspended from an archway as they ride under it.

confianza, confidence, familiarity, informality.

conjunto, small orchestra or group of costumed dancers; a *conjunto Incaico* is a group of dancers representing the Incas.

conviviente, a man or woman living in consensual union, that is, unmarried either by the church or in a civil ceremony.

copita, small glass for drinking alcoholic beverages, a drink of some alcoholic beverage.

corral, pen or enclosure for animals, a barnyard (often used as a latrine).

corregidor, an official of the Spanish colonial government, the head of the *corregimiento*.

corregimiento, district governed by the *corregidor*.

cortamonte, tree-cutting ceremony. During *Carnavales*, the founders of neighborhood fiestas erect small trees in front of their houses and decorate them with fruit and other small gifts. The invited guests dance about the tree taking turns chopping at it with an axe, which is passed from couple to couple. The couple cutting down the trees becomes the *mayordomo* of the fiesta for the coming year and is obliged to erect another tree then.

corte de pelo, first hair-cutting ceremony.

cosecha, harvest.

costál, gunny sack, a sack used for holding agricultural produce (often made of wool).

costeño, a person from the coastal area of Peru.

criollo, a person from the coastal area (particularly the urban centers), the culture particularly associated with the coastal people, knavishness (*a la criolla*, to do something in a half-hearted way, or by taking a short cut).

curaca, an Inca chief or Indian colonial official.

curioso, curiosa, person possessing a special skill (particularly mechanical), a healer.

cuy, guinea pig, cavy.

cuyero, pen or place in which *cuyes* are kept.

chacra, cultivated field.

chapetón, costumed dancer imitating the Spanish conquerors during the Fiesta of St. Elizabeth.

chicha, corn beer (*chicha de jora*, made from sprouted corn, and nonalcoholic *chicha morada* made from boiled purple corn).

chicharrones, cracklings, deep-fried pork tidbits.

chicote, bullwhip.

china, Indian girl or young woman.

choclo, green ears of maize eaten on the cob.

cholo, a person who is neither Indian nor mestizo in a cultural sense (a term of address used among friends, usually men, but sometimes carrying derogatory meaning outside of this context).

choza, a poor, thatched hut.

chuchín, unirrigated farmlands.

chullpa, Inca burial house or tomb.

denuncia, a formal complaint to a government official.

departamento, department, the largest political subdivision of the nation.

depositario, caretaker of a chapel or saint.

devoto, devotee of a saint, one who pays part of the expense of a religious fiesta.

dicho, a saying.

diputado, deputy, representative in congress.

disculpa, apology.

distrito, district, the political subdivision of a province.

doctrina, Catholic doctrine.

egoista, self centered, one who supports public events only for selfish ends.

encomienda, trust or responsibility granted by the King of Spain to Spaniards in the new world during early colonial times for supervising the collection of tribute and conversion of the Indians (in modern usage, a package, letter, or request given to someone to deliver or to fulfill).

envidia, envy. *envidioso,* an envious person.

escapulario, the hood, cape, or small cloth image of a saint worn in recognition of devotion; also, a small card pinned to one's lapel in recognition of a donation made to some cause.

escolta, flag escort, color guard.

escribano, court clerk, provincial clerk.

estancia, place in the rural area, rural property.

evangelista, member of a fundamentalist Protestant sect, a Protestant.

faena, collective public work (same as *república*).

faja, sash.

faról, lantern made of paper used in fiestas, often mounted on poles.

fogón, raised cooking platform for a wood or charcoal fire.

gasto, expense.

gente decente, decent people, upper class.

gente del barrio, people of the barrio.

gente de la chacra, people of the field.

gente de poncho e llanqui, people of poncho and sandal.

gente humilde, humble people.

gentiles, heathens, particularly non-Catholics (referring to the Incas or pre-Christian inhabitants of Peru).

gobernador, governor of a district.

gratificación, tip, bribe.

gringo, person of fair complexion and brown or blond hair, a European or North American, a term of address used with a person with such physical characteristics.

guaje, shout or cry.

guardia, policeman (*guardia civil,* civil guard).

hacienda, a manor with a resident serf population.

hermandad, a lay religious brotherhood.

hilandera, a woman spinner of wool.

Huaylino, Huaylina, man or woman born in the District of Huaylas.

huayno, type of native Andean music based on a pentatonic scale, a dance accompanying the music, sometimes spelled, *Wayno.*

incumplido, unreliable.

indígena, Indian.

indio, Indian.

injerto, person of Chinese (or Japanese) and mestizo (or white) ancestry.

inspección, area of supervision.

inspector, inspector, principal official of a *barrio* (same as *agente municipal*).

intendencia, political and administrative system instituted by the Bourbon kings of Spain in the eighteenth century to improve their control over the Spanish colonies in America.

jipe, jipejapa, fiber of the high-crowned hats worn in Huaylas.

jornalero, day laborer.

Junta de Regantes, the local governing board of the irrigation system.

juventud, youth, the young people (*La Juventud,* a club).

kermés (*kermís, kermesse,* or *quermese*), fund-raising dinner.

lampa, short-handled hoe, shovel.

látigo, bullwhip.

legajo, file.

leonera, a quarrelsome lot (literally, a den of lions).

Libro de Actas, book in which minutes of meetings, etc., are recorded.

licenciado, discharged soldier, veteran.

luto, mourning (*estar de luto,* to be in mourning; *medio luto,* half-mourning).

llanqui, sandal made of an automobile or truck tire.

lliclla, a *bayeta* cloth used by women to carry things on their backs.

macho, he-man, virile, brave, tough, a male animal.

madrina, godmother (term of address or reference).

maestro, schoolteacher, an artisan or work foreman.

maguey, the flower stalk of the *agave americana* (see *penca*).

maíz, Indian corn, maize.

manjar blanco, blancmange, a rich sweet dessert or spread made of sugar and boiled milk.

manto, cape or robe of the statue of the Virgin.

marinera, Peruvian dance particularly associated with the coastal regions but also danced in the sierra (of European origin).

mayordomo, sponsor of a fiesta.

medias (a medias), to farm on a sharecropping basis and divide the crop equally.

mestizo, Spanish-speaking person of mixed Indian and European ancestry.

minka (minga), cooperative exchange labor between households, often festive (see *rantín*).

mirones, onlookers.

misti, mestizo, "white," upper class.

mita, public labor system of the Incas used during the colonial period by the Spaniards to exploit the mines and other resources of the country.

mitayo, person forced to work under the *mita* system.

montaña, heavily forested eastern slopes of the Andes.

moroso, person who fails to participate in *repúblicas,* delinquent in his responsibilities.

mote, boiled grains of corn.

municipalidad, municipality, the Concejo Distrital, the municipal office.

nacimiento, birth.

nogál, walnut, walnut-colored dye used for ponchos.

notable, notable person, person of upper-class status.

obraje, colonial textile mill.

oca, oxalis crenata, an edible tuber native to the Andes.

oficio, official notice or announcement.

ojota, sandal.

olluco, ullucus tuberosus losan, an edible Andean tuber.

padrinazgo, godparenthood or sponsorship, the relationship between god-parent and godchild.

padrino, godfather (term of address or reference).

paisano, fellow countryman (term of address or reference).

palla, costumed woman dancer in the Fiesta of St. Elizabeth.

pan serrano, parched corn or *cancha* (literally, sierra bread).

pañolón, large shawl worn by the women.

papel sellado, official, numbered document paper used for all formal public documents.

pareja, a couple, a dancing partner.

partera, midwife.

partidario, sharecropper.

partir (al partir), system of sharecropping in which the crop is equally divided between *partidario* and owner.

pasha, a costumed male performer in the Fiesta of St. Elizabeth.

patrón, boss, a large landowner.

Patronato Escolar, organization of parents of school children, School Patrons Association.

penca, agave americana, the leaf of the agave, the agave itself.

personero, officer of a Communidad Indígena.

peruanidad, Peruvianness.

picante de cuy, fried guinea pig with a hot, spicy sauce.

picup, phonograph (derived from the English, pick-up, referring to the arm of the phonograph).

pisco, Peruvian grape brandy.

platea, seat on the main floor of a theater (*media platea,* a place on the main floor of a theater in which one may place his own chair).

pollera, a homespun *bayeta* skirt.

poto, a gourd drinking cup.

prefecto, the highest executive official at the department level of government.

procurador, procurator or caretaker of a chapel or saint.

progresista, a progressive person, forward looking and active.

protector, protector or trustee.

provincia, province, the political subdivision of a department.

provinciano, a person born outside of Lima, referring particularly to highlanders.

pueblo, town, people.

puesto, police station.

pulido, a nickname.

puna, treeless pasture lands above 12,000 feet.

quebrada, gorge, ravine.

quemazón, burning of dry plants on the eve of the Feast of St. John.

quinoa, chenopodium quinoa, native Andean grain.

rancha, a form of potato blight.

rantín, cooperative exchange labor between households, an often festive work bee (see *minka*).

real, ten cents, a colonial money unit.

reducción, the Spanish colonial policy under Viceroy Toledo in the latter half of the sixteenth century when efforts were made to establish the Indians in newly-created towns.

remate, auction or sale, the end (*rematista,* the highest bidder at an auction).

repartidor de aguas, water distributor.

repartimiento, Indians assigned to work under an *encomienda* in colonial times.

república, collective, public work sponsored by official administrative institutions in the district.

republicano, one who works in a *república.*

rompe, the first night of celebration of a fiesta, particularly the night of the sixth of July during the Fiesta of St. Elizabeth.

roncadora, a long flute, played in accompaniment with the *caja* (large drum) by the same man.

rubio, blond, fair complexion, light colored.

sala, living room

salud, health (a toast).

Semana Santa, Holy Week.

senador, senator

serrano, highlander, mountaineer.

shaqui, thick soup, particularly of peas or beans.

síndico, district official in charge either of income (*rentas*) or expenses (*gastos*), a member of the Concejo Distrital.

sol, basic monetary unit of Peru (at the time of the research the *sol* was valued at S/26.80 to one U.S. dollar).

subprefecto, administrative head of a province.

superarse, to improve oneself, to get ahead.

tablada, bamboo frame decorated with bread, fruit, and other sundries given by a *mayordomo* of a neighborhood fiesta during *Carnavales.*

teniente alcalde, lieutenant mayor, member of the *Concejo Distrital.*

teniente gobernador, lieutenant governor.

terciopelo, variety of maize grown in Huaylas with a tricolored grain (used especially for *cancha*).

terno, list of candidates for a public office.

terruño, native land, place of birth.

tierra, land, native land, or place of birth.

tintorillo, "ink dipper," a self-trained legal expert who exploits the ignorance of others.

típico, typical.

toma, irrigation sector, water distribution point.

tumbamonte, same as *cortamonte.*

uso, spindle whorl.

vals criollo, creole waltz, which is popular among Spanish-speaking Peruvians.

vara, influence or "pull."
varayoq, political and religious official of an Indian community.
verruga, Andean disease carried by a variety of mosquito.
visibles, important people of upper-class status (literally, visible people).
vivo, knavish, knave, alert.
vocal, trustee of a committee or organization.

washco, cane alcohol mixed with water or a soft drink.

zambo, person of Negro and mestizo ancestry.

Bibliography

Acosta, Zenobio. 1959. *Cuaderno de Difusión Cívica Popular*. Lima: Imprenta Lulli.

Adams, Richard N. 1953. "A Change from Caste to Class in a Peruvian Sierra Town," *Social Forces*, XXXI, 238–244.

———. 1959. *A Community in the Andes: Problems and Progress in Muquiyauyo*. (American Ethnological Society Series) Seattle: University of Washington Press.

Alba, Augusto, *et al.* 1945. "La Provincia de Huaylas en la Historia" in *Monografía de la Provincia de Huaylas*, ed. by Filiberto Garcia-Cuellar. Edición Extraordinaria de *Antena* (Caraz), VII.

Alers, J. Oscar. 1965. "Population and Development in a Peruvian Community," *Journal of Inter-American Studies*, VII, No. 4.

Alers, J. Oscar, Mario C. Vázquez, Allan R. Holmberg, and Henry F. Dobyns. 1965. "Human Freedom and Geographic Mobility," *Current Anthropology*, VI, No. 3, 336.

Alers-Montalvo, Manuel. 1960. "Social Systems Analysis of Supervised Credit in an Andean Community," *Rural Sociology*, XXV, No. 1.

Allred, Wells M. 1960. "System of Government in Peru," *Philippine Journal of Public Administration*, IV, No. 1, 46–60.

Andean Air Mail and Peruvian Times. 1950–1961 (Lima).

Andrews, David H. 1961. "Integration in a Peruvian Indigenous Community." Paper delivered at the 60th Annual Meeting of the American Anthropological Association, Philadelphia, November 16–19.

———. 1963. *Paucartambo, Pasco, Perú. An Indigenous Community and a Change Program*, Ph.D. Thesis, Cornell University, pp. 372ff.

Arciniega, Rosa. 1941. *Francisco Pizarro*. Santiago de Chile: Editorial Naciemento.

Arguedas, José Maria. 1953. "Folklore del Valle del Mantaro," *Folklore Americano,* I, No. 1, 101–124.

———. n.d. *Yawar Fiesta.* Lima: Populibros Peruanos.

Atun Huaylas. 1947–1962, selected numbers (Caraz).

Austin, Allan. 1964. *Research Report on Peruvian Local Government.* New York: Institute of Public Administration.

Babchuk, Nicolas. 1962. "Participation and Observation in the Field Situation," *Human Organization,* XXI, No. 3, 225–228.

Banco Central de Reserva del Perú. 1963. *Programación del Desarrollo: Actividades Productivas del Perú.* Vols. I and III. Lima: Banco Central de Reserva del Perú.

Banfield, Edward G., and Laura R. Banfield. 1958. *The Moral Basis of a Backward Society.* Glencoe, Ill.: The Free Press.

Barclay, George W. 1958. *Techniques of Population Analysis.* New York: John Wiley & Sons, Inc., pp. 266–268.

Basadre, Jorge. 1946. *Historia de la República del Perú.* Vol. II, 1866–1908 (3rd ed.). Lima: Editorial Cultura Antártica.

Beals, Ralph. 1952. "Social Stratification in Latin America," *American Journal of Sociology,* LVII, No. 4.

Belaunde, Victor Andrés. 1957. *Peruanidad.* ("Publicaciones del Instituto Riva-Aguero.") Lima: Ediciones Libreria Studium.

Belaunde Terry, Fernando. 1965. *El Perú Construye: Mensaje del Presidente de la República al Congreso Nacional, 28 de Julio, 1965.* Lima: Editorial Minerva.

Beltrán Cáceres, Miguel E. n.d. *Legislación Indígena.* Cuzco: Editorial Garcilaso.

Bennett, Wendell C. 1944. *The North Highlands of Peru.* (Anthropological Papers of the American Museum of Natural History, XXXIX, Part 1.) New York: American Museum of Natural History.

Bodenlos, Alfred, and John Straczk. 1957. "Base Metal Deposits of the Cordillera Negra," *United States Geological Survey Bulletin,* No. 1040, 3–10, 147–149.

Bourricaud, Francois. 1962. *Changements à Puno: Etude de Sociologie Andine.* Paris: Institut des Hautes Etudes e L'Amerique Latine.

Bradfield, Stillman. 1963. *Migration from Huaylas: A Study of Brothers.* Ann Arbor: University Microfilms, Inc.

Caballero, G. M. n.d. "Homenaje a la Virgen de la Asunción," *Huaynos Populares.* Lima.

Castillo, Hernán, Teresa Egoavil de Castillo, and Arcenio Revilla. 1963. *Carcas: The Forgotten Community.* (Socio-Economic Development of Andean Communities, Report No. 1.) Ithaca, N.Y.: Department of Anthropology, Cornell University.

Castillo, Hernán, *et al.* 1964a. *Chaquicocha: Community in Progress.* (Socio-Economic Development of Andean Communities, Report No. 5.) Ithaca, N.Y.: Department of Anthropology, Cornell University.

——. 1964b. *Mito: The Orphan of Its Illustrious Children.* (Socio-Economic Development of Andean Communities, Report No. 4.) Ithaca, N.Y.: Department of Anthropology, Cornell University.

Chadbourn, Cheryl. 1962. *Concepts of Disease in a Peruvian Indian Community.* (Columbia-Cornell-Harvard-Illinois Summer Field Studies Program, Mss.) Ithaca, N.Y.: Department of Anthropology, Cornell University.

Communidad Indígena de Huaylas, Padrón General. 1942, 1954, 1958, documents.

Corporación Peruana del Santa. 1958. *Planta Siderúrgica-Central Hidroeléctrica.* Lima: Iberia, S.A.

Cotler, Julio. 1959. *Los Cambios en la Propriedad, La Comunidad y la Familia en San Lorenzo de Quinti.* (Instituto de Ethnologia y Arqueología Publications.) Lima: Imprenta de la Universidad Nacional Mayor de San Marcos.

Crow, John. 1952. *Epic of Latin America.* New York: Doubleday and Co.

Dean, John P., and Alex Rosen. 1955. *A Manual of Intergroup Relations.* Chicago: University of Chicago Press.

De Armas Medina, Fernando. 1953. *La Cristianización del Perú, 1532–1600.* (Escuela e Estudios Hispano Americanos Series.) Seville: Concejo Superior de Investigaciónes Científicas.

Distrito de Huaylas. 1889–1961. *Libro de Actas.*

——. 1905–1961. *Dataria Civil.*

——. 1957. "Relación de ciudadanos que el Concejo Distrital de Huaylas ha premiado con un 'Diploma de Honor' a todos aquellos que se han destacado en las diferentes actividades desarrollados en el Distrito." Ms.

——. 1959–1960. *Legajo de Bandos.*

Dobyns, Henry F. 1963. "An Outline of Andean Epidemic History to 1720," *Bulletin of the History of Medicine,* XXXVII, No. 6.

——. 1964. *The Social Matrix of Peruvian Indigenous Communities.* (Cornell-Peru Project Monograph.) Ithaca, N.Y.: Department of Anthropology, Cornell University.

Dobyns, Henry F., and Ella Carrasco R. 1962. "Un Análysis de la Situación de las Comunidades Indígenas en el ambiente Nacional." (*Folletos del Proyecto Perú-Cornell,* No. 3.) Lima: Projecto Perú-Cornell.

Dobyns, Henry F., and Mario C. Vázquez. 1964. *The Cornell-Peru Project Bibliography and Personnel* (Cornell-Peru Project Pamphlet, No. 2.) Ithaca, N.Y.: Department of Anthropology, Cornell University.

Dobyns, Henry F., and Mario C. Vázquez (eds.). 1963. *Migración e Integración en el Perú.* Lima: Editorial Estudios Andinos.

Doughty, Paul L. Field Notes, Huaylas, Peru. Unpublished notes on file with the Department of Anthropology, Cornell University.

——. 1960. "A study of Mestizos in the Peruvian Sierra," Unpublished MS, Department of Anthropology, Cornell University.

——. 1961. "Light and Power in the Cordillera Negra: Huaylas—the Town That Wouldn't Wait," *Andean Air Mail and Peruvian Times* (Lima), XXI, No. 1061 (April 14).

——. 1961. "Knowledge of the United States and the Image of John F. Kennedy in Huaylas, Ancash, Peru," in "Rural Peruvian Views of President J. F. Kennedy." (Cornell-Peru Project, mimeographed.) Ithaca, N.Y.: Department of Anthropology, Cornell University.

——. 1963. 'Peruvian Highlanders in a Changing World: Social Integration and Culture Change in an Andean District. Ph.D Thesis, Cornell University.

——. 1963. "El Caso de Huaylas: Un Distrito en la Perspectiva Nacional," in H. F. Dobyns and M. C. Vázquez (eds.), *Migración e Integración en el Perú*. Lima: Editorial Estudios Andinos, pp. 111–127.

——. 1964. "La Migración Provinciana, Regionalismo, y el Desarrollo Local," *Economia y Agricultura* (Lima), I, No. 3.

Escobar M., Gabriel. 1947. "Sicaya, Una Comunidad Mestiza de la Sierra Central del Perú." Unpublished Bachelor's Thesis, Universidad de Cuzco.

——. 1959. *La Cultura: Factores Institucionales*. Lima: Plan Regional para el Desarrollo del Sur del Perú, XXII, No. 51, pp. 1–21.

——. 1964. "El Mestizaje en la Región Andina: El Caso del Perú," *Revista de Indias del Instituto Gonzalo Fernandez de Oviedo* (Madrid).

Escobar, Gabriel, and Richard P. Schaedel. 1959. *La Cultura: Sistemas de Valores*. Lima: Plan Regional para el Desarrollo del Sur del Perú, XXII, No. 50, pp. 11–15.

Estete, Miguel de. 1862. La Relación del viaje que Hizo el Señor Capitán Hernando Pizarro por Mandado del Señor Gobernador Su Hermano, desde el Pueblo de Cazamalca a Parcama, y de allí a Jauja. Reproduced in *Incas* archive of the Human Relations Area Files, New Haven.

——. 1872. *Report of Miguel de Estete on the Expedition to Pachacamac*. (Clements R. Markham, Translator and Editor.) London: The Hakluyt Society, No. 47, pp. 77–78.

Fajardo, J. V. n.d.(a). *La Constitución Política del Perú*. Lima: Editorial Mercurio.

——. n.d.(b). *La Ley Orgánica de Municipalidades*. Lima: Editorial Mercurio.

——. n.d.(c). *Código de Aguas e Irrigación*. Lima: Editorial Mercurio.

Filgar. 1945–1946. "Judas Encarcelado en Huaylas y Juzgado en Caraz" in

Monografía de la Provincia de Huaylas, ed. by Filiberto García-Cuellar. Edición Extraordinaría de *Antena* (Caraz), VII.

Flores V., Rodomiro. 1948. "Estampas Huaylinas: La Fiesta de Santa Isabel," *Atun Huaylas* (Caraz), II, No. 13 (April 30), pp. 29–30.

Ford, Thomas R. 1955. *Man and Land in Peru.* Gainesville: University of Florida Press.

Foster, George M. 1960. *Culture and Conquest: America's Spanish Heritage.* (Viking Fund Publications in Anthropology, No. 27.) Chicago: Quadrangle Books.

——. 1960–1961. "Interpersonal Relations in Peasant Society," *Human Organization,* XIX, No. 4, pp. 174–178.

Fried, Jacob. 1961. "The Indian and Mestizaje in Peru," *Human Organization,* XX, No. 1.

Friedl, Ernestine. 1959. "The Role of Kinship in the Transmission of National Culture to Rural Villages in Mainland Greece," *American Anthropologist,* LXI, No. 1, pp. 30–37.

García Calderón, F. 1879. "Ancachs," *Diccionario de la Legislación Peruana.* 2nd ed. Lima.

García-Cuellar, Filiberto (ed.). 1945. *Monografía de la Provincia de Huaylas.* Edición Extraordinaría de *Antena* (Caraz), VII.

Ghersi B., Humberto. 1955. "El Indígena y el Mestizo en Marcará," Unpublished Ph.D. dissertation, Instituto de Etnologia y Arqueologia, Universidad Nacional Mayor de San Marcos.

——. 1960. "El Indígena y el Mestizo en la Comunidad de Marcará," *Revista del Museo Nacional* (Lima), XXVIII, XXIX.

Gillin, John. 1945. *Moche: A Peruvian Coastal Community.* (Smithsonian Institution Institute of Social Anthropology Publications, No. 3.) Washington, D.C.: U.S. Government Printing Office.

Golenpaul, Dan (ed.). 1961. *Information Please Almanac: Atlas and Yearbook 1962.* New York: Simon and Schuster.

Gonzalez Prada, Manuel. 1960. *Pájinas Libres.* Vol. I. Lima: Ediciones Páginas Libres.

Goodenough, Ward H. 1963. *Cooperation in Change.* New York: Russell Sage Foundation.

Gridilla, P. Alberto. 1933. *Huaraz.* Huaraz: La Epoca.

——. 1937. *Ancahs y sus Antiguos Corregimientos* in *La Conquista.* Vol. I. Arequipa: Editorial La Colmena, S.A.

Guevara, J. Guillermo. 1959. *La Rebelión de los Provincianos.* Lima: Ediciones "Folklore."

Hammel, Eugene A. 1962. *Wealth, Authority, and Prestige in the Ica Valley, Peru.* (University of New Mexico Publications in Anthropology, No. 10.) Albuquerque: The University of New Mexico Press.

Hoever, Rev. Hugo H. (ed.). 1961. *Saint Joseph Daily Missal.* New York: Catholic Book Publishing Co.

Holmberg, Allan R. 1960. "Changing Community Attitudes and Values in Peru: A Case Study in Guided Change," in Council on Foreign Relations, *Social Change in Latin America Today.* New York: Vintage Books.

Holmberg, Allan R., Henry F. Dobyns, and Mario C. Vázquez. 1961. "Methods for the Analysis of Culture Change," *Anthropological Quarterly,* XXXIV (April), p. 39.

Holmberg, Allan R., *et al.* 1965. "The Vicos Case: Peasant Society in Transition," *The American Behavioral Scientist,* VIII, No. 7.

Huaylas: Organo del Círculo Huaylino, No. 1, 1930. Lima: Imprenta C. A. Castrillón.

International Labour Organization. 1953. *Indigenous Peoples: Living and Working Conditions of Aboriginal Populations in Independent Countries.* Geneva: International Labour Office.

El Jilguero del Huascarán. n.d. *Serrania* (Phonograph record, Odeon LD-1268.) Lima: Industrias Electricas y Musicales Peruanas, S.A.

Kasakoff, Alice B. 1960. "Class and the Schools in Huaylas, Peru." (Cornell-Harvard-Columbia Summer Field Studies Program, mimeographed.) Ithaca, N.Y.: Department of Anthropology, Cornell University.

Kinzl, Hans, and Erwin Schneider. 1950. *Cordillera Blanca: Perú.* Innsbruck: Universitat-Verlag Wagner.

Kubler, George. 1946. "The Quechua in the Colonial World," in *Handbook of South American Indians,* ed. by Julian Steward. Vol. II. (Bureau of American Ethnology Bulletins, No. 143.) Washington, D.C.: U.S. Government Printing Office.

———. 1952. *Indian Caste of Peru, 1795–1940.* (Smithsonian Institution, Institute of Social Anthropology Publications, No. 14.) Washington, D.C.: U.S. Government Printing Office.

Kwong, Alice Jo. 1958. "The Chinese in Peru," in *Colloquium on Overseas Chinese,* ed. by Morton Fried. New York: Institute of Pacific Relations.

Lewis, Oscar. 1951. *Life in a Mexican Village: Tepoztlán Restudied.* Urbana: University of Illinois Press.

Libreria e Imprenta "Guia Lascano" (eds.). 1964. *Constitución de la República del Perú.* Lima: Guia Lascano, pp. 52–53.

Linton, Ralph. 1936. *Study of Man.* New York: Appleton-Century-Crofts, Inc.

Little, Arthur D., Inc. 1960. *A Program for the Industrial and Regional Development of Peru: A Report to the Government of Peru.* Lima: Talleres Gráficos Pacific Press, S.A.

Loomis, Charles P., *et al.* 1953. *Turrialba.* Glencoe, Ill.: The Free Press.

Lopreato, Joseph. 1962. "Interpersonal Relations in Peasant Society: The Peasant's View," *Human Organization,* XXI, No. 1, pp. 21–24.

Malpica, Carlos. n.d. *Los Dueños del Peru.* Lima: Fondo de Cultura Popular.

Mangin, William P. 1955. "Estratificación Social en el Callejón de Huaylas," *Revista del Museo Nacional* (Lima), XXIV, pp. 174–89.

——. 1959. "The Role of Regional Associations in the Adaptation of Rural Population in Peru," *Sociologus,* IX, No. 1.

——. 1967. *Las Comunidades Alteñas de América Latina.* (Instituto Indigenista Interamericano, Serie Monográfico, No. 5.) México, D.F.

Mariátegui, José Carlos. 1952. 7 Ensayos de Interpretación de la Realidad Peruana. Lima: Biblioteca "Amauta."

Martín Pastor, Eduardo. 1938. *De La Casa Vieja de Pizarro al Nuevo Palácio de Gobierno.* Lima: Ministerio e Fomento y Obras Públicas, pp. 8–14.

Martinez, Eneas. 1961a. "Arbol Geneológico de Doña Inés Huaylas y del Inca Garcilaso de La Vega." *Forjando Ancash* (Lima), II, No. 8.

——. 1961b. "Conquista de Los Atun Huayllas por el Inti Patza Cutec." *Forjando Ancash* (Lima), III, No. 9, pp. 30–31.

Martinez G., S. n.d. *Manual y Reglamento de Jueces de Paz.* Lima: Mercurio.

Mason, J. Alden. 1957. *The Ancient Civilizations of Peru.* Edinburgh: Penguin Books.

Matos M., José, *et al.* 1959. *Las Actuales Comunidades de Indígenas: Huarochiri en 1955.* Lima: Instituto de Etnologia y Arqueología, Universidad Nacional Mayor de San Marcos.

Mayer, Kurt B. 1955. *Class and Society.* New York: Random House.

Maynard, Eileen. 1964. *Patterns of Community Service Development in Selected Communities of the Mantaro Valley, Peru.* (Socio-Economic Development of Andean Communities, Report No. 3.) Ithaca, N.Y.: Department of Anthropology, Cornell University.

McDowell, Bart, and John E. Fletcher. 1962. "Avalanche!" *National Geographic Magazine,* CXXI, No. 6, pp. 854–880.

Merton, Thomas K. 1957. *Social Theory and Social Structure.* 2nd ed. Glencoe, Ill.: The Free Press.

Middendorf, E. W. 1895. *Peru.* Vol. III. Berlin: Robert Oppenheim (Gustav Schmidt).

Mintz, Sidney W., and Eric R. Wolf. 1950. "An Analysis of Ritual God-Parenthood (Compadrazgo)," *Southwestern Journal of Anthropology,* VI, No. 5, pp. 341–368.

Morales G., Emilio S. 1958. "Mi Huaylas," MS.

Murdock, George P., *et al.* 1950. *Outline of Cultural Materials.* 3rd ed. New Haven, Conn.: Human Relations Area Files, Inc.

Nuñez del Prado, Oscar. 1955. "Aspects of Andean Native Life," *Kroeber Anthropological Society Papers,* No. 12, pp. 1–21.

Organización de los Estados Americanos. 1961. *Integración Económica y Social del Perú Central.* Washington, D.C.: Pan American Union, pp. 89–109.

Owens, R. 1963. *Peru.* London: Oxford University Press.

Palma, Ricardo. 1953. *Las Tradiciones Peruanas.* Madrid: Aguilar, S.A. de Ediciones.

Patch, Richard. 1960. "Bolivia: U.S. Assistance in a Revolutionary Setting," in Council on Foreign Relations, *Social Change in Latin America Today.* New York: Vintage Books.

The Peruvian Economy. 1950. A report prepared by the Division of Economic Research. Washington, D.C.: Pan American Union.

Perú, Dirección National de Estadística. 1933. *Extracto Estadístico y Censo Electoral de la República.* Lima: Imprenta del Ministerio de Hacienda.

Perú, Instituto Nacional de Planificación, Dirección Nacional de Estadística y Censos. 1964. *Sexto Censo Nacional de Población, 2 de Julio de 1961: Resultados de Primera Prioridad.* Lima: Dirección Nacional de Estadística y Censos.

Perú, Ministerio de Educación Pública, Dirección de Educación Primaria. 1955. *Planes y Programas para la Educación Infantil, Las Clases de Transición y la Educación Primaria.* Lima: Dirección de Educación Primaria.

Perú, Ministerio de Gobierno. 1878. *Resumen del Censo General de Habitantes del Perú hecho en 1876.* Lima: Imprenta del Estado.

Perú, Ministerio de Guerra. 1922. *Conscripción Viál: Resolución Suprema de 17 de Diciembre de 1912, Ley No. 4113.* Lima: Imprenta del Estado.

Perú, Ministerio de Hacienda y Comercio. 1944. *Censo Nacional de Población y Ocupación, 1940.* Vols. I and III. Lima: Imprenta Torres Aguirre, S.A.

Perú, Ministerio de Hacienda y Comercio, Dirección Nacional de Estadística y Censos. 1962. *Resultados Preliminares del Censo de Población de 1961.* Lima: Ministerio de Hacienda y Comercio.

Perú, Ministerio de Trabajo y Asuntos Indígenas, Dirección General de Asuntos Indígenas. 1961. *Padrón General de Comunidades Indígenas Reconocidas Oficialmente al 30 de Junio de 1961.* Lima: Imprenta del Ministerio de Hacienda y Comercio.

———. 1964. *Atlas Comunal.*

——. n.d. Archives of the *Dirección General de Asuntos Indígenas Expidiente 19,* document.

Pitt-Rivers, Julian. 1961. *People of the Sierra.* Chicago: University of Chicago Press.

Plan Regional Para El Desarrollo del Sur del Perú. Funciones y medios de Gobierno local Informes, XXIII, No. 52. 1959. Lima: Servicio Cooperativo Peruana Norte-americano de Educación.

Porras Barrenchea, Raúl. 1936. *El Testamento de Pizarro.* ("Cuadernos de Historia del Perú, Documentos Inéditos," I.) Paris: Imprimeries les Presses Modernes.

La Prensa. 1960. Lima (August 14), p. 4.

Pritchett, V. S. 1965. *The Spanish Temper.* New York: Harper and Row.

Raimondi, Antonio. 1873. *El Departmento de Ancachs y Sus Riquezas Minerales.* (Publicado por Enrique Meiggs.) Lima: Imprenta El Nacional.

——. 1943. "Viaje al Departamento de Ancash, 1860–1861," in *Notas de Viaje Para Su Obra "El Perú."* (Publicado por Alberto Jachamowitz.) Vol. II. Lima: Imprenta Torres-Aquirre.

Reichel-Dolmatof, Gerardo, and Alicia Reichel-Dolmatof. 1961. *The People of Aritama.* Chicago: University of Chicago Press.

Ritter, Ulrich Peter. 1965. *Comunidades Indígenas y Cooperativismo en El Perú.* ("Estudios sobre la Economia Iberoamericana," Tomo I.) Bilbao: Ediciones Deusto.

Rodriguez, Justiniano. 1958. *La Virgen de la Asunción de Atun Huaylas.* Lima: Mercagraph, S.A.

Ross, Murray G. 1955. *Community Organization: Theory and Principles.* New York: Harper and Bros.

Rowe, John Howland. 1947. "The Distribution of Indians and Indian Languages in Peru," *Geographical Review,* XXXVII.

——. 1946. "Inca Culture at the Time of the Spanish Conquest," in *Handbook of South America Indians,* ed. by Julian Steward. Vol. II. (Bureau of American Ethnology Bulletins, No. 143.) Washington, D.C.: U.S. Government Printing Office.

——. 1957. "The Incas under Spanish Colonial Institutions," *Hispanic-American Historical Review,* XXXVII, No. 2, pp. 155–99.

Rycroft, W. Stanley (ed.). 1946. *Indians of the High Andes.* New York: Committee on Cooperation in Latin America.

Sabogal Wiesse, José R. 1961. "La Comunidad Andina de Pucará," *América Indígena,* XXI, No. 1, pp. 39–64.

Saenz, Moises. 1933. *Sobre el Indio Peruano y su Incorporación al Medio Nacional.* México: Secretaria de Educación Pública.

Sancho de la Hoz, Pedro. 1917. "Relación para S. M. de lo Sucedido en la Conquista y Pacificación de Estas Provincias de la Nueva Castilla . . .," in *Las Relaciones de la Conquista del Peru*. Lima: Coleción de Libros y Documentos Referentes a la Historia del Perú, V, p. 135.

Schaedel, Richard P., *et al.* 1959. *La Demografia y los Recursos Humanos*. Lima: Plan Regional para el Desarollo del Sur del Perú, IV, No. 8, pp. 15–26.

———. 1959a. *La Organización Social en el Departmento de Puno*. Lima: Plan Regional Para el Desarollo del Sur del Perú, XXII, No. 49.

———. 1959b. *Los Recursos de la Región: Recomendaciones para su Desarollo*. Lima: Plan Regional Para el Desarollo del Sur del Perú, XXVII, No. 58, pp. 131–147.

Silva Santisteban, Fernando. 1964. *Los Obrajes en el Virreinato del Perú*. Lima: Museo Nacional de Historia.

Simmons, Ozzie G. 1955. "The Criollo Outlook in the Mestizo Culture of Coastal Peru," *American Anthropologist*, LVII, No. 1, pp. 107–117.

Snyder, Joan C. 1960. "Group Relations and Social Change in an Andean Village." Unpublished Ph.D. dissertation, Department of Anthropology and Sociology, Cornell University.

Spitzer, Allen. 1958. "Notes of a Mérida Parish," *Anthropological Quarterly*, XXXI, No. 1, pp. 1–20.

Stein, William W. 1961. *Hualcan: Life in the Highlands of Peru*. Ithaca, New York: Cornell University Press.

Stewart, Watt. 1951. *Chinese Bondage in Peru*. Durham, N.C.: Duke University Press.

Stiglich, Germán. 1923. "Huailas," *Diccionario Geográfico del Perú*. Lima: Imprenta Torres Aguirre, pp. 191–192.

Tello, Julio C. 1960. *Chavín: Cultura Matríz de la Civilización Andina*. (Revised by Toribio Mejia Xesspe.) Lima: Imprenta de la Universidad Nacional Mayor de San Marcos.

Thompson, Donald E. 1962. "Additional Stone Carving from the North Highlands of Peru," *American Antiquity*, XXVIII, No. 2, pp. 245–246.

Toor, Frances. 1949. *The Three Worlds of Peru*. New York: Crown Publishers.

Tschopik, Harry, Jr. 1947. *Highland Communities of Central Peru: A Regional Survey*. (Smithsonian Institution, Institute of Social Anthropology, No. 5.) Washington, D.C.: U.S. Government Printing Office.

———. 1948. "On the Concept of Creole Culture in Peru," *Transactions of the New York Academy of Sciences*, Second Series, X, No. 7, pp. 252–261.

———. 1951. *The Aymara of Chucuito Peru*. (Anthropological Papers of the

American Museum of Natural History, XLIV, Part 2.) New York: American Museum of Natural History.

Varallanos, José. 1959. *Historia de Huánuco*. Buenos Aires: Imprenta Lopez.

——. 1962. *El Cholo y El Perú*. Buenos Aires: Imprenta Lopez, pp. 1–36.

Vargas Ugarte, Rubén, S.J. 1949. *Historia del Perú, El Virrienato, 1551–1600*. Lima: Talleres Gráficos A. Baiocco y Cia., S.A.

Vázquez, Mario C. 1951. "La Cultura 'Chola' o 'Cholo' en el Perú." Paper delivered at the Primer Congreso Internacional de Peruanistas, Lima.

——. 1952. "La Anthropología Cultural y Nuestra Problema del Indio," *Perú Indígena*, II, Nos. 5 and 6.

——. 1961a. *Hacienda, Peonage y Servidumbre en los Andes Peruanos*. ("Monografias Andinas," No. 1.) Lima: Editorial Estudios Andinos.

——. 1961b. "Local Authority in a Peruvian Andean Hacienda." Paper delivered at the 60th Annual Meeting of the American Anthropological Association, Philadelphia, November 16–19.

——. 1961c. "Educación Formal en una Comunidad Rural Indígena: Vicos." (Cornell-Peru Project, mimeographed.) Lima: Projecto Perú-Cornell.

——. 1963. "Proceso de Migración en la Comunidad de Vicos, Ancash," in H. F. Dobyns and M. C. Vázquez (eds.), *Migración e Integración en el Perú* ("Monografias Andinos," No. 2). Lima: Editorial Estudios Andinos, pp. 93–102.

——. 1964. *The Varayoc System in Vicos*. (Comparative Studies of Cultural Change.) Ithaca, N.Y.: Department of Anthropology, Cornell University.

Velasco Nuñez, Manuel D. n.d. *Compilación de la Legislación Indigenista Concordada*. Lima: Editora Médica Peruana, S.A.

Veliz Alba, María. 1947. "El Recibimiento de la Virgen," in *Mitos, Leyendas y Cuentos Peruanos*, ed. by José Maria Arguedas and Francisco Izquierdo Rios. Lima: Ministerio de Educación Pública.

Von Hagen, Victor W. 1956. *Highway of the Sun*. London: Victor Gollancz.

Whetten, Nathan L. 1948. *Rural Mexico*. Chicago: University of Chicago Press.

Index